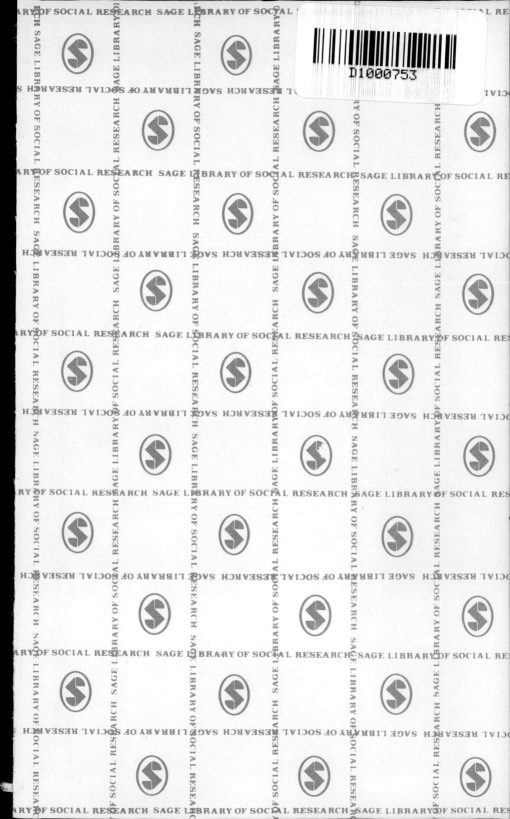

BUREAUCRACY OR PARTICIPATION

Volume 51, Sage Library of Social Research

Sage Library of Social Research

BUREAUCRACY OR PARTICIPATION

THE LOGIC OF ORGANIZATION

BENGT ABRAHAMSSON
Introduction by MORRIS JANOWITZ

Volume 51
SAGE LIBRARY OF
SOCIAL RESEARCH

 SAGE PUBLICATIONS   Beverly Hills   London

For information address:

SAGE PUBLICATIONS, INC.
275 South Beverly Drive
Beverly Hills, California 90212

SAGE PUBLICATIONS LTD
28 Banner Street
London EC1Y 8QE

Printed in the United States of America

Library of Congress Cataloging in Publication Data

Abrahamsson, Bengt, 1937-
    Bureaucracy or participation.

    (Sage library of social research; v. 51)
    Translation of Organisationsteori.
    Includes index.
    1. Management.   2. Employees' representation in
management.   3. Organization.   I. Title.
HD38.A2513   658.31'52   77-10023
ISBN 0-8039-0836-9
ISBN 0-8039-0837-7 pbk.

THIRD PRINTING

CONTENTS

ABOUT THE AUTHOR

BENGT ABRAHAMSSON is Associate Professor (Docent) of sociology at the University of Uppsala, Sweden, and Lecturer at the University of Stockholm. He was Post-Doctoral Fellow at the University of Chicago 1968-1969, and Editor of *Acta Sociologica* (Journal of the Scandinavian Sociological Association) 1972-1974. Dr. Abrahamsson has written extensively on professions, the military and politics, the sociology of education, social psychology, the sociology of work, and bureaucracy. Among his publications are "The ideology of an elite: Conservatism and national insecurity," in J.A.A. van Doorn (ed.), *Armed Forces and Society: Sociological Essays* (The Hague: Mouton, 1968); "Military professionalization and estimates on the probability of war," in J.A.A. van Doorn (ed.), *Military Professions and Military Regimes: Commitments and Conflicts* (The Hague: Mouton, 1968); *Military Professionalization and Political Power* (Beverly Hills: Sage Publications, 1972); and "Rationalism and systems thinking in organization theory," *Faculty of Social Sciences at Uppsala University, Acta Universitatis Upsaliensis* (Uppsala 1976).

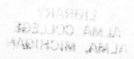

INTRODUCTION

Bengt Abrahamsson's study is a rigorous and bold effort to present a systematic overview of the idea and reality of "bureaucracy." He reviews with clarity the classic writings on bureaucratic organization, as well as the more contemporary perspectives, and incorporates a wide body of empirical research into his analysis. His goal is a more deliberate and reasoned approach to dealing with the policy issues which he sees as required to "refute" the manifold manifestations of the "Iron Law of Oligarchy."

This study is also a noteworthy step in the continuing "struggle" to internationalize sociology. The author is a Swedish sociologist with a wide knowledge of the scholarship and research on bureaucratic organization. It is a book written in the active neutrality of the Swedish model—a critical but sympathetic search for objective understanding based on the widest possible international perspective. He is consciously dedicated to the search for areas of common agreement in the differing scholarly traditions, but is equally aware that the search for convergence does not necessarily, nor should it be expected to, produce a unified reformulation.

The author is well known for his realistic research into military organization and military professionalism. His study of military institutions is no doubt one of the best preparations for this field. He is fully aware of the political assumptions and political consequences of various types of bureaucratic organization; his trenchant criticisms have pointed out that professionalism and expertise, in general and especially in the case of the military, hardly insure political neutrality.

Abrahamsson is dedicated to the central importance of the term bureaucracy for analyzing an advanced industrial society. He strives to make this a concept relevant to all sectors of society. However, the core of the analysis focuses on industrial organization, since the central issues are those of the democratic control of the work place and of the industrial sector of modern society.

His review of the existing alternative formulations of organizational theory leads to an emphasis on organizational goals and organizational leadership. He makes use of the term mandators—those persons who create organizations and assemble the essential resources. His perspective converges with that of sociologists and organization theorists who are interested in the linkages between the internal organizations of bureaucracies and the larger environment—that is, those who see the study of bureaucracy as an essential aspect of macrosociology.

In order both to create efficiency and to control the "Iron Law of Oligarchy," he argues in favor of greater democratization—that is, broader employee participation is required. His perspective is global. The goals of democracy are twofold: equality of influence in decision-making, and equality of economic and material resources. In turn, the analysis of the merging forms of participation in the industrial sector are twofold: one is political and the other socio-technical. The socio-technical deals with the microlevel, the dynamics of the immediate work place. While strategies at this level are of lesser importance than political participation, they cannot be overlooked or dismissed since they deal with real issues. At the crucial level, political participation is designed to produce basic changes in the position of the employee in the factory system. For Abrahamsson, mainly by inference, political parties and interest groups are insufficient. The internal organization of the work place and its democratization remain the essential strategy in the long-term goals of societal change.

Abrahamsson engages in a careful examination of the empirical research dealing with the difficulties of stimulating effective worker participation in the industrial plant. The importance of the analysis rests in the fact that this sociologist, committed to an extension of worker participation, presents a realistic assessment of participatory democracy. He is explicit in his conclusion—"it carries the risk of permanenting inequalities that already exist; indeed they may be reinforced." But on balance, he sees no alternative, and he believes that the potentials for reasoned change outweigh the negative elements.

For me, his analysis indicates the clear limits on internal industrial participation in achieving the good society, and his conclusion highlights the necessity of invigorating the organized competing political parties as the final safeguard. But clearly this analysis, based on an international perspective, has sharpened and made more comprehensible the issues which social scientists, leaders, and effective citizens must face.

Morris Janowitz

ACKNOWLEDGMENTS

For comments and criticisms of the manuscript for the Swedish edition of this book I am greatly indebted to Torsten Björkman, Alfred Bret-schneider, Annika Brickman, Edmund Dahlström, Björn Eriksson, Axel Hadenius, Horst Hart, Ulf Himmelstrand, Kaj Håkanson, Åke Sandberg, and Haluk Soydan. Chapter 13 was made possible partly due to the kind cooperation of the chairmen of the communal assemblies in Belgrade and Pančevo, Mr. Zivorad Kovaćević and Mr. Vitomir Sudar-ski, and to the assistance of Milan Miloradović and Aleksandar Milo-savljević, directors of "Galenika," Zemun. In general, much of my interest in problems of organization and bureaucracy stems from my frequent contacts with Yugoslav friends and colleagues, in particular Tanja Petovar, Veljko Rus, and Rudi Supek.

Sandra Albrecht read the English manuscript, checked my translation and suggested a number of highly useful changes of content and style. My sincere thanks to her, and to all the others, for their help and constructive criticism. The faults are all mine.

March, 1977
Stockholm

Bengt Abrahamsson

FOREWORD

The perspective on organizations which will be developed in this book can be briefly summarized in the following way: Organizations are deliberately designed social structures which have been established by a certain person, group or class, in order to implement certain goals. These persons, groups, or classes shall be called the *mandators* of organizations.

Organizations are instruments for the pursuit of rational action motivated by personal, group, or class interests. They are means for getting work done, i.e., means for production, whether material or immaterial.

The instrumental aspects of organization will be emphasized in the discussion to follow. My general thesis is that these aspects—important as they are for our understanding of organizations and the behavior of interest groups—are not adequately represented in the mainstream of organizational sociology today. In particular, I am questioning the fruitfulness and adequacy for empirical research of the propositions and assumptions of the human relations and Barnard-Simon-March traditions. In these traditions, tendencies toward organicism, and emphasis on internal "plant variables" (such as cohesion, cooperation, morale, satisfaction, and productivity), and an individualistic approach to man's motivation to organize, contribute to a view of the organization as an actor-in-itself while distracting our attention from the organization as a power resource and as a means for the domination of others.

In Sherman Krupp's formulation, it is the "friendly face" of organizations which is emphasized in the writings of, for example, Mary Parker Follett, Elton Mayo, Roethlisberger and Dickson, Chester I. Barnard, Herbert A. Simon, and James G. March. But friendly to whom? The fact that an organization may be used for the domination and control of people—either inside or outside of the organization—is generally understated in the writings of these organizational analysts. "The predatory side of organizations somehow disappears in the analysis," to quote Krupp (1961 : 85).

Although the discussion below is largely based on rationalistic assumptions, it should be clear that no unlimited rationality, or "free will," of organizational actors is assumed. This perspective requires that we look beyond the boundaries of the organization and take account of the wider societal forces giving rise to interests, and thereby to organizations. A detailed treatment of these macromechanisms is outside the scope of the present book, but a recognition of their existence is a necessary basis for the full understanding of organizational processes. Thus, economic, technological, and political forces are the bases for the emergence of interest groups. These forces also set the limits for the use of organizational resources. That is, they constitute the *conditions* for rational action and define the area within which the motives of organizational actors may be implemented. (This discussion is developed more fully in Part II, Ch. 10, esp. Figure 10.1.)

Organizational theory encompasses three highly important problem areas. First is the problem of how to make the organization *efficient*. This is often dealt with in the framework of administration theory and will be the subject of Part II of this book. Second, there is the problem of making the organization *representative* for the interests and objectives of its mandators. This is the subject of theories of democracy and self-management, which will be presented and commented on in Part III.

In order to increase the organization's efficiency, the mandator usually appoints an administrative cadre, i.e., an *executive* which is entrusted with the responsibility of working for the goals and interests of the mandator. Here, i.e., in the intersection between the demands for efficiency and representativeness, a new problem area emerges: the problem of administrative groups which work for their own goals rather than those of their masters, and who gradually become less representative for their mandators' interests. This is the problem of *bureaucracy*.

Since, in many ways, the problem of bureaucracy is of central importance to organizational theory, it is essential to introduce it at an early stage in the discussion. Thus, it is the subject of Part I.

PART I

THE EMERGENCE OF BUREAUCRACY:

OUTER FORCES OR INNER LOGIC?

Chapter 1

BUREAUCRACY: Some General Remarks

What is Bureaucracy?

The concept of bureaucracy, in itself, condenses a development of almost two centuries of political-scientific and sociological analysis of problems of administration and government. It has been an important subject of interest to a large number of classical social theorists such as John Stuart Mill, Gaetano Mosca, Karl Marx, V. I. Lenin, Max Weber, Rober Michels, Talcott Parsons, and Joseph A. Schumpeter. The everyday, pejorative meaning of "bureaucracy" is roughly "illegitimate power." The term connotes an administration standing above and beyond the reach of the people, an administration which sometimes collaborates with power-groups beyond democratic control. As I hope to show, this everyday use of the word, which is also common in daily political debate, corresponds fairly well with how the term is used by several classical sociological authors.

This political application of the term "bureaucracy" is well exemplified in an article by two Swedish trade union writers, Rudolf Meidner and Anna Hedborg (*Tiden,* No. 2, 1974). In their opinion, the expansion of the public sector in Sweden involves certain risks. The development towards larger organizational units and towards increasingly centralized administration may lead to greater bureaucratization. In such a development, the citizenry may become more and more alienated from those services, such as health care, public education, and other publically financed activities that have been established solely for its benefit.

> Many decisions which people were earlier able to check and over-see have now been transferred to regional and administrative levels less close to the citizenry than before. The form of centralization which is represented by big communes, central hospitals, and standard norms for achieving economic support conveys to many people a feeling of being dominated and being kept isolated from a process in which they themselves could affect the situation, and in which they could understand why one solution is chosen rather than another. . . . There are certain dangers involved when one party—such as the Social Democratic party—is responsible for administrative operations over a long period of years: . . . The primary representatives of the party may be conceived of . . . as essentially top bureaucrats, having loyalties primarily tied to administrative strata rather than to political visions (pp. 80-83).

Interpretations of "bureaucracy," and the assessments of both the social functions and political role of bureaucracy, are as numerous as there are writers on the subject. Therefore, it is quite difficult to give a reasonably clear and concise answer to the question of what bureaucracy actually is. In Nordic folklore, one encounters the mythical being "huldra," a beautiful young woman who tempts the forest wanderer to approach her and then suddenly disappears by turning her back on him. In social science, the concept of bureaucracy has played a role similar to that of the huldra: fascinating and seductive, but evading capture in the very moment when the observer-analyst believes he has grasped its true character. Martin Albrow, who has written perhaps the most complete review of the term "bureaucracy" as it is used in political science and sociology, gives us an impressive number of applications of the term from which to choose:

(1) State administration. "Bureaucracy" has been used for denoting the prominent position given by the centralized state power to permanently employed public officials, and has been applied as an instrument of critique against this state power. This critique has generally come from liberal political scientists like John Stuart Mill, who in several of his major writings opposed the concentration of knowledge and admin-

istrative experience in a particular stratum of public officeholders. Mill further pointed to the risks of bureaucratic abuse of power. "Where everything is done through the bureaucracy, nothing to which the bureaucracy is really adverse can be done at all" (Albrow 1970, Ch. 1, esp. p. 22 with excerpts from *Principles of Political Economy, On Liberty* and *Considerations on Representative Government*). Classical Marxist treatment of bureaucracy is also related to state power. However, Marxist analysis of bureaucracy deals specifically with the administration of the *bourgeois* state, and thus, the problem of doing away with bureaucracy is directly linked to the theory of how this state is to be eliminated.

(2) Group of officials. "Bureaucracy" can denote a group of individuals who carry out administrative tasks, or administration carried out by persons who are employed specifically for this type of job regardless of whether it is public or private. When Max Weber discussed the general phenomenon of bureaucratization (not to be confused with his ideal type of bureaucracy, see item (4) below), he referred to the growth of forms of administration characterized by contract employment of officials. This kind of administration should be distinguished from administration through *collegia,* traditional leaders, notables, or groups of ordinary citizens (Albrow 1970: 40-49, 98-100).

(3) Administrative autocracy. Still another definition is that of an administration in which the officials exert power in order to implement their own interests. For example, Harold Laski in the *Encyclopedia of the Social Sciences* (1930: 70-74) defines bureaucracy as "a system of government, the control of which is so completely in the hands of officials that their power jeopardizes the liberties of ordinary citizens" (cf., the discussion by Albrow, 1970: 92). This definition comes close to the concept of technocracy, i.e., a group of technical experts who can exert power because of their special knowledge and central positions within a social institution.

(4) Rational organization. Here, the term "bureaucracy" is used to describe all forms of rational organization. This usage is in accordance with Max Weber's ideal type, i.e., it denotes a form of organization characterized by a hierarchy of offices, careful specification of office functions, recruitment on the basis of merit, promotion according to merit and achieved competence, positions salaried according to hierarchical level, and a coherent system of discipline and control (Weber 1968: 956-558).

Weber's interpretation has inspired a multitude of empirical studies, debates and critiques. Social scientists have devoted great effort to investigating whether organizations with traits such as those specified by Weber are also optimally efficient. "It is not surprising," says Albrow, "that this concept of bureaucracy . . . has appealed to management theorists since the idea of efficiency has been central to much of their writing" (1970: 88). The results of theoretical as well as empirical research in this field have often shown organizations of this kind to be lacking in efficiency. For some important statements, see item (5) below.[1]

As I shall later develop in greater detail, the Weberian ideal type has served as a point of departure for important segments of administrative theory. Because of this, the concept has tended to lose its original function as an inherent element of a general and broad historical analysis concerning forms of social government. Instead, it has been employed for technological purposes, serving especially as a source of inspiration for American organizational sociology.

(5) Organizational inefficiency. Robert K. Merton and Michel Crozier are perhaps the two most prominent representatives of the school of thought which emphasizes "how informal and unanticipated processes, generated by ostensibly rational organization, may occasion administrative delay and public complaints of red tape" (Albrow 1970: 90). Organizational means and methods marked by restraint, discipline, and routine are sometimes perceived as goals by the officeholders. This process may cause the emergence of a bureaucratic personality type (Merton 1957). Crozier, as well, uses the term "bureaucracy" to denote "an organization which cannot correct its behavior by learning from mistakes" (1964: 187).

(6) Modern organizations. Since modern organizations often exhibit the characteristics pointed out by Weber in his ideal type formulation, it may be tempting to equate bureaucracy with organizations in general. Probably the most well-known spokesman for this view is Talcott Parsons, who in his *Structure and Process in Modern Societies* see bureaucracy as roughly equivalent to "relatively large-scale organizations with specialized functions" (1960: 2; for some further examples, see Albrow 1970: 100-102).

(7) Modern society. As Albrow points out, it is sometimes difficult to establish the borderline between an organization and society-at-large. "Hierarchy, rules, division of labor, careers, qualifications seem to pervade modern society, and are not simply housed in separate organizations" (1970: 102). The number of organizations increases in society. If one sees organization and bureaucracy as parallel concepts (as some prefer, see item (6) above) it is easy to view society as a bureaucracy.

"The growth of organizations involves the bureaucratization of society, and that is tantamount to society becoming bureaucracy" (Albrow 1970: 105). Other exponents of this line of reasoning are Robert E. Presthus in his book *The Organizational Society* (1962), and William H. Whyte in *The Organization Man* (1956).

Semantic confusion is close at hand when one is confronted by such a multitude of definitions. Descriptive and normative meanings are mixed together. The concept of bureaucracy is multisided. It is used as a summary term for a category of persons with special administrative tasks, as a specific form of organization, and polemically and pejoratively as a criticism of certain trends in modern society. With these differing views in mind, one needs to ask the question, what strategy may be used in order to make a reasonable pattern from this confusion of definitions?

Albrow's Solution: Reject the Term "Bureaucracy"

In my view, Albrow's excellent, broad, and impressively learned book ends in an abrupt and rather defeatist manner. A major thesis of Albrow's is that the term "bureaucracy" is used, and has been used, as a label for a multitude of phenomena which have very few components in common.

In his book, he searches for a common denominator, which he feels might be found among the applications of the term made by different authors on the subject. Yet, he finishes his work by concluding that no such common denominator can be identified. Albrow does admit, however, that the concepts interlock and that they are "related, logically and historically" (1970: 125), but he goes on to say that "there is no element common to them all which could form part of a useful definition" (p. 125). Although various interpretations do overlap, Albrow apparently means that they nonetheless differ enough to have few detectable similarities. Granted, they have the same name, but just as a name may denote a family relationship, "bureaucracy" only signifies that a group of phenomena are in some way related. Here, however, the similarity ends. The only common denominator which Albrow is able to find is that the term represents "the whole gamut of issues concerning the relations of individuals to abstract organizational features." He goes so far as to recommend that social scientists stop using the word "bureaucracy." This should not be misinterpreted, however, as a recommendation to stop studying the areas which are covered by the various definitions. One ought to "avoid the use of the term 'bureaucracy' while pursuing research in the areas in which it has been employed" (1970: 125).

In Defense of the Concept of Bureaucracy

I believe there is much to be lost by throwing the term "bureaucracy" overboard. Instead of this term, we would have to use several others, each one representing a part of the problem area covered by "bureaucracy." But then we would not have any terms for *the problem area itself*. This problem area, as we have seen, is vaguely defined by Albrow and may be more precisely delineated. Albrow's approach is historical-descriptive. He tries to answer the question "how has the term 'bureaucracy' been employed in various theoretical systems and during different historical epochs?" He finds, not surprisingly, that "bureaucracy" has been employed quite generously in a large variety of contexts. For this reason, Albrow seems to feel, we should be highly sceptical of the term. He seems to suggest that by lending itself so freely to widespread use, the term "bureaucracy" can hardly be of any scientific value.

There are several objections to Albrow's position. The very terminological generosity shown in his book, and exemplified in his avoidance of *evaluating* the many and diverse applications of "bureaucracy," is what serves in the final chapter as an alibi for making a totally empty house. Instead of cleaning up among the conceptual debris, an operation which would be very natural after making such careful inventory, he simply throws it all out. This is hardly constructive, but might have been justified if it had been shown to contribute to theoretical precision and clarity.

I believe, however, that the opposite situation resulted. It is true that the term "bureaucracy" has been used to cover a multitude of organizational phenomena. But this does not imply that all such phenomena *should* be subsumed under the same label, nor that the use of the term in all these cases is *justifiable* or *scientifically fruitful*. The strategy of enumeration and examination used by Albrow is certainly reasonable, but it need not necessarily mean that all of the applications of the term must be *accepted*. Just as reasonably, Albrow's book might have ended with a discussion exhibiting the various uses of "bureaucracy" from the viewpoint of theoretical relevance and applicability in social science analysis. On this basis, an attempt could have been made to possibly exclude some of the conceptual variance. With the remainder, one might have been able to find common conceptual elements.

If Albrow is correct in his statement that no element common to *all* uses of "bureaucracy" can be found, it seems even more important to attempt to group together those interpretations that actually *have* something in common. Such an approach might contribute to increasing the precision of the concept instead of leaving one to disregard closer specifications as being impossible. In my view, the most reasonable recommendation is to examine in which contexts "bureaucracy" is not fruitful, and to explain why this is so. Then, what should be sought after is a definition which *if left out of* the discussion of bureaucracy would drastically reduce the meaningfulness of the term. In other words, we seek *a definition that is central and strategic to the debate on bureaucracy*.

It is my belief that the establishment of such a definition is possible. This, however, requires two operations. First, one must critically scrutinize the various definitions of "bureaucracy" (for these definitions, see items (1)-(7) above) with regard to their usefulness. Second, one must make a distinction between the abstract and concrete aspects of the concept of bureaucracy. To a great extent, the conceptual confusion in the field derives from the fact that these two dimensions are not kept separate.

I shall begin with the latter issue. Often, the central problem that is dealt with in theories of bureaucracy is the contradiction between two goals. On the one hand, organizations should be *effective,* but on the other hand, they should be *representative* as well, i.e., the organizations should work for the goals of their mandators. (On this concept, see p. 26 below.) "Bureaucracy" analyzed on this abstract level, represents a *tendency within an organization's administration to disengage itself from those very interests which it is supposed to work for,* i.e., the interests of those persons who are the legitimate mandators of the administration.

Such an "abstract" formulation of the problems of analysis to be found in theories of bureaucracy does not in itself require a rejection of Albrow's statement that the various definitions of bureaucracy lack common elements. It is quite conceivable that the problem area might be determined in the way I have just done, but that different definitions still do not overlap terminologically. To use a metaphor, the definitions could be "islands" in a common "sea." But even this is disputable. Looking at bureaucracy on a very concrete level, the definitions, with two exceptions to be discussed shortly, all contain some term connecting "bureaucracy" with characteristics of the administra-

tive system in organizations, or to activities carried out by it. By "administration" is meant those organization officials who are responsible
for the implementation of daily decisions, and those rules to which
they are subject or which they are expected to follow.

Common to almost all conceptualizations of bureaucracy is the fact
that these conceptualizations are used for the analysis of *the execution
of tasks* in the service of some person or group of persons. It is the
characteristics and problems of this executive stratum which are at the
center of the various theories of bureaucracy, and which are singled
out as analytical phenomena when various writers use the term "bureaucracy" (bureaucracy encompassing here (1) state administration
through officials, (2) a specific group of employed officeholders, (3)
administrative autocracy, (4) rational organization characterized by
officials ranked hierarchically, (5) inefficiency within an organization's
administration). *The administrative system* is the concrete dimension of
"bureaucracy" in the sense that it can be described through the use of
various statistical and sociological methods of measurement. The administrative system in an organization may be surveyed through descriptions of, for example, the number of officials, their social recruitment, their education, their place in the salaried hierarchy, their formal
and informal relations, task content, etc.

Essentially, the concept of bureaucracy is exhausted by these two
dimensions, the abstract and the concrete. This means that if these
two aspects are *not* included in the use of the term, it becomes almost
useless for theoretical purposes. For example, if left out, it could not
then be applied in the discussion of the three theories which will be
dealt with in Chapter 2, i.e., the Marxist conception of bureaucracy,
Weber's theory of bureaucracy, and Michel's discussion of elite formation in organizations. These three major theories would certainly fall
outside a concept which is reduced in this way.

There is another compelling reason for keeping "bureaucracy" as
a concept in the social sciences. If we rid courselves of this concept, we
lose an important means of communication with the intellectual, scientific, and political tradition represented in the social sciences by John
Stuart Mill, Karl Marx, Max Weber, and many others. The contributions
of these authors would appear historically and socially isolated, having
no clear connection with today's problems of organizational management and organizational democracy.

Let us assume that we eliminate from our language the word "democracy," a term equally ambiguous as the one which is the object of

the present discussion. We would then need new terms for different aspects of the people's sovereignty, for questions related to direct and indirect representation, equality, freedom of communication and association, etc. The works of Plato, de Tocqueville, Rousseau, Lenin, and Myrdal, to name just a few, would soon seem outdated and in large measure unintelligible.

It is now possible to return to the first of the two previously mentioned operations needed to establish a definition of "bureaucracy," i.e., the discussion of the usefulness of the various definition of bureaucracy with which the chapter began. Against the background of what has been sketched above, two determinations of "bureaucracy"—item (6), bureaucracy as equal to every modern organization, and item (7), bureaucracy as "modern society"—become difficult to accept. The terms "formal organization" and "complex organization" are already coined for the phenomena discussed by Parsons, and I cannot see what would be gained by applying "bureaucracy" also to the *general* subject of organization. For the problem of bureaucracy is only a *partial* aspect of the problem of organization, and its concrete sense it applies only to a particular subgroup within the organization. It is for the same reason that one must also object to the practice of stretching the term even further to let it represent "society as a whole." As we have already seen, this determination is based on equating "organization" with "bureaucracy." If we go this far, we are back in the misdirected terminological overgenerosity of which I have spoken above, and which leads the discussion on bureaucracy back into the conceptual debris.

The Problem of Representative Administration: the Self Indulgent Executive

"Each form of administration," says Max Weber, "demands some form of authority, since its government requires that some kind of power to give order is delegated to a certain person" (1956: 545). When the power to give orders in the organization is transferred to the administrative system, the mandator loses the possibility of exerting direct, continuous control over the organization. The transfer of executive power may take place with or against the will of the mandator. Some dictatorial person or junta may illegitimately try to control the executive, and either by persuasion or use of force cause the executive to rise against its masters. From the viewpoint of analysis of bureaucracy, however, it is far more interesting that the transfer of power typically takes place with the explicit consent of the mandator and, in fact, often with his active solicitation. In such cases, power is delegated to the administration with the goal of making the organization more effective as an instrument for the program and purposes of the manadator. As soon as power is delegated, however, the mandator may find that the administrative apparatus is no longer an obedient instrument. On the contrary, the administration may utilize its new freedom to choose lines of action other than the ones originally intended by the mandator. In the absence of continuous control, the administration can gradually strengthen its positions until, one day, it surfaces as the organization's ruling group and actual holder of power.

As one of many possible examples of this kind, let me use Stalin's seizure of power within the Russian Communist party during the 1920s to illustrate my case. The annual party congresses elected a central committee with wide-ranging authority to make decisions on party policy and to administer the party organization. The central committee, in its turn, elected the politburo. According to the original intentions, the latter was to only decide on especially urgent matters that might occur between the sessions of the central committee, which met every one to two weeks. Gradually, however, the work load of the central committee increased. Its members became more and more involved in the governmental tasks and increasingly had to spend their time away from Moscow. The central committee, therefore, "gradually and informally" delegated some if its decision-making authority to the politburo (Deutscher 1959: 75).

Stalin acted as the general secretary of the party, and together with Zinovjev and Kamenev, was able to control the politburo. The other members were Trotsky, Tomsky, Bucharin, and Lenin. The latter, however, was ill and did not participate in the politburo meetings. No coalition able to outvote the "triumvirate" could therefore be formed. But for that matter, differences of opinion among the opposition generally excluded such agreements anyway. For their part, the "triumvirate" also dominated the central committee as well as the control commission which functioned as the supreme disciplinary court of the party. The main conflict which eventually developed within the politburo was the one between Trotsky and the Stalin triumvirate. Stalin had the advantage of being able to control the recruitment to the party—a fact which, in the end, was decisive. Deutscher writes:

> [Stalin] used his wide powers of appointment to eliminate from important posts in the centre and in the provinces, members who

might be expected to follow Trotsky; and he filled the vacancies with adherents of the triumvirate or preferably of himself. He took great care to justify the promotions and demotions on the apparent merits of each case; and he was greatly assisted by the rule, which Lenin had established, that appointments should be made with reference to the number of years a member had served the Party. This rule automatically favoured the Old Guard, especially its caucus.

It was in the course of this year, the year 1923, that Stalin, making full use of this system of patronage, imperceptibly became the Party's master. The officials whom he nominated as regional or local secretaries knew that their positions and confirmation in office did not depend on the members of the organization on the spot but on the General Secretariat. Naturally they listened much more attentively to the tune called by the General Secretary than to views expressed in local Party branches. The phalanx of these secretaries now came to "substitute" itself for the Party, and even for the Old Guard of which they formed an important section. The more they grew accustomed to act uniformly under the orders of the General Secretariat, the more it was the latter which virtually substituted itself for the Party as a whole (Deutscher 1959: 105).

Somewhat later in his exposé Deutscher adds:

In truth, the Bolshevik bureaucracy was already the only organized and politically active force in society and state alike. It had appropriated the political power which had slipped from the hands of the working class; and it stood above all social classes and was *politically* independent of them all (1959: 130).

There are also other ways in which the administrative machinery may become involved in conflicts over the aims and interests which it was constructed to serve. The executive may develop into a force obstructing change and innovation precisely because of its ambitions to do its duty and fulfill its obligations to the mandator. Attachment to routine and habit, to rules and paragraphs, may become substituted for the long-term goals of the organization. That is to say, means become ends, discipline and order attain a value of their own, and administrative efficiency is transformed into perfectionism and overconformity (Merton 1957). "Bureaucracy" becomes synonymous with "rigidity," and the organization finds itself having difficulties in adjusting to changes in its environment (Crozier 1964: Ch. 7). In this way, the links with the aims and interests of the mandator are weakened, not by violent conflict, but rather by slow, steady erosion.

In the debate on bureaucracy, it is hard to find any theme which outranks this one in importance: i.e., the theme concerning the contradiction between (1) the aspirations of a certain group or class to have an active and effective administration at its disposal, and (2) the simultaneous requirement that this administration take maximum notice of the opinions of the masters. Thus the central object of the analysis of bureaucracy may be stated as *the problem of getting the administrators to govern the organization according to the wishes and ambitions of its mandator*. If this problem area is eliminated from the theory of bureaucracy, this theory, and indeed the very concept of "bureaucracy," becomes next to meaningless. The analyses of bureaucracy try to solve the contradiction between two goals that are extremely difficult to achieve simultaneously, i.e., (a) administrative efficiency and (b) representative administration. (The solutions are very often sought after within the field of participation theory, a subject with which I shall deal in Part III of this book. This problem of efficiency and representation, as we shall find in Chapter 2, is a main element within the Marxist conceptualization of bureaucracy, as well as in the non-Marxist social science treatment of the concept.

The Concepts of Mandator and Executive

As has already been stated, the analyses of bureaucracy typically deal with one and the same concrete object: the administrative system in the organization. By "administrative system"[2] I mean those persons who compose the executive group of the organization, the means of production which they have at their disposal, and their formal and informal interrelationships which are, to a substantial degree, determined by particular rules and norms. The administrative system is attached to the organization primarily because of its relationship with the mandator, i.e., those who have established the organization as a means for achieving certain goals.[3]

I shall deal with this relationship in a more detailed fashion in later sections (pp. 52-65 and Part II). In connection with this, I shall also discuss the question, inspired e.g. by March and Simon, of how modern administration theory approaches the problems of power and interest representation in organizations. In order to prepare the reader for this discussion, I shall now briefly touch upon a few items of a more formal nature. First, how does one operationally define the mandator of the organization, i.e., the party who sets up the general tasks to be carried out by the administration? Second, by what rules is the mandate transferred to the administration from its superordinates? Among other things, these rules have the function of being the basis for holding the administration responsible for the proper functioning of the organization. Thus, in this section, the emphasis is to be put on constitutional aspects. It is not uncommon for the reality of an organization to look quite different from its formal-juridical blueprint. However, it would be a mistake to ignore those formal aspects, as they are the expressions of the expectations of the mandator, and other power groups as well, vis-à-vis the administrative system.

An organization is a social unit, deliberately constructed for achieving certain goals or, more generally, for working for certain programs or lines of action. Organizations constitute resources which are means for the implementation of certain interests. Some people, usually those who have taken the initiative to establish the organization and/or have raised the funds necessary for its existence, have a more specific and usually different interest in the organization's well-being and effectiveness than do others.[4] This group of people may be labeled the *mandator* of the organization. Mandators are of different kinds, depending upon which variety of organization we choose to study and partly upon which theoretical interests and points of departure we may have. Mandators may be voters (mandators to representative assemblies and to the state), capital owners (mandators to the management of private enterprises), members of a political party (mandators to the party leaders), etc.

It is important to differentiate between the concept of mandator and another term which is used quite frequently by Scandinavian organizational writers, i.e., "stakeholder" (*intressent*). (The translation is taken from Rhenman (1968) and will be used in the discussion to follow below. The term is used by Rhenman in a way similar to "participant" in the theory of March and Simon (1958), two authors to whom Rhenman is much indebted.) The concept of stakeholder is in many ways problematical, and a *caveat* is called for. According to Rhenman, the stakeholders of an organization may be seen to subsume a wide variety of groups and institutions. In fact, the theory does not specify any limit to the number of stakeholders. As examples, Rhenman mentions owners, creditors, suppliers, employees, the state, communes, and the organization's managing group. In Rhenman's model (to be discussed more fully on pp. 117-119) these are characterized as having roughly equal power. The firm is seen as the object of everybody's concern. Conflicts and disagreements may, of course, arise. The organization, however, strives to maintain stability. In order to do this, it tries as far as possible to fulfill the requirements of the different stakeholders. Through compromise, the system seeks to establish solutions which minimize conflicts (Rhenman 1968: Ch. 3).

By using the concept "mandator," I wish to stress the fact that the power relations in an organization are rarely as pluralistic and counterbalanced as implied by Rhenman. This, of course, is hardly a novel argument, as Rhenman's theory of interest balance has been subjected to fundamental criticism by, among others, Göran Therborn et al. in *En ny vänster* (*A New Left*, 1966: 169 ff). One may question, furthermore, whether controversies between groups which are dependent upon an organization are solved primarily through compromises or whether they are settled in a more brutal manner.

Rhenman's conceptualization is made possible partly due to the fact that it ignores the historical dimension. It says nothing about the reasons why certain groups have become "stakeholders" in an organization, and how this process is related to the organization's own previous activity. If, for example, an enterprise has a monopoly situation in the product market, customers are restricted, assuming they cannot choose to ignore the product altogether, to its offers for sale and thereby *have to* become "stakeholders" in the company. Yet, this is hardly a voluntary decision. The same is true when an enterprise is in a monopoly situation with regard to the supply of employment opportunities. The employees then necessarily become "stakeholders" unless they choose to move to another place or to stay unemployed. In both of these cases, the term "stakeholder" conceals the fact that the organization exerts power, and that this exertion of power is seldom regretted by the mandator. In fact, *the explicit purpose of the mandator is often to create, via the utilization of the organizational resource, such situations of dependence.* "Thus, an increase in monopoly by a firm increases the scope and effectiveness of management authority" (Krupp 1961: 177).

Since the mandator, as a rule, cannot administer the organization entirely on his own, he requires a group of persons who are able to both supervise production (whether material or nonmaterial) and oversee organizational activities in such a way as to stay within the interests of the mandator. Simply stated, the mandator requires a group of persons who constitutes the organization's executive group. The members of the executive are usually of two kinds. Some are elected for certain terms and are, more than others, expected to be the true interpreters of the mandator's intentions. Others are hired to carry out executive tasks. (Very often, persons in the latter category can count among their merits the fact that they have had good connections with the mandator before their employment. For example, they may have worked as supporters of a political party or as members of a trade union.) Within business enterprises, the elected members of the executive make up the management board, whereas the hired executives are in positions of managing directors and their subordinates. A parallel distinction can be made in the state organization between the concepts "government" and "public officials."

Who is a mandator? As already mentioned, such person or group can often be identified as the initiator of the organization and/or the partial or complete financer of its activities, e.g., through the purchase of shares, payment of membership dues, or other modes of voluntary economic support. However, the criterion of "initiator" is often insufficient since an organization may and often does have a life-span longer than that of the people who were its originators.[5] The economic criterion is likewise dubious since economic enterprises, as well as voluntary interest associations, often acquire economic support from sources other than the mandator. Note the fact that the income of enterprises primarily derives from the selling of products and services, and that the financing of interest associations is often accomplished by utilizing state and communal funds.

Which definition, then, may be employed? One possibility is to start with the distinction between formal rights and actual power within the organization. That is to say, one can determine who is the mandator of an organization in terms of formal rights, leaving as an empirical question the extent to which these formal rights coincide with actual power. Almost without exception, organizations have some kind of constitution (e.g., bylaws, a charter) which states who is the mandator and how the tasks of the organization are to be defined. The mandator may therefore be operationally defined as the person (or collective of persons) who has the formal right to appoint and dismiss the executive group: capital owners, members, voters, etc.

One advantage of this definition is that it is fairly easy to apply in empirical research situations. Another more important advantage is that this definition does not classify everyone who is working within the organization as a "member" of it (cf., pp. 167-169). Rather, it views one's membership as being contingent upon the degree to which a certain actor has acquired the right to take part in the appointment of the executive.

Formal rights, of course, are not the same as actual power. The intentions that a mandator may have had in setting up an organization may become eroded, transmuted, displaced, and perhaps even openly counteracted. The executive group may divert itself from the goals and purposes of the mandator, thus slowly abdicating its original function as representatives of the mandator. We shall shortly return to this problem as it constitutes the main theme in the analysis of bureaucracy and lies at the center of most of the important contributions to this debate.

On Rules and Relations

The relations within the administrative system, as well as between the administration and the rest of the organization, are determined and restricted by different kinds of formal and informal rules. I shall limit myself here to the formal rules since the informal ones depend to a large degree on conditions specific to each organization, making a classification somewhat difficult.

There are at least four kinds of rules which regulate the daily activities of the executive. First, there are *goal formulations* which state the general aims and purposes of the organization, and indicate the recommended directions to be taken by the executive. Second, there are *procedural rules* which indicate those routines which are to be followed in the execution of tasks, and which lay down the manner in which the coordination between the various officeholders is to be accomplished. For example, there are rules for the handling and the registration of important documents, routines for employing and dismissing personnel, rules dealing with accounting procedures, etc. Third, there is a special group of rules which *delimit the area of executive competence* and define those kinds of decisions which the executive is not entitled to make. These rules, for example, may prohibit the sale of property belonging to the mandator, or deal with entering into coalitions with other organizations. Fourth, there are rules which are formalizations of *requirements* directed against the organization *from external power centers,* such as state and judicial authorities. These rules usually come in the form of laws, and concern, for example, the right to classify written material, the organization's responsibilities to its employees, and the rights and duties of public officials.

Summary

Theories of bureaucracy deal with different aspects of the general problem area as sketched out above, i.e., the contradiction between administrative efficiency and representative administration. Their concrete object and unit of study is the administrative system in a particular organizational structure. This structure varies according to the interests of the analyst. To some, it is the state apparatus, while to others, it is complex organizations in general.

Different theories view the functions of bureaucracy differently, and oftentimes their evaluations of the role of the administrative system vary considerably. It is precisely this fact that makes a synthesis of the debate on bureaucracy so exceedingly difficult. That is, the *evaluations* of bureaucracy are at the center of the different theories, and it is these very evaluations which are often sharply at variance with one another.

We can now turn to the study of three theoretical systems whose evaluations of bureaucracy diverge in several important respects. We shall deal with the conceptualizations represented, first, by classical Marxism, second, by Max Weber, and third, by Robert Michels. The title of Part I refers to the different explanations of the emergence of bureaucracy given by these three schools or research traditions. According to the Marxist view, bureaucracy is connected with the capitalist state, and the emergence of bureaucracy is seen as contingent upon the economic, social, and political changes which brought about the rise of this state. Whereas the Weberian view emphasizes the importance of economic and other power resources for the emergence of bureaucracy, at the same time it stresses the importance of various conditions directly related to mechanisms internal to the organization. Finally, Michels' theory strongly stresses an inner-logical, immanent explanation for the emergence of bureaucracy. He sees the organization itself as the carrier of forces towards increased power concentration and oligarchy. All three of these traditions, however, have in common the fact that they view bureaucratic tendencies, i.e., the transfer of administrative power to a special stratum of experts, as a definite challenge to democratic principles. They all see the problems inherent in an attempt to eliminate bureaucracy,[6] and furthermore, they see that the key to the elimination of bureaucracy is to be found in an understanding of how bureaucracy emerges.

NOTES

1. A consistent theme in Albrow's treatment of Weber is Albrow's thesis that these results may not be used to criticize Weber. According to Albrow, Weber was not interested in the question of the efficiency of rational organization. "It would be quite misleading," says Albrow, "to equate Weber's concept of formal rationality with the idea of efficiency." (1970: 63). "The novel, unique, and for later commentators disturbing feature of Max Weber's account of bureaucracy was his utter disregard for the problems of efficiency" (1970: 66).

Granted, one cannot equate formal rationality (one of Weber's main concepts) and efficiency. Nonetheless, Albrow's thesis is put too categorically. Weber himself emphasized that the bureaucratic type of administration was capable of reaching the "highest degree of efficiency" and used formulations which can hardly be interpreted otherwise than as support by Weber for the thought that bureaucracy is superior in a technical sense. As Sten Johansson has succinctly pointed out, the German terms used by Weber to describe his theoretical creation, beautifully illustrate this. According to Weber, bureaucracy gives maximum profit with regard to "Präzision, Schnelligkeit, Eindeutigkeit, Aktenkundigkeit, Kontinuerlichkeit, Diskrätion, Einheitlichkeit, straffe Unterordnung, Ersparnisse und Reibungen, sachlichen und persönlichen Kosten" (Johansson 1970: 54; Weber 1968: 973).

2. The term "system" is here used only as a summary formulation for several organizational elements that should be treated together. It does not serve as a point of departure for a general system-theoretical analysis of administration. As will become clear in Part II, I am not convinced about the advantages of such an analysis. The view of organizations as "wheels within wheels within wheels" seems to me to divert one's attention from what is perhaps most central in all organizational analysis, i.e., the study of power and influence applied in a conscious and rational manner.

3. The development and shaping of these goals, like the use of organizational resources, should not be construed as a limited problem of rational choice. On the contrary, economic, political, and other factors set explicit limits on how freely goals and means may be chosen. However, subjective aspects do have to be included in organizational theory, as a partial explanation of the behavior of collective actors. "The action possibilities of each person and the number of possible action alternatives are subordinated to and encircled by external objective conditions. It is within the framework of this relatively strictly determined area that the behavior motives of the actors and their subjective orientation play a definite role" (Berntson 1974: 35). (See further Part II, Ch. 10).

4. More about the concept of effectiveness will follow later (pp. 142-143 and 148 ff.) However, two determinations of this concept should be pointed out immediately. According to one of these determinations, effectiveness is equal to the degree of goal implementation; according to the other, the organization is effective to the extent that the value of its output exceeds the value of its input.

5. There is cause here for stressing that the criterion "initiators" should not be confused with the initial *goals* which were perhaps important when the organization was formed. Although the original initiators may be identical to the mandators of the organization today, the original motives for the creation of the

organization may differ quite a bit from the motives that are salient to the mandator today. (Regarding the difficulties of defining an organization in terms of its goals, see Silverman 1970: 9; also Part II of this book, pp. 142ff.).

6. A note is justified here concerning the use of the terms "bureaucratism" and "bureaucratization." Sometimes these terms appear as synonyms. Poulantzas, for example, uses them both as representing "the political impact of bourgeois ideology on the state" (1975: 332). The most common use of these two terms, however, is that "bureaucratism" is employed in a clearly pejorative sense, whereas "bureaucratization" is used descriptively to represent a growing dominance of rational-bureaucratic forms of government. In his historical survey of the use of the concept of bureaucracy, Albrow stresses the fact that "bureaucratism" has often been given the meaning "bureaucratic abuses," whereas "bureaucratization," in reference to Weber, signifies the successive growth of bureaucratic types of organization (Albrow 1970: 45-46).

Chapter 2

THEORIES OF BUREAUCRACY

The Emergence of Bureaucracy —
Outer Forces or Inner Logic?

One of the dominating impulses behind many different treatments and theories of bureaucracy is the conviction that it is a negative social element; that it is a repressive force and a parasite (Marx, *Kritik des Hegelschens Staatsrechts*; Lenin, *The State and Revolution*); that it is undemocratic and an outgrowth of illegitimate power concentration (Mill, *On Liberty,* and other writings; Michels, *Political Parties*); that it constitutes a "new class" greedy for power (Djilas, *The New Class*); that it is dysfunctional and leads to the ossification of organizational forms (Merton, "The bureaucratic personality," Crozier, *The Bureaucratic Phenomenon*). Weber, too, in some contexts found reason to emphasize the risk that bureaucracy may develop into an illegitimate political force (e.g., in his article, "Parliament and government in a reconstructed Germany").

The *normative* nature of theories of bureaucracy should be especially emphasized. Bureaucracy is described as an unnatural and undemocratic force. Therefore, it should be eliminated, or its negative effects at least attenuated. But how is this to be brought about? For the analysts of bureaucracy, the answer to this question is closely related to the question of the emergence of bureaucracy. In the genesis of bureaucracy, the key to its eradication is contained. And since opinions on the causes of bureaucracy vary strongly between the different authors on the subject, it is hardly surprising that the suggestions concerning how society is going to rid itself of bureaucracy also differ, sometimes dramatically.

One writer (Heiskanen 1967) has criticized theories of bureaucracy for being "underdeveloped": "The generalizations, hypotheses, and suggested theories are on so low a level of generality and so dispersed theoretically from each other that they do not have much value over and above that of sheer descriptions" (p. 115; cf. also p. 108). His aim is to coordinate all formulations on bureaucracy under one common theoretical roof in order to finally arrive at a unified theory of bureaucracy. In his discussion, he suggests measures which are "needed in order that the theories of bureaucracy could move toward theoretical unification and proper scientific explanations" (p. 114). One such measure is trying to treat both "bureaucratization" and "debureaucratization" within "a common frame of reference" (p. 113).

This, I believe, is altogether impossible. As the following sections will hopefully serve to demonstrate, the views and ideas of different authors concerning the emergence of bureaucracy are so distant from each other as to render unification impossible. Among other things, such a unification would have to reconcile the Marxist view of bureaucracy, connected as it is with the bourgeois state, with Michels' idea that oligarchy is immanent in the organizational principle as such. Furthermore, it would have to combine optimistic perceptions of man's capacity for self-government with pessimistic conceptions which emphasize man's continued subordination under elites; etc. Additionally, because theories of the emergence of bureaucracy differ widely, the same is true about ideas of "debureaucratization." The latter are usually contained in the former.

As we shall find, these different images of bureaucracy are also connected with different perceptions concerning the autonomy of bureaucracy, i.e., the extent to which it may be independent of its mandators. Within the Marxist tradition, bureaucracy, as a matter of definition, is seen as tied to the capitalist state, and is therefore a "bourgeois" phenomenon. Whereas in Michels' writings various administrative deformation processes tend to bring about an autonomous social category, i.e., an oligarchy, Weber is more ambiguous. He sometimes describes bureaucracy as an animated machine, activated only by specific orders. Sometimes he sees it as possessing a considerable power of its own, a power deriving from its expertise and specialized knowledge.

Marx and Lenin on Bureaucracy

Karl Marx' conception of bureaucracy and his views concerning its social functions have to be related to his interpretation of the character of the state. The basic theses are developed in his critique of Hegel's *Grundlinien der Philosophie des Rechts* (Marx, *Kritik des Hegelschen Staatsrechts*) where Marx attacks the Hegelian idea of the state as representative of the common interest. The contradiction between Hegel and Marx is described by Albrow in the following way:

> In the great ideological systems one may distinguish two major theories of the distribution of power in society. In the one, those who held power were justified in either religious or secular metaphysical terms. They had a mission to perform for God or society and their servants, the public officials, shared in that purpose. In the other, power was the product of a group's place in the economic order of society. Officials were simply the agents of government, the instruments of the dominant class. We can see these two essentially simple standpoints elaborated by Hegel and Marx respectively (Albrow 1970: 31).

According to Hegel, administration through officials is a link between, on the one hand, the state, and on the other hand, the various groups and strata in society: State bureaucracy is "the medium through which this passage from the particular to the general interest becomes possible," as Mouzelis (1967: 8) expresses it. Above the particular interests of corporations and local communities the supreme reason is located. It is embodied in the leadership of the state, the state executive with the monarch as the supreme head.[1] What, then, does Hegel include in the concept of executive?

> In its broadest sense it includes the activities of the police and the judiciary, but since these bear more directly on the affairs of civil society they are included within it. The state executive *sensu stricto* is organized hierarchically and comprises (a) ordinary civil servants at the bottom, (b) higher advisory officials above them, and (c) supreme heads of department 'who are in direct contact with the monarch' (Pelczynski 1964: 126).

The public officials are the servants of the state and not servants of the king himself. Hegel's conception of the rational state includes as one important element the idea of "a corps of public servants, independent of the good will of the monarch and his Ministry, dedicated to the interest of the state and with a loyalty transcending that to any particular person" (Pelczynski 1964: 102).

In contrast to this, Marx maintained that the state does not represent any "common interest," but rather, the interests of the ruling class. The state and its executive constitute an instrument through which this elite class expresses its power. Bureaucracy fulfills the function of contributing to the consolidation of class differences, and of supporting the power of the ruling class. "In bureaucracy the identity of the interests of state and of the particular private purpose is so established that the interests of state become a particular private purpose confronting other private purposes" (quoted from Albrow 1970: 69). At the same time, bureaucracy has the task of concealing the actual power relationships, and to function as "the general interest smoke screen between exploiters and exploited" (Mouzelis 1967: 9). Bureaucracy contributes to the alienation of the people: "Bureaucracy becomes an autonomous and oppressive force which is felt by the majority of the people as a mysterious and distant entity—as something which, although regulating their lives, is beyond their control and comprehension, a sort of divinity in the face of which one feels helpless and bewildered" (Mouzelis 1967: 10; cf. also Albrow 1970: 68-70).

THE EMERGENCE OF BUREAUCRACY

For Marx, bureaucracy is a social force through which the interests of capitalism and the bourgeoisie are implemented. The issue of the emergence of bureaucracy and of its continued existence is hence inextricably connected with the wider topic of the character of the capitalist state. Here we find the point of departure for the Marxist analysis of bureaucracy, starting with very broad formulations by Marx himself, and developed in greater detail by Lenin, and later by Poulantzas. Here we also find the reason for the continuous controversy within Marxism concerning the problem of whether the executive groups in the Soviet Union and other socialist states have become a "new class" or not. According to the classical view, this is not possible. According to certain "revisionist" theories, however, the existence of the "new class" is an empirical fact. We will return to this question below (p. 44).

According to Marx, the state is "nothing more than the form of organization which the bourgeois necessarily adopt . . . for the mutual guarantee of their property and interests" (*The German Ideology*, quoted from Albrow 1970: 70). In his critique of the Gotha program, Marx underscores the fact that the state can never be seen as "an independent entity that possesses its own intellectual, ethical, and libertarian bases" (Albrow 1970: 70).

Perhaps the most influential further development of these thoughts is Lenin's *The State and Revolution*. In this book, Lenin comments on Marx' work *Louis Bonaparte's 18th Brumaire*. He also discusses the problem of transcience from bourgeois to proletarian state and comments on the connection between the ruling class and the state's executive power.

> The centralized state power that is peculiar to bourgeois society came into being in the period of the fall of absolutism. Two institutions are most characteristic of these state machine: bureaucracy and a standing army. In their works, Marx and Engels repeatedly mention the thousand threads which connect these institutions with the bourgeoisie. The experience of every worker illustrates this connection in an extremely striking and impressive manner. . . . The bureaucracy and standing army are a 'parasite' on the body of bourgeois society—a parasite created by the inherent antagonisms which rend that society, but a parasite which 'chokes all its pores' of life (Lenin, *Selected Works*, Vol. VII: 29).

Somewhat later in the book, Lenin explicates his thesis about the association between the bureaucracy and bourgeois interests. In a commentary to the debate between Kautsky and Pannekoek, he states that the experience of the Paris Commune of 1871 clearly shows that the state functionaries in a socialist system will relinquish their roles as "bureaucrats" or "public officials." The problem raised by Kautsky and Pannekoek concerns the bureaucratization of the workers' political and trade union organizations. Lenin recognizes that such bureaucratization affects these organizations as well, but puts the blame for this on the impact of the capitalist system. The following quotations also clearly shows that Lenin perceives a basic element in bureaucracy (or "bureaucratism") to be its isolation from the majority of the people.

> Under capitalism democracy is restricted, cramped, curtailed, mutilated by all the conditions of wage-slavery, the poverty and misery of the masses. This is why and the only reason why the

officials of our political and industrial organizations are cor-
rupted—or, more precisely, tend to be corrputed—by the conditions of capitalism, why they betray a tendency to become
transformed into bureaucrats, i.e., into privileged persons di-
vorced from the masses and *superior to* the masses.

This is the *essence* of bureaucracy, and until the capitalists have
been expropriated and the bourgeoisie overthrown, *even* proletarian officials will inevitably be "bureaucratized" to some extent (Lenin, *Selected Works,* Vol. VII: 107).

The bureaucracy is an administrative category separated from the
masses by means of particular prerogatives, playing the role of representatives for the capitalist class.

The State and Revolution, however, was completed before the big
societal and political transformations in Russia after 1917. It would be
interesting to study what Lenin's view of bureaucracy looked like after
the end of these revolutionary events. To what degree had the attacks
against the old order also meant an end to the bourgeois character of
the administration and its ties with the aristocracy? Had the revolution
been successful in the sense which Lenin saw as one of the most important, i.e., the broadening of the administration of society and making it a task for all citizens, thereby exterminating the "parasite" of
bureaucracy?

At the 8th Congress of the Bolshevik party in 1919, Lenin read a
report on the work in progress concerning the revision of the party
program. Among other things, he dealt with the problem of the so-
called "bourgeois experts" and their relatively privileged positions. It
was true, Lenin said, that the revolution had meant a substantial reduction in the salary differences between experts and workers. Before the
revolution, the experts were paid roughly twenty times more than the
workers; after the revolution, the relationship was something around
five to one. However, this still meant that the experts were overpaid
and that the principle of equal pay was set aside. In spite of this, the
differences could easily be explained by the need for the development
of the productive forces, and this was impossible without the "bourgeois experts" (Lenin, *Selected Works,* Vol. VIII: 350). Furthermore,
they could not be made to work effectively if persuaded by force.

We must not practice a policy of petty pinpricks with regard to
the experts. These experts are not the servitors of the exploiters,
they are active cultural workers, who in bourgeois society served

the bourgeoisie, and of whom all socialists all over the world said that in a proletarian society they would serve *us*. In this transition period we must endow them with the best possible conditions of life. That will be the best policy. That will be the most economical management (p. 351).

The need for economic and cultural rearmament was thus subordinated to the specific question of the position of the "bourgeois experts." A year earlier, Lenin had admitted that this was "a step back," although a necessary one considering "the principles of proletarian power" (in the essay, "The immediate tasks of the Soviet government," written in the spring of 1918; *Selected Works,* Vol. VII: 323).

What, then, was the situation of the bureaucracy, i.e., the executive stratum which had enjoyed a highly privileged position during the Tsarist regime and which Lenin had accused of being "isolated from and standing above the masses?" Had the revolution been forced to accept an administration run by bourgeois officials? Lenin, in his commentary to the party program, dealt with this question in the following way:

> The next question which . . . falls to my share is the *question of bureaucracy and of enlisting the broad masses in Soviet work*. We have been hearing complaints about bureaucracy for a long time; the complaints are undoubtedly well founded. We have done what no other state has done in the fight against bureaucracy. The apparatus which was a thoroughly bureaucratic and bourgeois apparatus of oppression, and which remains such even in the freest of bourgeois republics, we have destroyed to its very foundations. [One example is provided by the courts, which were transformed into people's tribunals.]

> The employees in the other spheres are more hardened bureaucrats. The task here is more difficult. We cannot live without this apparatus; every branch of government creates a demand for such an apparatus. Here we are suffering from the fact that Russia was not sufficiently developed capitalistically. [In Germany conditions were different, since the bureaucrats there were better educated.]

> [During the revolutionary upheavals, the bureaucrats from the Tsaristic time had been shaken up and placed in new posts. But they did not remain there. They tried to regain their old positions.] The Tsarist bureaucrats began to enter the Soviet institutions and practice their bureaucratic methods, they began to as-

sume the colouring of Communists and, for greater success in their careers, to procure membership cards of the Russian Communist Party. And so, having been thrown out of the door, they fly in through the window! (*Selected Works,* Vol. VIII: 353).

According to Lenin, the bureaucracy could be defeated only if the whole people could be mobilized to participate in the administration of the state. In bourgeois republics, this was not only practically impossible but the law itself prevented it. In Russia the legal obstacles had been cleared away by the revolution, and yet the working masses did not participate in the management of the affairs of the state. Why? Lenin contends that the solution to this problem lies in an improvement of education, a rise in the cultural level of the people, and a better organization of the working class. "Bureaucracy has been defeated. The exploiters have been eliminated. But the cultural level has not been raised, and therefore the bureaucrats are occupying their old positions. They can be forced out only if the proletariat and the peasantry are organized far more widely than has hitherto been the case, and only if real measures are taken to enlist the workers in the work of government" (*Selected Works,* Vol. VIII: 354).

Bureaucracy had been defeated, yet the *bureaucrats* had remained in their old positions. This, in a nutshell, shows the immense practical problems which stand in the way of representative administration— problems deriving from a crippled national economy, cultural underdevelopment, and century-old, firmly established privileges. The law may be changed, the principles of popular administration may be laid down, and a certain reshuffling in the old bureaucratic stratum may be carried out. But as long as new administrators cannot be recruited from the previous underprivileged classes, the old ones will continue to "fly in through the window."

A possible interpretation of Lenin's seemingly paradoxical formulation is that the earlier *function* of bureaucracy, i.e., being an instrument of the bourgeois class, had ceased, but that the *effects* of the bureaucratic system survived, e.g., in the practice of recruitment of personnel to the Soviet administration. According to the theory, a bureaucratic structure could no longer exist once the proletariat had established its power. Since the previous ruling class had been defeated, the necessary material and political basis of bureaucracy had vanished. The *tendencies* of bureaucratization were still a troublesome fact, however, and Lenin discussed them in several contexts. (For one example, see p. 45 below). These tendencies could be seen as depending on various "hibernating" characteristics of the individuals who formed the basis of the old bureaucracy, i.e., the information about the state which they had previously acquired; different kinds of strategic administrative knowledge; their bourgeois social background; and their generally privileged social position.

It is obvious that concession to the effect that a bureaucratic structure exists in the socialist society has far more serious consequences for classical Marxist theory than a recognition of the problem of "in-flying bureaucrats" or the existence of "petty-bourgeois elements" in the administration. The former recognition leaves the door open for accusations that state government is dominated by a "new class," and that the party and state officials no longer work for the true interests of the people.[2]

AUTONOMY OF THE BUREAUCRACY

Following Marx' own views, the Marxist tradition treats bureaucracy as one element in the power exertion of the ruling class. Bureaucracy is perceived as organically tied to the capitalist state. This is perhaps the most fundamental component in the Marxist conception of bureaucracy. *Bureaucracy cannot be treated as an independent unit of analysis*. It must be scrutinized against the background of its direct or indirect connections with the bourgeoisie. A revolt by the bureaucracy which strikes at the root and basis of the ruling class is not possible, according to this view.

Empirically it may appear as if, now and then, the bureaucracy gets involved in conflicts against the capitalist class. The bureaucracy is not a part of this class in the sense that it owns means of production. Contradictions between the real owners and their administrators may therefore arise. But if such conflicts develop, they can never go beyond certain limits which are determined by "the existing forces and relations of production" (Mouzelis 1967: 9). The state apparatus, including the bureaucracy, constitutes "the organized power of economically based classes" (Albrow 1970: 70). To the extent that this power is undermined by economic and political events, the position of the bureaucracy will also become weakened.

As Albrow points out, it would have been fatal to Marx' theory, had he acknowledged the existence of bureaucracy as an autonomous social force (or, even more serious, as a particular class) with possibilities of appropriating autonomous power.

Any suggestion that the body which merely implemented the formal arrangements of government could become a determining influence on the future of society would have run counter to the belief that nothing could prevent economic forces producing the polarization of society into bourgeois and proletariat (Albrow 1970: 70).

Here we find the reason why orthodox Marxism rejects the idea of bureaucracy as a "new class." This idea has acquired perhaps its most well-known spokesman in Milovan Djilas (1957), but is also represented by Bruno Rizzi (*The Bureaucratization of the World,* 1939) and by several writers within the Yugoslav anti-etatist tradition (e.g., Marković 1972; Stojanović 1970; Horvat 1969: 195ff.). The de facto utilization of the means of production by the bureaucracy and the possibilities by the party officials to dictate the principles of social development (often in contradiction to democratic principles) is used by them as their point of departure for a criticism of etatistic traits in socialist societies.

According to Marković, the dominance by the state and party apparatus has a number of fatal consequences for democracy, among others "the keeping back of initiatives at the economic microlevel, the formalization of political activities resulting in a widespread passivity among the masses, and a subordination of all areas of creativity to politics, careerism, moral dissolution, etc." (1972: 126). The etatist system is dominated by a bureaucracy, which is defined as "a unified, closed working group consisting of professional politicians who control all decision-making and enjoy considerable economic and political privileges" (1972: 126). The elimination of the role of professional politician therefore becomes an important condition for the realization of democracy. "If professional politics were to disappear as a special task area within the social distribution of work, the nature of the political organizations could be fundamentally changed. A party ... could gradually be replaced by a plurality of flexible political organizations. ... The significant characteristic of the political organizations would be the absence of permanent party machinery and party bureaucracy" (1972: 224).

If we, like Marković, recognize bureaucracy as an autonomous political force, it will no longer be possible to associate it with the bourgeois state as a matter of definition. Regardless of whether one goes so far as to see bureaucracy as a new class or more generally points out its possibilities of working for its own particular interests, the making of assumptions concerning the potential autonomy of bureaucracy confronts the Marxist theory of bureaucracy with two difficult questions. First, as Albrow points out, the question of whether the thesis of a polarization of society into two antagonistic classes is tenable. Second, the question of whether socialist society can get free from accusations that a parasitic stratum has emerged, a stratum of officials which appropriates all or part of the surplus value for themselves, and which acquires material and social privileges at the expense of the working class.[3]

When the revolution is still in its infancy, the thesis of an association between the bureaucracy and the capitalist state involves no serious theoretical problems. Indeed, it might well be the case that the smashing of the capitalist state brings an end to the privileges of the administrative group. Politically a polemic point may be made in showing the relationship between, on the one hand, the state power that one wants to abolish and, on the other, authorities which function repressively and generally parasitically—"standing army, police, bureaucracy, clergy, and judicature—organs wrought after the plan of a systematic and hierarchic division of labor" (Marx 1933: 37).

Lenin saw that the bureaucratic apparatus did not diminish, but on the contrary, tended to consolidate itself. How did he explain these tendencies, which so clearly deviated from his theory in *The State and Revolution*? As we have seen above, his solution was first and foremost to stick to the theory. The bureaucracy *had* been defeated, but the time was not yet ripe to completely transfer the administration into the hands of the people. Mouzelis comments on Lenin's "The Tax in Kind": "Lenin explains it [i.e., the remaining bureaucracy] as a sign of the 'immaturity of socialism.' The civil war and the ensuing chaotic state of the economy partially account for it. Moreover such factors as the nonsocialist relations of production between the workers and the peasants, the still existing small bourgeoisie and the tsarist bureaucrat with his feudal mentality, constitute a fertile soil for the further strengthening of bureaucracy" (Mouzelis 1969: 12).

The key to the abolishment of bureaucratic malfunctions was to be found in the development of the productive forces.

According to Lenin, the cure for this bureaucratization will come automatically when economic development is achieved. In the long term, it is increasing industrialization which will constitute the objective basis for a final victory over bureaucracy (Mouzelis 1969: 12).

To the extent that the means of production are socialized and production becomes more effective, the petty-bourgeois strata will diminish in number and the "tsarist bureaucrats" will die away. Socialist relations of production will clear away bourgeois-capitalist bureaucratic remains.

TROTSKY ON THE AUTONOMY OF BUREAUCRACY

About a decade after Lenin's death, Trotsky published his critical evaluation of the young Soviet state in his book, *The Revolution Betrayed* (1936/1969). In this book he refers to Lenin's words about the disappearance due to the revolution of the "parasite on the body of bourgeois society" (1969: 41). According to the party program, the state as a bureaucratic apparatus was to begin withering away on the very first day of proletarian dictatorship. "This is what the Party program says: and it has still not been cancelled. Strange: it sounds like a voice of a ghost from out of the mausoleum. . . . Bureaucracy has not only refused to disappear, as it could have done by entrusting its role to the masses, but it has become an uncontrolled power which dominates the people" (1969: 42).

But is this the same as saying that the bureaucracy has become a new class? To Trotsky's mind, this would not be scientifically defensible.

> The attempt to depict the Soviet bureaucracy as a class of "state capitalists" obviously cannot withstand criticism. Bureaucracy owns neither shares not state bonds. It is recruited, replenished, and renewed as an administrative hierarchy, independently of property relationships. The individual bureaucrat cannot transfer the right to exploit the state apparatus to his heirs. *Bureaucracy enjoys its privileges in the form of power abuse* (1969: 179-180; italics mine).

Thus, we observe how Trotsky takes great care not to fall into the trap of defining a new, third class between capital owners and the proletariat. Bureaucracy is not a class, since it does not own the means of production. The difference in actual political practice between *ownership* and the ability to *control the use* of these means may appear small. As Albrow has pointed out (1970: 70), however, it is highly significant for the interpretation of, and belief in, the polarization thesis.

Although denying that bureaucracy has become a new class, Trotsky does not dispute its autonomy. On the contrary, he explicitly stresses it.

The means of production belong to the state. But the state "belongs" to the bureaucracy, so to speak. . . . In its intermediary and regulatory function, in its concern for preserving the social rank hierarchy, and in its exploitation of the state apparatus for personal purposes, the Soviet bureaucracy resembles any other bureaucracy, especially the fascist one. But it is also widely different. Under no other regime has bureaucracy reached such a degree of autonomy from the dominating class (1969: 179). . . . As a conscious political force, the bureaucracy has betrayed the revolution (1969: 181).

Although formally adhering to the classical Marxist tradition by denying the autonomous class-in-itself perspective on bureaucracy, Trotsky is clear in his judgment. Bureaucracy has the character of an independent, exploitative force. Also, according to Trotsky, socialist production relations are far from sufficient for clearing away the administrative remnants of bourgeois-capitalist society.

THE ELIMINATION OF BUREAUCRACY

The answer of classical Marxism to the question of how bureaucracy is to be eliminated, has already been suggested. Since bureaucracy, as a matter of definition, is connected to the bourgeois state, a proletarian revolution against the latter will also create the conditions necessary for the elimination of bureaucracy.

The discussion of bureaucracy by Lenin is carried out within a general theoretical framework dealing with the change of the character of the state resulting from the transformation of society to communism. Kupferberg (1974) summarizes:

After the revolution, a proletarian state is established. A proletarian class dictatorship will, during the transformation period, by the help of the state officials defend and promote the class interest of the proletariat until communism has finally become implemented. When these preconditions have been fulfilled, the class dictatorship can be abolished. However, the state will not immediately cease to exist, but rather will "die away" as the tasks of administration are distributed among all members of the society.

The state will remain as an instrument to support "bourgeois law" during the transient phase which Lenin called socialism. The state will be responsible for the regulation of distribution, "to each one according to his work." But as soon as the distribution of

labor has been abolished, development of the productive forces
has taken place, and work is no longer a means of existence but
man's most important need, the necessity of this "bourgeois law"
and the last remains of the state apparatus will be eliminated.
Society can, then, distribute resources "to each one according
to his needs."

The struggle against bureaucracy is one of the first tasks of the revolution. In his analysis of the Paris Commune, Marx had indicated the
most important steps in this struggle.

The first decree of the Commune . . . was the suppression of the
standing army and the substitution for it of the armed people.

The Commune was formed of the municipal councillors, chosen
by universal suffrage in various wards of the town, responsible
and revocable at short terms. The majority of its members were
naturally working men, or acknowledged representatives of the
working class. The Commune was to be a working, not a parliamentary body, executive and legislative at the same time. [The
police and the officials were transformed into responsible agents
of the Commune and were revocable at all times.] From the
members of the Commune downwards, the public service had to
be done at *workmen's wages*. The vested interests and the representation allowances of the high dignitaries of the State dis-
appeared along with the high dignitaries themselves. Public
functions ceased to be the private property of the tools of the
Central Government (Marx 1933: 40).

"This," says Lenin in *State and Revolution*, "is a case of 'quantity becoming transformed into quality': democracy, introduced as fully and
consistently as is generally conceivable, is transformed from bourgeois
democracy into proletarian democracy: from the state (*i.e.,* a special
force for the suppression of a particular class) into something which is
no longer really a state" (*Selected Works* VII: 41).[4]

Thus, the basic modes for replacing a state machinery which has
been crushed by the revolution, are (1) that each public official should
be eligible for immediate recall; (2) that the salaries of public officials
should not exceed the wages of ordinary workers; and (3) that administrative tasks should be simplified and allowed to rotate among all members of the commune. (Technical specialists constitute a special category. Therefore, engineers and agricultural experts are not included in
the category "administration" [*Selected Works,* VII: 92]). Lenin made
the following arguments:

(1) and (2) Eligibility and Wage Equality

All officials, without exception, elected and subject to recall *at any time,* their salaries reduced to the level of 'workmen's wages'— these simple and 'self-evident' democratic measures, while completely uniting the interests of the workers and the majority of the peasants, at the same time serve as the bridge between capitalism and socialism. . . . 'The Commune,' Marx wrote, 'made that catchword of bourgeois revolutions, cheap government, a reality by destroying the two greatest sources of expenditure— the standing army and state functionaries' (*Selected Works,* VII: 42-43).

(3) Administrative Tasks Should Be Simplified and Allowed To Rotate Among All Citizens

For, in order to abolish the state, the functions of the Civil Service must be converted into the simple operations of control and accounting that can be performed by the vast majority of the population, and, ultimately, by every single individual (*Selected Works,* VII: 71; cf. Max Weber's definition of "direct democracy," 1968: 948). If, indeed, *all* take part in the administration of the state, capitalism cannot retain its hold. The development of capitalism, in turn, itself creates the *prerequisites* that *enable* indeed "all" to take part in the administration of the state. Some of these prerequisites are: universal literacy, already achieved in most of the advanced capitalist countries, the "training and disciplining" of millions of workers by the huge, complex and socialized apparatus of the post-office, the railways, the big factories, large-scale commerce, banking, etc. etc. . . . *All* citizens become employees and workers of a *single*, national state syndicate. All that is required is that they should work equally—do their proper share of work— and get paid equally. The accounting and control necessary for this have been so utterly *simplified* by capitalism that they have become the extraordinarily simple operations of checking, recording and issuing receipts, which anyone who can read or write and who knows the first four rules of arithmetic can perform (*Selected Works,* VII: 92-93).

In communist society, where no exploitation and no class differences exist, bureaucracy becomes superfluous. Bureaucracy is "absorbed" by society (Mouzelis 1976: 11), and the administrative tasks lose their exploitative character. In the new society, the administrative system occupies itself with the administration of things and not, as was the case with bourgeois bureaucracy, the administration of people.

The development of the productive forces creates, first, the possibilities of education for all, and, second, the preconditions for the simplification of administrative operations so that an elementary knowledge of writing and arithmetic is sufficient for mastering them. It is in this way, according to Lenin, that it becomes possible to distribute administrative tasks among all citizens (with the exception of the technical specialists whose services society could not do without), and as a consequence, to give everyone equal remuneration for his services.

I will not discuss in this context the reasonableness of the preconditions on which Lenin bases his program for the elimination of bureaucracy, nor will I comment on the observable deviations of today's Soviet society from Lenin's model. However, I do want to stress that the solutions to the problems of bureaucracy must be one of the most important undertakings in any attempt to realize a system capable of self-government. The problems brought up by Lenin, and which were based on Marx' analysis of the Paris Commune, reappears with full force among proponents the syndicalist movement (see, e.g., Håkanson 1974) and also among several social scientists who have been occupied with criticizing and suggesting changes in the Yugoslav associationist-socialist system (see, e.g., Marković 1972: esp. Chs. 5, 7, and 12; Horvat 1969: chs. 3-5). The questions which they have tried to answer, among others, are,

(1) Does the development of the productive forces really imply that the administrative tasks are simplified?[5]

(2) Is it possible to obtain optimum efficiency in a system of equal pay?[6]

(3) How is one to avoid the drawbacks inherent in the rotation of tasks, i.e., the lack of continuity in work and the loss of the valuable experience which the administrators would get through the very process of working?[7]

(4) Will the technical specialists, who probably could not be incorporated into the equal pay system, but who rather would have to be stimulated through the use of economic incentives, get an unacceptably privileged position in society?

(5) How is one to avoid the professionalization of administrative and political positions? That is, how does one avoid the risk that these officials will acquire the same advantages as the technical specialists?

Thus, briefly, the problems that confront Lenin's model of debureau-cratization are dependent to a great degree on what Lenin saw as the long-run solution for the elimination of bureaucracy, i.e., the intensification of the productive forces. On the one hand, we find that a precondition for this intensification would be the proper cultivation of technical, scientific, and administrative competence. But on the other hand, we see that in order to make this cultivation as effective as possible, at least a certain amount of distribution of work tasks would become necessary. This, of course, involves risks of professionalization, permanence in positions, economic advantages and other social privileges. Furthermore, officials may attempt to consolidate their own positions by making their tasks appear too complicated to be executed by others (cf. Germain 1969: 4 ff.).

A NOTE ABOUT CHINA

To a substantial degree, the development in China during and after the Cultural Revolution may be seen as a conscious fight against tendencies of bureaucratization and as a struggle toward administrative arrangements which maximize the contact between the ruling and the ruled. These words, the ruling and the ruled, are partially misleading due to the nature of static dichotomies. The problem which is actually being confronted is the attempt to clear away the *limits* between these two categories, in the spirit of Marx (the Paris Commune) and Lenin (*The State and Revolution*).

In contrast to what is common in Western, Weberian-inspired ideas, the Maoist conception of organization does not primarily stress efficiency and the maximum use of technical knowledge, but rather, the importance of engaging "the masses" in organized work. Martin K. Whyte describes the differences between the two conceptualizations regarding organizations in the following way:

> While Weber focussed most of his attention on the administrators within bureaucracies rather than on the entire personnel, the Maoists focus most of their attention on how subordinates are tied into the organization. . . . [The major emphasis] on involvement rather than on internal efficiency is seen as producing, as a by-product, greater actual efficiency (1973: 156-158).

The term "mass line" covers a number of different procedures which the organization is expected to employ in order to counteract the tendencies towards an increasingly hierarchical arrangement in organizations. Political functionaries, for example, are encouraged to use a certain portion of their time in order to work together with people at the base of the organization. The latter, in their turn, are expected to take an active part in the decision-making within the organization (Whyte 1973: 156-158). According to official ideology, organizations should strive to minimize rules and procedures so that persons with new ideas and suggestions for the improvement of the work processes will feel free to try out their ideas. At certain intervals, campaigns are initiated to "reshuffle" organizations and to "break through" unnecessary rules and patterns of action. These procedures do not exclude a strong regulatory role for the party, but the centralized leadership of the party "must be viewed in relationship to the strong emphasis which is put on the mass line, on the principle of serving the people, and on the practice of criticism/self-criticism. These patterns are designed to prevent both party leaders and the party from dissociating themselves from the people on the basis of its monopoly of power, and to prevent them from acquiring privileges of different kinds" (Dahlström 1975: 12).

The Chinese example may be seen as an attempt, on a grand scale, to dissolve the contradiction between administrative efficiency and representative administration. It is an attempt to utilize local initiative and local knowledge, thereby preserving efficiency via massive participation of the people in administrative and decision-making tasks. The use of these resources is, to a great extent, the subject of local determination.

Max Weber: The Theory of Administrative Evolution

Max Weber perceived the capitalist order of production as *one* important driving force for the emergence of bureaucratic patterns of organization. According to him, bureaucracy was a product of a general development of society towards rational, goal-oriented organized behavior. In this development, capitalism played a major role. In contrast to Marx and Lenin, Weber did not see bureaucracy as a specific bourgeois phenomenon tied to capitalism and thus destined to vanish with the disappearance of capitalism. Rather, bureaucracy was seen as an independent entity, surviving in society, be it capitalist or socialist.

In his treatment of the emergence of bureaucracy. Weber worked with a multifactor model wherein economic variables constituted the most crucial elements. Since the rise of bureaucracy is conditioned by those factors which have created the "modern" society, i.e., capitalism, centralization tendencies, and "mass democracy," it is a phenomenon which cannot be eliminated. It is an indispensable component of a society built on a complex distribution of labor, centralized administration, and money economy. It simply cannot be done away with. "If bureaucratic administration is, other things being equal, always the most rational type from a technical point of view, the needs of mass administration make it today completely indispensable. The choice is only that between bureaucracy and dilettantism in the field of administration" (Weber 1968: 223).[8]

Bureaucracy has become a permanent social force. Its superiority derives from its character of being an impersonal apparatus, technically competent, precise and disciplined. But could this apparatus, exactly because of its competence, become the master of its masters, overthrowing its mandators? Where did Weber actually stand on this issue of the possible autonomy of bureaucracy and its ability to act on its own behalf? What did he say on the issue of bureaucratic autonomy, which Marxism denies as a matter of definition? As we shall see, it is difficult to find in Weber's writings any definite opinion on this point. In certain contexts he strongly stressed the subordination of bureaucracy ("straffe Unterordnung") and its capability of being an obedient instrument to any holder of power. In other contexts, however, he saw it as a sovereign power in itself with own "vested interests" for the preservation of the social system.

WEBER ON THE EMERGENCE OF BUREAUCRACY[9]

According to Weber, there are several historical examples of bureaucratic forms of administration. One such example is that of Egypt during the period of the New Kingdom where the need for centralized control of water regulations and the construction of an irrigation system demanded a vast staff of officials. Other examples can be found in the later Roman Principate, in China during the time of Shi Hwangti and up to 1900, and in the Roman Catholic church, particularly after the thirteenth century (Weber 1968: 964, 972). However, the bureaucratic systems in these cases had certain feudal nepotistic characteristics, and were also partially based on remuneration in natura to the officials. They are not, therefore, pure examples of bureaucracies.

Bureaucracy, in the form we know it today, appeared in the European states in increasingly pure form concurrently with the growth of the absolute kingdoms. An important precondition for the spread and consolidation of bureaucracy was the creation of a *money economy,* the rules of which became more strongly emphasized when the European states began to develop in a capitalist direction. "The large modern capitalist enterprise" is perhaps Weber's foremost example of the application of bureaucratic principles of administration (1968: 964).

> The development of the *money economy* is a presupposition of a modern bureaucracy insofar as the compensation of officials today takes the form of money salaries. The money economy is of very great importance for the whole bearing of bureaucracy, yet by itself it is by no means decisive for the existence of bureaucracy. . . . [At this point there follow the examples of early bureaucracies which were mentioned above.] A certain measure of a developed money economy is the normal precondition at least for the unchanged survival, if not for the establishment, of pure bureaucratic administrations (Weber 1968: 963-964).

A distinctive trait of Weber is his reluctance to designate a particular factor as *the most important* or *key factor* in a causal sense.[10] Even in his explanation of the emergence of bureaucracy, he is, as was shown in the quotation above, anxious to avoid emphasizing the money economy as the most important cause, even though it is obvious that few factors outrank it in importance. It may be that a money economy is not an "indispensable precondition" for bureaucratization, says Weber. Yet bureaucracy as a permanent structure is "knit to the one presupposition of the availability of continuous revenues to maintain it." When such income cannot be taken from private profits (as in modern enterprises, for example) or from land rents (as in the case of big estates), then a permanent *taxation system* is necessary in order for a system of bureaucratic administration to prevail. And, "for well-known general reasons, only a fully developed money economy offers a secure basis for such a taxation system" (1968: 968). A society where remuneration to the working people is given in the form of money, and where the tasks and undertakings of the state have to be financed through taxation, requires a staff of administrative officials which can exercise a degree of control while performing book-keeping and money-collecting activities.

It is not only within private capitalist enterprises and modern state administrations that Weber observes tendencies of bureaucratization. He also stresses how the modern army, the church, and the universities have gradually lost their traditional, archaic characteristics. He finds

Max Weber: Legal Authority: The Pure Type

The purest type of exercise of legal authority is that which employs a bureaucratic administrative staff. Only the supreme chief of the organization occupies his position of dominance (*Herrenstellung*) by virtue of appropriation, of election, or of having been designated for the succession. But even *his* authority consists in a sphere of legal competence. The whole administrative staff under the supreme authority then consists, in the purest type, of individual officials . . . who are appointed and function according to the following criteria:

(1) They are personally free and subject to authority only with respect to their impersonal official obligations.

(2) They are organized in a clearly defined hierarchy of offices.

(3) Each office has a clearly defined sphere of competence in the legal sense.

(4) The office is filled by a free contractual relationship. Thus, in principle, there is free selection.

(5) Candidates are selected on the basis of technical qualifications. In the most rational case, this is tested by examinations or guaranteed by diplomas certifying technical training, or both. They are *appointed,* not elected.

(6) They are remunerated by fixed salaries in money, for the most part with the right to pension. . . . The salary scale is graded according to rank in the hierarchy; but in addition to this criterion, the responsibility of the position and the requirements of the incumbent's social status may be taken into account.

(7) The office is treated as the sole, or at least the primary, occupation of the incumbent.

(8) It constitutes a career. There is a system of "promotion" according to seniority or to achievement, or both. Promotion is dependent on the judgment of superiors.

(9) The official works entirely separated from ownership of the means of administration and without appropriation of his position.

(10) He is subject to strict and systematic discipline and control in the conduct of the office.

(Weber 1968: 220-221)

that they are increasingly administered by impersonal and rational rules aimed at attaining maximum efficiency. Weber's exposition is a methodical review of factors which generally work in the direction of bureaucratization, an inventory filled with numerous examples of how organizations become bureaucratized. In addition to a money economy, on which I have already commented, the following factors as well are part of Weber's sketch.

Standing armies. Power motives and expansionist strivings of national states produce a necessity for permanent military forces. Since money has to be collected to finance the armies and the war enterprises, a corps of functionaries comes into existence for this purpose. Weber also posits the idea that armies tend to become more and more organizationally differentiated, in and of themselves, and subsequently, more bureaucratized.

Material wealth. Greater material affluence and a raised standard of living are accompanied by the need for the public sector to play an increasingly active role in the management of the state. A growing number of social services begin to be seen as indispensable, with the result being that bureaucratic forms of management are employed to fulfill needs that previously were performed either locally or through the private sector (Weber 1968: 972).

Modern means of communication. The administration of modern Western society is possible only if the state takes control of telegraph communications, mail distribution, and the railroads (Weber 1968: 973).

Political factors. Universal suffrage and the rise of the institution of mass political parties, both of which are associated with general voting rights, are factors of utmost importance for the spread of bureaucracy. Here, Weber is close to being categorical and far less restrictive than in his previous causal explanations.

> Bureaucracy inevitably accompanies modern *mass democracy,* in contrast to the democratic self-government of small homogeneous units. . . . Mass democracy, which makes a clean sweep of the feudal, patrimonial, and—at least in intent—the plutocratic privileges in administration unavoidably has to put paid professional labor in place of the historically inherited "avocational" administration by notables [as, e.g., the landlords of eastern Prussia] (Weber 1968: 983-984).

In his reflections on the need of the modern party institutions for professional administrators, Weber strongly resembles Robert Michels (see pp. 67 ff.). Michels, however, ties his analysis of the bureaucratic tendencies in party organizations to strong deterministic presuppositions concerning the inevitability of the concentration of power into an oligarchy. Although Weber was far from silent about the power abuse and antidemocratic aspects of bureaucratization, he was nonetheless cautious about implying that bureaucratized politics must *necessarily* lead to a reordering of the administration in the direction of oligarchy. Nevertheless, it is obvious that Weber was aware that the *size* of political organization in itself is a force towards increased bureaucratization. Both direct democracy and government by notables are "technically inadequate" in "organizations beyond a certain limit of size, constituting more than a few thousand full-fledged members" (1968: 291). The participation of every individual in the governing of an organization is possible only in small associations of an egalitarian nature. In such associations, direct democracy can be implemented via various technical arrangements, for example, by rotating officials, by having short mandate periods, and by utilizing the notion of recallability (1968: 289, 948; cf. also Lenin's blueprint for debureaucratization in *The State and Revolution*, see pp. 48-49 above). However, the larger the organization becomes, the greater is the difficulty in sustaining these principles. According to Weber, excellent examples of this relationship between an organization's size and its tendency toward bureaucratization can be found in the case of the German Social Democratic Party, and the American Democratic and Republican parties (1968: 971).

In his writings on the importance of the size factor, Weber comes close to the "inner-logical" explanations of the emergence of oligarchy as espoused by Michels in his book, *Political Parties*. Weber's writings, in contrast to Michels', stress the idea that immanent factors only represent one element in the explanation of the rise of bureaucracy. To Weber, the macrorelationships involving economic, political and technological transformations, were equally as important for the emergence and existence of bureaucratic forms of administration as were immanent factors. Weber's concept of bureaucracy cannot be properly understood unless seen within the erudite, historically insightful, and broadly displayed sociological and political-scientific framework which he provided. Unfortunately, this framework has all too often been ignored by organizational sociologists. A few words about this are in order.

BUREAUCRACY, CAPITALISM AND
ORGANIZATIONAL SOCIOLOGY

As has been often pointed out (for one example, see Sunesson 1974: 59-68), the sociology of organizations which has arisen and developed during this century has largely consisted of commentaries to, and modifications of Weber's ideal-typical concept of bureaucracy. On school of thought within organizational sociology has questioned whether bureaucracy is actually as rational as Weber claimed (Merton 1957; Crozier 1964). Other social scientists, partly inspired by Weber, have tried to develop various typologies of organizations (e.g., Blau and Scott 1963; Etzioni 1961; Burns and Stalker 1961). Still others have focussed on the individual and his adjustment to the organization (see Argyris 1964; and the literature on self-governing work groups, e.g., Lysgaard 1961) and industrial democracy (e.g., Thorsrud and Emery 1964; Karlsson 1969; Dahlström 1969; and others). These contributions, which are all closely related to administrative theory, might be termed un-Weberian in the sense that they concentrate almost exclusively on relationships and problems internal to the organization. On this basis, Sunesson (1973, 1974) emphatically rejects "organization theory" as historically uninformed and macrosociologically naive. He further claims that Weber's intention in developing the concept of bureaucracy

> was not "organizational sociology" in any sense of the word, but was associated with assumptions about a dominating *type of state,* i.e., a capitalist state, and an organizational system naturally related to it. Thus, for Weber, the concept of "bureaucracy" was closely connected to a definite historical process (1974: Ch. 2, p. 5).

This interpretation, I believe, makes a travesty of Weber's work. Admittedly, modern organizational sociology deals with perspectives which by Weberian standards are indeed somewhat narrow. But one may justify such restricted approaches as a logical means for fulfilling Weber's intentions when he formulated his concept of the ideal-typical bureaucracy. That is to say, these organizational sociologists simply utilize Weber's formulation as a point of departure from which to proceed on a path which fulfills the spirit of Weber's notion of bureaucracy. Weber examined bureaucracy as a form of organization especially suited for, and functionally adapted to an economically developed, technically complex modern society. It is from this point that modern organizational sociology departs, and subsequently explores the logical extensions of Weber's work. For example, modern social scientists often use Weber's framework to discuss and analyze various types of organization and their relationship to efficiency. Weber's concept of bureaucracy is a *construct,* a unit of comparison, an idealized "norm" against which different forms of organization can be compared and contrasted and against which deviations can be measured. The Weberian ideal type has prepared the foundation for an organizational sociology on the microlevel, a science of organization which no longer must begin with an all-encompassing analysis of the total society, a science of organization which does not need to resort to deliberations concerning the character of the state and the social order.

The practical consequences of Weber's analysis of bureaucracy have been considerable. He made it a legitimate undertaking to look at bureaucracy as a general phenomenon and not as something unique to state administration. Through him, and the somewhat less influential Michels, the groundwork was prepared for the "anatomical," micro-directed analysis of organizations, the application of which is the science of administration (see Part II of this book). One may regret the fact that in this process, organizational analysis has turned away from certain "classical" perspectives, but one can hardly maintain that this is un-Weberian. That is to say, Weber's analysis does *not* imply that it is necessary to connect the research on bureaucracy with research on the state, and perhaps not even with macrorelations, since we have seen that he himself made use of "inner-logical" explanations.

Furthermore, Weber's theory of bureaucracy does *not* say that the concept of bureaucracy has to be tied to the *capitalist* order of production, as Sunesson maintains. It is true that Weber explained the emergence of bureaucracy by reference to the nature of the capitalist system, but, as we have seen Weber referred to this as merely *one of several* causal factors. Indeed, bureaucracies might well exist in societal forms *other* than those of the capitalistic world. Weber pointed to the *interconnection* between a capitalist economy and bureaucracy. "On the one hand, capitalism in its modern stages of development requires the bureaucracy, though both have arisen from different historical sources. Conversely, capitalism is the most rational economic basis for bureaucratic administration and enables it to develop in the most rational form" (Weber 1968: 224). But Weber also argued that even if capitalism were abolished, bureaucracy would nonetheless remain. Thus he states in one of his political writings during the First World War:

A progressive elimination of private capitalism is theoretically conceivable, although it is surely not so easy as imagined in the dreams of some literati who do not know what it is all about; its elimination will certainly not be a consequence of this war. But let us assume that some time in the future it will be done away with. What would be the practical result? The destruction of the steel frame of modern industrial work? No! The abolition of private capitalism would simply mean that also the *top management* of the nationalized or socialized enterprises would become bureaucratic. Are the daily working conditions of the salaried employees and the workers in the state-owned Prussian mines and railroads really perceptibly different from those in big business enterprises? It is true that there is even less freedom, since every power struggle with the state bureaucracy is hopeless and since there is no appeal to an agency which as a matter of principle would be interested in limiting the employer's power, such as there is in the case of a private enterprise. *That* would be the whole difference.

State bureaucracy would rule *alone* if private capitalism were eliminated. The private and public bureaucracies, which now work next to, and potentially against, each other, and hence check one another to a degree, would be merged into a single hierarchy. This would be similar to the situation in ancient Egypt, but it would occur in a much more rational—and hence unbreakable—form (1968: 1401-1402).

It is obvious that Weber disliked such a development and that he saw bureaucracy in a society based on socialist economy as becoming a monolithic, immovable structure. In his early works as well, Weber portrayed bureaucracy as being independent of the economic system once it had been established. To Weber, the indispensability of bureaucracy is a fact in all industrially developed societies: "It makes no difference whether the economic system is organized on a capitalistic or a socialistic basis" (1968: 223).

A misconception similar to Sunesson's appears in Nicos Poulantzas' book *Political Power and Social Classes* (1975). Poulantzas argues that Weber, along with the Marxist classics, "establishes a necessary relation between bureaucratism/bureaucracy and the capitalist mode of production" (p. 342). However, against the background of the quotation from Weber above, this certainly cannot be correct. Weber established a sufficient, and not a necessary, relationship between bureaucracy and capitalism. Wherever capitalism flourishes, bureaucracy emerges. However, bureaucracy can also emerge, or continue to exist, under other conditions, e.g. socialism.

THE AUTONOMY OF BUREAUCRACY

A basic trait in Weber's theory is that it gives bureaucracy the character of an *impersonal apparatus* whose existence is motivated by technical competence, predictability of action, precision, stability, etc. In this sense, bureaucracy allows an exceptionally high degree of calculability (1968: 223-224). The loyalty of the official is not paid to any particular person, as in traditional or charismatic organizations, but rather, to the *impersonal and functional purposes* of the organization itself. The official is characterized by "a specific duty of fealty to the purpose of the office (*Amtstreue*)" (1968: 959; cf. also 988).

It is especially clear in Webe_'s article, "Parliament and government in a reconstructed Germany," that he wanted to depict bureaucracy as a *machine,* perhaps an animated machine, but nevertheless as a structure based on "objectified intelligence."

> An inanimate machine is mind objectified. Only this provides it with the power to force men into its service and to dominate their everyday working life as completely as is actually the case in the factory. Objectified intelligence is also that animated machine, the bureaucratic organization, with its specialization of trained skills, its division of jurisdiction, its rules and hierarchical relations of authority (1968: 1402).

After such a statement, one may feel that the answer to the question of whether bureaucracy can be an autonomous political force should be easy. Similar formulations appear in other writings by Weber. For example, in a description of modern capitalist industrial enterprise, he noted that to be run properly it would presuppose a bureaucracy, a legal and administrative system, the function of which may be predicted "by virtue of its fixed general norms, just like the expected performance of a machine" (1968: 1394).

If bureaucracy is indeed a machine, it must be tended to. Someone must program it, give it proper tasks, lubricate it, and if necessary, repair it (i.e., issue new rules and regulations) and replace parts which are worn out or which no longer function properly (i.e., dismiss and hire personnel). It seems virtually impossible that Weber could have perceived bureaucracy as an autonomous social unit. The question, then, regarding control of the bureaucracy seems rather easy to answer:

Bureaucracy subordinates itself to anyone who is able to master the economic and legal techniques necessary for its proper functioning.

It is easy to find statements by Weber which support this contention. For example, Weber makes a clear distinction between "superordinates" (i.e., the masters) and "apparatus" (i.e., the bureaucracy, 1968: 953). He argued that the "objective indispensability" of the bureaucratic "mechanism" makes it easy to get it to work "for anybody who knows how to gain control over it" (1968: 988). The coup d'état, and not the revolution, becomes the typical means for obtaining control over the leadership of the state. Bureaucracy cannot be disposed of (1968: 224), and therefore, groups in revolt need only to *take over* the previous machinery to successfully gain control. Those who seize this power may need to replace various top officials (1968: 989), but thereafter, the bureaucracy is prepared to serve its new masters. It is able to serve any interest.

> [One has to remember] that bureaucracy as such is a precision instrument which can put itself at the disposal of quite varied interests, purely political as well as purely economic ones, or any other sort (1968: 990).

Even though Weber's standpoint may, to a certain extent, resemble that of Marxism in that they both stress bureaucracy's subordination to its masters, I feel that it is the differences between the two systems that is most striking. For example, Marx and Lenin emphasized bureaucracy's dependence on and attachments to the bourgeois state. Weber, on his part, energetically and eloquently stressed that the masters of bureaucracy may be motivated by *any* interests. Be these interests bourgeois or socialist, state or private, the bureaucracy will obediently follow their orders. Lenin, following Marx, emphasized that the proletariat's taking of power requires that the state apparatus be crushed. For Weber, shifts of power were merely a question of replacing a few public servants at the top of the hierarchy. (Cf. Kautsky's argument in the dispute with Pannekoek; see Lenin, *Selected Works,* VII: 103-111. Kautsky argued that the gaining of socialist power should not have as its purpose the abolishment of the state functions and dismissal of public officials, since these officials would be needed for the reconstruction of the new society. Nor should the state departments be dissolved. Lenin's standpoint was that such departments should be replaced by expert commissions and Soviets of workers and soldiers.)

However, Weber's opinion on the question of bureaucratic autonomy and the possibilities for bureaucracy exerting power on its own
cannot, and should not, be summarized in such a simple way as I have
done here. It is evident that he was ambiguous with regard to this issue,
and that he could see the possibility of a bureaucratic machine revolting
against its masters. The reason for this can be found in the fact that
bureaucracies possess superior technical and practical knowledge as
well as the ability to dominate the gathering and dissemination of vital
information. "Bureaucratic administration means fundamentally domination through knowledge" (1968: 225).

The notion that bureaucracy *has* power due to the fact that knowledge *is* power, is clearly in line with Weber's general view that power is
controlled by *individuals*. As one commentator has pointed out (Sunesson 1974: 22), social institutions are seen by Weber as a form of aggre-
gated action. The power of bureaucracy becomes an expression of ac-
cumulated administrative knowledge transformed into praxis. Such
influence may be exerted against the superordinate of the bureaucratic
system and against the organization's environment. That is, to the extent that the bureaucracy has interests of its own, the possibility exists
that this knowledge will be used in a way that is beneficial, first, to the
group of bureaucrats, and only second, if at all, to its mandators. In
his general theory of bureaucracy, Weber was not sure as to how much
power bureaucracy is actually able to command. What he evidently
meant, however, was that it is not possible to off-handedly predict
such behavior.

> It must also remain an open question whether the *power* of
> bureaucracy is increasing in the modern states in which it is
> spreading. The fact that bureaucratic organization is technically
> the most highly developed power instrument in the hands of its
> controller does not determine the weight that bureaucracy as
> such is capable of procuring for its own opinions in a particular
> social structure (1968: 991).

Perhaps the best summary of Weber's view on the power of bureaucracy is to say that its influence is contingent upon the specific circumstances present. *If* bureaucracy chooses to act politically, its masters
could easily become victims, since they lack the necessary expertise to
effectively control the reigns of the bureaucracy. It is easier for the the
career official to pursue his opinion vis-à-vis the chief of state than it is
for the official's nominal superior, i.e., the cabinet minister (1968:

224). This is due to the simple fact that the latter lacks the adequate know-how. The superordinates of the bureaucracy are always (note the word) subordinated in relationship to experienced officials, the superordinate playing the role of a "dilettante facing the expert" (1968: 991). This is regardless of who the "superordinate" is: the general public, the parliament, etc.

The bureaucrat may keep information secret if he finds this suitable for his purposes. Weber points to the example of Prussia where public statistics existed, but where only those data which were harmless to bureaucracy were made public. Bureaucracy dislikes public scrutiny. "Bureaucracy naturally prefers a poorly informed, and hence powerless, parliament—at least insofar as this ignorance is compatible with the bureaucracy's own interests." Here, Weber becomes unusually categorical: "*Against* the bureaucracy the ruler remains powerless" (1968: 993).

One possible explanation for Weber's fuzziness on the issue of the power of bureaucracy is that he concentrated so strongly on the studies of the *character* and *inner properties* of bureaucracy that he came to overlook the issue of the *conditions* for bureaucratic insubordination. However, a qualification to this statement must be made. He did, at least in one case, explicitly bring up the problem of the power of bureaucracy. It was in reference to the situation in Germany immediately after the First World War, and in this particular instance he was pointedly clear about the fact that bureaucracy had developed a power position of its own. The main cause of this, as he saw it, was that the parliament lacked the ability to supervise the administration. The state officials could not be subjected to public questioning (1968: 1418), and the actions of the administration were not subject to inspection (1968: 1418-1419). After Bismarck's resignation, Germany was ruled by bureaucrats with the result that all political talent was eliminated. Openness, elimination of "official secrets" and the introduction of effective parliamentary control were necessary for reducing the influence of the bureaucracy to its rightful proportions. As conditions were, the system allowed "qualified bureaucrats who nevertheless have no traits of statesman-like talent to maintain themselves in leading political positions until some intrigue forces them out in favor of similar personages" (1968: 1410).

THE ELIMINATION OF BUREAUCRACY

On this point, Weber is exceptionally clear. He felt that, from a technical viewpoint, the bureaucratic type of administration is indeed capable of reaching the maximum degree of efficiency (1968: 223). Thereby it is "the most rational known means of exercising authority over human beings." It is fruitless to try to avoid bureaucracy. The only choice is between bureaucracy and dilettantism. To fight bureaucracy one needs bureaucracy. "When those subject to bureaucratic control seek to escape the influence of the existing bureaucratic apparatus, this is normally possible only by creating an organization of their own which is equally subject to bureaucratization" (1968: 224).

That the existence of bureaucracy means definite problems in the implementation of democracy is certainly unquestionable. As organizations emerge and grow large, a bureaucratic administration becomes necessary, hindering direct democracy from being practiced. In whatever organization it exists, direct democracy becomes unstable in that there always exists a tendency for the resourceful to take over the administrative functions for their own purposes (1968: 949). It is, however, theoretically conceivable to dispose of bureaucracy by returning to a social system composed of very small organizations (1968: 224), yet it is evident that Weber did not see this as a real alternative. While bureaucracy *can* be controlled under certain circumstances through parliament,[11] the contradiction between democracy and bureaucratic rule nonetheless appears to be permanent (1968: 991).

Robert Michels: The Natural Law of Power Concentration

At a quick glance, it may seem that Robert Michels does not belong in this discussion. Michels primarily wrote about tendencies toward the concentration of power and minority rule; in explicit words, he only superficially dealt with "bureaucracy," and then, only as a concept which can be equated with state administration. But the discussion on Michels' most important contribution, *Political Parties,* is still quite relevant. As it was first issued in Germany in 1911, Michels' book may be seen as a parallel to Weber's treatment of the emergence of bureaucracy. Whereas the size and complexity of an organization is emphasized in Weber's work as a *contributing* cause of its bureaucratization, these factors assume a far greater importance in Michels' theory. Both the originality and the limitations of Michels' treatment of oligarchic tendencies stem from his almost manic attachment to, and purification of, the thesis of the inevitability of oligarchic tendencies, "the iron law of oligarchy" (1958: 393-409). It is original in that the mechanisms of the deformation of power in big organizations have not by any previous social scientist been given such a significant formulation. Its limitations are due to Michels' hard-headed fixation on his basic thesis. By doing so, he establishes an effective block to any deliberation of how oligarchic tendencies might possibly be modified.

When Michels talks of oligarchy, he comes very close to the explication of the essence of bureaucracy which I have tried to make in Chapter 1. As he intended to show, Michels' law of oligarchy is an expression of the inevitable and unrestrained tendency that the conflicts between the demands of efficiency and democracy are always solved to the advantage of those forces acting on behalf of efficiency, and therefore at the cost of democracy. There is strong reason to emphasize the term "forces," since Michels has often been misunderstood. His exposition of oligarchical tendencies has sometimes been seen as a description of how leading strata political organizations consciously, and as part of a personal striving for power, try to consolidate and reinforce their positions. This is only partially correct. The dominating characteristic of Michels' book is the dogged stressing of the *necessity* and the *regularity* of something which is built *into the organizational principle itself.* Oligarchy irresistibly follows from people's attempts to organize in associations and unions. (Similar theses have later been put forward by, among others, Whyte, 1965; and Presthus, 1962.) *Political Parties* is written partly as a polemic against those who believe that oligarchy can be avoided. For example, Michels triumphantly points to the fact that the first workers' organizations in Germany, Allgemeiner Deutscher Arbeiterverein, was ruled autocratically by Ferdinand Lassalle, who made use of "a power comparable with that of the doge of the Venetian Republic" (1958: 201). Furthermore, the general assembly of the First International was subordinated to "the iron will of one single man, Karl Marx" (1958: 204). The International, according to Michels, was seen by many as the negation of socialism because it introduced the authority principle into workers' politics.

Michels major polemical point is his demonstration that the tendencies toward power concentration are significant characteristics even in organizations which have very explicit democratic goals. His foremost example is that of the German Social Democratic Party, but he also takes great pains to show that syndicalism, as well as anarchism, are not immune to the tendencies toward oligarchy (1958: Part V, Chs. III and IV).

On the rare occasions when the term "bureaucracy" appears in Michels' work, it is used as a label for the officials employed by the state and the political organizations. Both the state and the political parties try to acquire as broad a base as possible. As an element of this policy, they recruit a great number of administrators, who because of their economic dependence on the organization, act for their benefit. Thus, not only do the state and political organizations need administrators, but the creation of big administrations is the functional answer to the career needs of many intellectuals. Another demand for extensive administration arises because of the large number of tasks which the modern organization needs to perform. Here Michels refers back to his general discussion about the causes of oligarchy (1958: 196).

Michels' section on bureaucracy is clearly subordinated to his general theory of oligarchy, and it is obvious that Michels views bureaucracy as only one element in the concentration of power and influence within a small stratum of leaders. In Michels' *Political Parties* both oligarchy and bureaucracy are terms generally used to represent *elite rule*.

THE EMERGENCE OF ELITE RULE

Leadership, says Michels, is a necessary phenomenon of all social life. It is pointless to ask whether it is a good or bad phenomenon. All that science can do is to establish the law of the inevitability of oligarchy, and then to try to determine and explain the causes of oligarchic tendencies (1958: 418). Wherever we encounter organization, we find oligarchy as well.

> *Organization implies the tendency to oligarchy.* In every organization, whether it be a political party, a professional union, or any other association of the kind, the aristocratic tendency manifests itself very clearly. . . . *As a result of organization,* every party or professional union becomes divided into a minority of directors and a majority of directed (1958: 37; italics mine).

> *Who says organization, says oligarchy* (1958: 418; italics mine).

Michels' line of reasoning is close to the thinking of elite theoreticians such as Mosca and Pareto. In partial resemblance to them, especially to Pareto, he attributes some of the causes for the emergence of elite rule to psychological factors of the upwardly mobile strata.

Oligarchy stems from the psychological transformations of the leading personalities within the parties. In contrast to the other elite theoreticians, however, Michels also carefully surveys a number of internal organizational variables, such as factors connected with tactical and technical necessities. This survey, in turn, becomes part of a debate against those "utopians," primarily socialists, who believe that direct democracy and broad membership participation is possible in a political organization. The tactical and technical factors which are mentioned by Michels as reasons for the development of an elite stratum, and which subsequently make direct democracy impossible, are the following:

(a) The *number* of members. To organize meetings in which up to 1000 members participate is highly difficult, says Michels, "especially in northern climes, where the weather makes it impossible to hold open-air meetings for the greater part of the year" (1958: 30). Furthermore, no speaker can make himself heard to more than 10,000 members, "even if we imagine the means of communication to become much better than those which now exist" (1958: 31). (In just a few years this statement was to be profoundly falsified because of radio communications.)

(b) The need to decide on *matters of dispute* among members. Controversies between two parties within the organization can not be settled by participation of the entire collective in the process (1958: 31).

This leads to a need for a system of delegation, i.e., a system where appointed persons represent the mass of members and execute their will. This need for delegation also arises from every organization's need for

(c) *expertise*. The technical specialization which inevitably results from large-scale organization creates the need for a staff of experts. In referring to Heinrich Herkner, *Die Arbeiterfrage* (1908) Michels also stresses the fact that the workers' organizations are forced toward professionalization because of their having to defend themselves against the expert power which the employers' organizations are able to mobilize, their employees being "university men" (1958: 33; also, cf. pp. 38-39).

There is another factor, however, which is perhaps more important still. In work conflicts and strikes, the rapid mobilization of the collective forces of the organization becomes a necessity. According to

Lassalle, the organization should be able to act like a "hammer" in the hands of its leadership. Thus, the concentration of executive power is needed to allow for

(d) *quick decisions*. The modern party is a fighting organization and requires a certain degree of "caesarism" if orders are to be quickly communicated and executed (1958: 48). Michels points out the similarities between an actively fighting political party and a military organization, and points to the irony in the "military" terminology he finds in the writings of leading German socialists, e.g., Kautsky (1958: 48).

Finally, there exists a vast mobility in the membership cadres of political organizations, which gives rise to the need for

(e) *continuity* in the leadership of the organization. Particularly in the trade unions, the mobility of members is considerable. In order to preserve continuity, a leadership stratum is required which can form "a more stable and more constant element of the organized membership" (1958: 85).

It is not entirely clear what Michels means when he speaks of "psychological factors" leading to oligarchy, but the examples he provides seem to point to the existence of certain permanent character traits both among the members and those in leadership positions.

(a) As soon as a delegate is elected, Michels says, he tends to perceive his post as a lifetime appointment, as his "property" (1958: 50). For this reason, organizations which take care to appear especially democratic try to introduce rules concerning short mandate periods (1958: 103). But tradition, the need for stability, and sometimes the leaders' own threats to abdicate often lead to a permanence for such positions.

(b) There is a born leader in every good speaker and journalist, Michels says. The oratoric quality of a political leader in a democracy is an extremely strong force in the direction of power concentration: "The essential characteristic of democracy is found in the readiness with which it succumbs to the magic of words, written as well as spoken" (1958: 75).

(c) The most important of these psychological factors has to do with the idea that members in an organization experience a need for a leader. Most people are politically detached. The

decisions made within a party are always made by a small handful of members, with the majority of the members being satis-
fied with participation in the political elections (1958: 54-55).
The majority usually appreciates the fact that there are persons
who want to devote their time to represent its interests (p. 58).

In Michels' treatment of the relationship between oligarchical tendencies and psychological factors, one can easily discover his basic
assumptions about human nature. They are, to be sure, pessimistic:
Egoism, particularism, and a quest for material gains are strong driving
forces behind the decisions of men who go into politics (1958: 54-55).
"The mass" can never gain influence over an organization because it is
amorphous and incompetent, therefore needing a distribution of labor,
specialization, and leadership (1958: 421). "Man as individual is by nature predestined to be guided, and to be guided all the more in proportion as the functions of life undergo division and subdivision" (1958:
422). As a rule, the contradiction between "democratic" and "aristo-
cratic" processes in organizations tends to be solved in favor of the
aristocracy.

The contrast between Michels' viewpoints and, for example, either
John Stuart Mill's view of democracy or the classical Marxist perception
of bureaucracy and the problems of administration, could hardly be
greater. Mill emphasizes the importance of everyone participating in the
organization, and, as an essential criterion of democracy everyone being
trained to protect their interests. Through this process the individual's
responsibility for the totality is developed. Similarly, Marx and Lenin
are optimistic about the possibilities of implementing broad participation in the leadership of the state, once the old state apparatus has been
abolished. To Michels, however, such a hope is vain. He contends that
socialists are wrong when they maintain that the difficulties of democracy stem from the fact that the masses, in earlier epochs, were re-
pressed through slavery and exploitation (1958: 420). Oligarchic tendencies are always present, and therefore cannot be attributed to any
particular epoch. Consequently, they can not be abolished through
social transformation in the form of a revolution.

THE AUTONOMY OF THE RULING ELITE

In discussing Michels' view of the autonomy of the executive stratum, it is necessary to differentiate between the *employed* and the
elected executive. The employed executive, or "bureaucracy," is viewed

by Michels as a subordinate category, strongly dependent on its masters. For example, the state bureaucracy takes on as its task the defense of the state in exchange for economic remuneration as well as the security offered by the state.

Public officials are dependent on their superordinates (1958: 200). The possibility that bureaucracy might revolt against its masters is not within the framework of Michels' theory. Such an omission is easily understandable. Since his theses concern tendencies toward concentration of power in the *political* leadership, i.e., the elected executive, he has to avoid giving the impression that such monolithic power can be shaken or counteracted by actions from other groups. (This problem resembles the difficulties found within the Marxist conception of bureaucracy when it confronts the possibility of an autonomous stratum of public servants. See pp. 43-46.) In passing, however, Michels takes care to note some dysfunctional tendencies of bureaucracy. For example, it is hostile to initiative, it represses individuality, it replaces goals with means, it leads to "moral poverty," etc. Thus, Michels carries out an analysis which in many respects anticipates Merton's well-known article, "Bureaucratic structure and personality" (1957; Michels 1958: 198-199).

THE ELIMINATION OF ELITE RULE

I have already reviewed the major aspects of Michels' viewpoint with regard to the possibilities of eliminating tendencies to oligarchy. Simply put, they are that organization implies oligarchy and that organization without immanent tendencies of elite formation are unimaginable. In short, elite rule cannot be abolished.

Despite the fact that Michels' main thesis is expressed quite emphatically, it would be incorrect to give the impression that he does not discuss at all how oligarchic tendencies may be modified. In the last pages of his book, he actually shows a degree of reverence for democracy, albeit in a very restricted manner. He feels that democratic movements are not completely ineffectual in checking the tendencies toward elite rule. Even if such movements never "discover" democracy, they nonetheless carry out valuable work during their search for it (1958: 423). For example, the workers' movements strengthen and stimulate the intellectual abilities of the individuals involved, along with their abilities to criticize and control, characteristics which may be further improved by education (p. 424). Michels' modifications, however, are presented in an abrupt and abbreviated manner, thus acquiring the character of quickly improvised qualifications. Through them, he tries to attenuate the rather doomsday-like forecast he has created in the rest of his book. The lasting impression of Michels' major work, however, is that democracy appears to be, for the most part completely lacking in the ability to check the automatic, natural-law forces of oligarchy.

Discussion

I have already pointed out (p. 36) that it seems impossible to reconcile the various conceptualizations of bureaucracy which have been reviewed above. True, they have certain important aspects in common. One, they deal with the same problem in that they work with the two conflicting goals of administrative efficiency and effective representation. Two, they have in common in their descriptive parts the treatment of different issues which pertain to the administrative system of organizations.

With these two similarities exhausted, the contrasts become the dominating features. There is a sharp confrontation between the classical Marxist view of bureaucracy, on the one hand, and Michels' theory of oligarchic processes, on the other. Both theories raise large, even absolutistic claims. The former maintains that the analysis of bureaucracy cannot be separated from the analysis of capitalist society and the state. That is, bureaucracy is the official servant of capitalism, thus the characteristics of bureaucracy are dependent on the bourgeois state. The latter theory categorically holds that organization in itself leads to oligarchy. Rule of the few and the transference of power from the original mandators of the organization to a small circle of leaders is immanent in the organization principle. Thus, the theory of bureaucracy as dependent on specific *external forces* is contrasted to the theory of bureaucracy as a general organizational phenomenon, stemming from *inner processes* in the organization. If one accepts the former, one must reject the latter, and vice versa.

My thesis in this final section is that neither the Marxist view of bureaucracy nor Michels' theory of immanence contain adequate explanations of the emergence and development of bureaucracy. Nevertheless, they form perspectives which, precisely because of their contradictory natures, increase the fruitfulness of the analysis of bureaucracy. To a large degree, the two perspectives have been brought together in a kind of compromise by Max Weber. To Weber, bureaucracy is contingent on *both* structural-macroscopic processes *and* on the internal processes within organizations. The latter, however, cannot be isolated from the former. What happens within organizations in the last instance is dependent on forces in the surrounding society. This does not necessarily imply that a study of a certain organization has to start with a comprehensive societal analysis, however.

In which ways are the Marxist and Michelsian theories problematic? I shall briefly try to mention some of the major arguments in the following two sections.

The Marxist Concept of Bureaucracy: Bureaucracy Associated with the Bourgeois State

The problems which arise in the Marxist view of bureaucracy can best be demonstrated by giving three different emphases to the thesis in the heading above, i.e., (1) the association of bureaucracy with the bourgeois *state*; (2) the association of bureaucracy with the *bourgeois* state; and (3) *the association* of bureaucracy *with* the bourgeois state.

THE ASSOCIATION OF BUREAUCRACY WITH THE BOURGEOIS *STATE*

If one argues that bureaucracy is a phenomenon which is tied exclusively to the administration of the *state*, it becomes difficult to explain in *other* organizations the tendencies of growing hierarchy, expert rule, systems of privileges, and increasing rigidity. As we have seen, Lenin's solution is to refer to the demoralizing impact of the "capitalist environment" when such tendencies of bureaucracy emerge in trade unions and political organizations. In their case, then, bureaucracy can be explained by pointing to the characteristics of *bourgeois society*. There does not exist in the classical Marxist tradition any particular theory of bureaucracy for organizations other than the state.

One reasonable explanation for the weakness of Marxist theory on this point is provided by Lennart Berntson in his book, *Political Parties and Social Classes* (*Politiska partier och sociala klasser*, 1974). Marxism is a theory for the analysis of social structure and class relationships on macro- and intermediate level, and it is not, at least in the form it was given by Marx, Lenin, Engels, and later Poulantzas, a theory for the explanation of phenomena on a microlevel (i.e., organizations, small groups, individuals). To exemplify this, a natural application of Marxist organizational analysis would be to study political parties. Berntson notes, however, that the study of these organizations "are outside the traditional object of historical materialism" (1974: 18). Thus, in his book, Berntson takes on the task of filling in the theoretical holes left by the Marxist tradition in the field of organization theory. He does this by analyzing the internal conditions of political parties against the background of the broader social theory and the theory of class relations.[12]

THE ASSOCIATION OF BUREAUCRACY
WITH THE BOURGEOIS STATE

How does classical Marxism explain the presence of bureaucracy after the revolution has been carried out? The theory may be resorted to in this case as well, since bureaucracy can be shown once to have constituted an integral part of capitalist society. If that society was inadequately developed, this fact provides further support for the notion that bureaucracy rests on the remnants of previous societal formations. The bourgeois repression apparatus had been destroyed, Lenin said in 1919, but the need for a state apparatus remained: "Here we are suffering from the fact that Russia was not sufficiently developed capitalistically." The bourgeois state with its mechanisms of administration and distribution was able to survive partly because of bureaucratic "elements."

The explanation is risky, however, since it implies that bureaucracy will in fact gradually decrease following the development of the productive forces in the socialist society. If this were in fact the case, one would expect that increased economic development, public education, etc., in a socialist society would be accompanied by an attenuation and gradual dissolution of the system of bureaucratic privileges. The fact that this did not take place was the basis of the critique by Trotsky and the leftist opposition to Stalin's growing power during the 1920s. According to the established party functionaries, explained Trotsky, "bureaucratism was nothing else than a leftover from the war period, i.e., a phenomenon in the process of dying away" (1923; see Trotsky 1972: 17). But according to Trotsky himself, bureaucratism is a phenomenon which stems from factors *within* the apparatus.

> The state apparatus is the most important source of bureaucratism. On the one hand, it sips off an enormous amount of the most active elements of the party and educates the most competent group among these in the administration of people and

things, and not in the political leadership of the masses. On the other hand, it must be paid great attention to by the party apparatus, and in this sense can exert influence because of its administrative methods (1972: 39).

The party was living at two different levels: "the top floor where things are decided on, and the ground floor where decisions are received and obeyed" (1972: 16).

Trotsky's argument resembles Michels' discussion in that it directs our attention to the inner mechanisms and tendencies of deformation in the state apparatus. However, there are two modifications of this statement which need to be made. First, Trotsky and his followers generally agreed with the theory which emphasized the primary role of the economy for the elimination of bureaucracy within the state and party machinery (i.e., an improvement of the economy would lead to, among other things, increased education). Second, Trotsky expanded the scope of his thesis when he stated that the Soviet Union was dependent on the spread of revolution to other countries and when he denied the possibility of "socialism in one country."

Both Trotsky's critique and Michels' discussion of oligarchy highlight the fact that an explanation of bureaucracy in terms of its dependence on a certain kind of society or state is not adequate. Such a macroanalysis often requires a complement in the form of assumptions regarding immanent processes.

THE *ASSOCIATION* OF BUREAUCRACY *WITH* THE BOURGEOIS STATE

It is possible that certain Marxists reject theories of "inner logic" because such theories make it more difficult to wed the problems of bureaucracy with the characteristics of the capitalist society. Take, for example, Sunesson (1973), who objects to the "general interpretations of the problem of bureaucracy made by L. Trotsky and bourgeois historicist elite theoreticians like Robert Michels" (p. 9). He attacks "the texts by the so-called Trotsky-ites" for dealing with the problem of bureaucracy as "separated from history, as a general organizational problem" (p. 6).

If the ideas of "inner-logic" are accepted, one cannot theoretically rule out the possibility that a bureaucratic stratum will arise as a natural consequence in a society based even on socialist principles. This recognition of the possibilities of an autonomous bureaucratic power center means that the door is open to possible accusations that the existing state and party apparatus actually *is* such a center of power. Such a recognition represents a fundamental flaw in the *theory*, because it makes the hypothesis about the polarization of society into two antagonistic classes less credible. That is, if the possibility of an autonomous bureaucracy is acknowledged, it also becomes possible that bureaucracy in a certain society may become, or has already become, a "new class."

If, on the other hand, such autonomy is accepted as possible, difficulties arise on several issues when the theory is confronted with reality. The military coup in Chile might be explained as an example of the power strivings of capitalism (the bourgeoisie, or U.S. imperialism) and not primarily as a "military" coup (see editorial in *Häften för Kritiska Studier,* No. 7, 1973), but can the same model be applied to other revolts by the military? For example, in Egypt (Naguib, Nasser), Peru (Velasco) and Portugal (the captains' movement, MFA), has it been the case that the military has acted as agents of the ruling class? The events in e.g. Portugal led to the legalization of the Communist party, the acceptance of strikes and unions, the increased influence of Socialists and Communists in the government, and the initiation of negotiation of independence with the African resistance movements in the Portuguese colonies. Certain interest groups in industry might have condoned the military coup because they saw both the possibility of a decrease in colonial military expenses and an increase in the accessibility to investment capital (*Dagens Nyheter,* May 17, 1974), but it is hard to see that the coup could have been particularly welcomed by the major part of the dominating power groups, who immediately lost the support they had been able to gain from the Caetano government. Therefore it seems that, to a large degree, the military revolt in Portugal can be explained by the particular grievances in the military itself.

The Marxist may object that the military revolt in Portugal is rather an example of what Poulantzas calls the "relative autonomy" of a bureaucratic group within "the capitalist class state." Which role does this class state play, according to Poulantzas?

> It can be stated as follows: it takes charge, as it were, of the bourgeoisie's political interests and realizes the function of political hegemony which the bourgeoisie is unable to achieve. But *in order to do this, the capitalist state assumes a relative autonomy with regard to the bourgeoisie.* This is why Marx' analyses of Bonapartism as a capitalist type of state are so significant. For

this relative autonomy allows the state to intervene not only in order to arrange compromises vis-à-vis the dominating classes, which, in the long run, are useful for the actual economic interests of the dominant classes or fractions; but also (dependent on the concrete conjuncture) to intervene against the long-term economic interests of *one or other* fraction of the dominant class: for such compromises and sacrifices are sometimes necessary for the realization of their political class interests (Poulantzas 1975: 284-285).

The employment of the concept "relative autonomy" is motivated by the ambition of correcting "a simplistic and vulgarized conception which sees in the state the tool or instrument of the dominant class" (Poulantzas 1975: 256). Bureaucracy, says Poulantzas, is also characterized by "relative autonomy," "by its character as a specific category through the intermediary of its relation with the state" (p. 337).

The term "relative autonomy" is a good safety valve for the Marxist theory of bureaucracy, since almost any action by a group or stratum might be explained as being advantageous to the interests of the bourgeoisie. Anyway, what can *not* be shown to be a "compromise" in "the long run" if only the run is long enough? Furthermore, Poulantzas does not give any example of when and how these interests would *not* be supported, thus giving the theory an empty and empirically untestable quality, due to the fact that the limits of his "relative autonomy" are not indicated. (I suppose that Poulantzas means that a socialist revolution would transcend these limits, but there are a lot of other possible threats against the interests of the bourgeoisie on which it would have been interesting to have his opinion.)

Sunesson (1974: 89) argues in the same vague and imprecise manner in his discussion about "concessions made by the state." The state allows "certain economic concessions" in order to reinforce the political interests of the capitalist class in the long run. This may be so. However, the interesting problem is to discuss in which concrete case a real, and for capitalism harmful, concession actually is being made by the state.

There is further reason to raise the question as to what extent Poulantzas actually brings about any modification of the "instrument thesis" in Marxism. Like Lenin, Poulantzas contends that bureaucracy has to be analyzed, as a matter of definition, in connection with the capitalist state. It is symptomatic of his position that he bluntly rejects, on a theoretical basis, the hypothesis about the possible autonomy of bureaucracy. When studying bureaucracy, he states, one has "no theoretical need to concede it its own political power" (1975: 337). Just like the state, bureaucracy is "simply the center of class power" (p. 337).

From the viewpoint of empirical research, such a strong aprioristic position does not seem too fruitful. Aside from its lack of testability, it carries the uncomfortable burden of the requirement that *all* actions by bureaucratic groups must be explained by referring to characteristics of the capitalist society. Poulantzas may want to object by saying that the analysis of specific bureaucratic phenomena without making this broader reference may make us not see the forest because of all the trees. While recognizing the need for being aware of the forest—i.e., the social macroconditions—I feel that, on a good many occasions, trees (i.e., the specific actions of bureaucratic groups) can be pretty interesting in themselves.

A NOTE ON MICHELS

For similar reasons, it is difficult to accept the whole of Michels' theory. To Michels, *all* organizations regardless of type or inner structure, have tendencies toward oligarchic control, i.e., toward a differentiation between the leaders and the led. Two points should be stressed. First, Michels carries out his work on the basis of an implicit direct-democratic model. Because of this, every form of representative system and system of delegates can be taken as evidence that an oligarchy exists, and since each organization of any reasonable size has to have some kind of representative system, every organization thereby becomes oligarchic. The need for delegation is demonstrated by the following example.

Assume that an association that is trying to reach a decision on a particular matter allots 10 hours for the discussion of the question. Assume further that each and every member of this association is guaranteed 10 minutes to make a personal speech on the matter. What, then, is the maximum possible size of the association? Answer: 600 minutes (= 10 hours): 10 minutes = 60. (This example is taken from Dahl, 1970: 67.) Yet in reality the membership would probably agree that the need for each of them to put forward his particular view appears less important than (a) saving time (10 hours is a very long time for discussion of almost any matter); and (b) bringing forward every argument which is necessary for the elucidation of the case. Since the number of possible arguments is usually much lower than the number of possible speakers, this procedure would not require everyone using his or her allotted ten minutes. Further, Michels directs our attention primarily to the *form* of decision-making and ignores the *content* of the decisions involved. It is quite possible that even a very small group in the leadership of the organization, because of good contacts with lower-level members, can reach decisions which are in accordance with the goals and interests of the mandators/participants.

The second point that should be stressed about Michels' theory is that it is virtually blind to the society which surrounds the organization, as well as to those historical processes which gave rise to the organizations initially. To Michels, there is no difference between the organizational *principle* on the one hand, and on the other, a specific *organization*. Thus he takes no interest in investigating the conditions underlying the emergence and development of a certain association, nor does he question to what extent this emergence is dependent on economic, technological, and political-social forces. The reason for this is that he already has the answer. Elite formation tendencies are treated as "given," and can be explained partly by technical and tactical factors and partly by psychological factors connected with the leaders and the led.

The Synthesis: Max Weber

To a substantial degree, the concepts of bureaucracy set forth by Michels and the Marxists are integrated by the contributions of Max Weber. As we have seen, Weber's theory, first, connects the developments of bureaucracy with the issue of the long-run material and political development of society. The capitalistic production system and economy are two of the most important factors in Weber's explanatory scheme. In those respects, there are important similarities between Weber and the Marxist tradition. Secondly, Weber points to the importance of immanent organizational factors which move the organization towards bureaucratization. An especially important factor is the increase in size of organizations, which leads to a need for "mass administration" and which makes direct democracy impossible. In these microaspects, there are clear parallels between Weber and Michels.

I have questioned the possibility of integrating all theories of bureaucracy within a common frame of reference. But is Weber providing us with the roof under which Marx and Michels might feel at home? No. As the reader may recall, I said previously that one criterion of an integrative theory is its possibility to explain both bureaucratization and debureaucratization. Even though Weber, in his stress on macroaspects and in his broad historical survey, has very much in common with the Marxist tradition, he differs nonetheless in at least one major respect. Weber's theory is a theory about the impossibility of eliminating bureaucracy, whereas Marx' theory explicitly explains how this elimination can and will be accomplished. As has been stressed several times above, Weber also contradicts Marx' theory at another point: He leaves open the possibility that bureaucracy may act autonomously, thereby rejecting the Marxist hypothesis of polarization.

The contrasts between Weber and Michels are less obvious. Like Michels, Weber is a "generalist," i.e., he investigates bureaucracy as a *general* organizational phenomenon. There are also similarities between Michels' formulation of his thesis as a natural law, and Weber's way of explaining the bureaucratic ideal type as the end point of an administrative evolution. The contrasts only become evident when one looks at the specific groups of explanatory factors which the two authors emphasize. Despite the formal elegance and eloquence of Michels' theory, it appears as lacking in detail in comparison to the enormous scanning of the broad historical processes put forward by Weber. Weber deals with processes where psychological factors and the character traits of individuals play a rather subordinated role, and where the general development of organizations—their increasing size and inner differentiation along with their problems of government—are never completely isolated from the background drawings of economic and political conditions.

NOTES

1. See T. M. Knox's translation of Hegel's *Philosophy of Right* (1942: 188-189).

2. See Håkanson (1973: 158 ff.). Håkanson's polemics against Bo Gustafsson's introduction to *Socialkapitalismen* (*Social Capitalism*) is based on the distinction between bureaucratic "structure" and bureaucratic "elements." One of Håkanson's arguments is that Gustafsson trivializes the content of a pamphlet by the Hungarian writer Eugen Varga (*The Russian Road to Socialism*) by ignoring that Varga gives *structural* reasons for the growth of bureaucracy under Stalin.

3. In Germain/Mandel (1969) who recognizes the possibility of general bureaucratization mechanisms and who is thus not limited to "bourgeois" societies, the concept of "workers' bureaucracy" is used as a label of administrative deformations of socialist states and workers' organizations (p. 3). Germain carries

out an analysis of bureaucratization processes within the workers' movement which in many respects resembles Michels' discussion of oligarchic phenomena in *Political Parties*. Thus, Germain points to the need of mass organizations for permanent administrative apparatuses, for the privileges which are usually attached to positions within these apparatuses, for the influence of experts, etc. Compare also Mandel 1971: "Lenin to a great extent underestimated . . . the danger that the apparatus might become autonomous and the danger of bureaucratization of the workers' parties" (p. 27).

Sunesson (1973: 6) attacks Germain/Mandel because the latter views the problem of bureaucracy as "separated from history, as a general organizational problem." This highlights the question of whether bureaucracy is an immanent organizational phenomenon (Michels) or whether its emergence is related to primarily external forces (e.g., the capitalist social order).

4. Lenin's determination of "democracy" contains various ambiguities and changes between the components of form and content. According to the quotation given here, the state "in its proper sense" will disappear when the proletariat takes power. However, as Håkanson (1973) points out, this takeover means that force still has to be asserted. The democracy sketched by Lenin is also a *state*. "It contains repression through means of violence. And in exactly the same way as the democratic republic within the framework of capitalism is democracy for the rich, the dictatorship of the proletariat is democracy for the proletariat with the exception of its previous repressors" (p. 353). Håkanson feels that as long as there exists an apparatus of repression, democracy is not fulfilled because the exertion of force blocks the implementation of certain important socialist values.

Within the framework of this chapter it is not possible to account for the different aspects of Lenin's views on democracy, and even less possible to review the turns in the discussion of it. The reader is referred to Håkanson's detailed analysis of *The State and Revolution* (1973: 107-110 and Ch. VII).

5. Marković thinks that while the administrative tasks have become more complicated, modern science and technology, especially cybernetics, have opened up possibilities for the elimination of bureaucracy and the implementation of self-government (1971: Ch. VII).

6. See Håkanson (1973: 80f.).

7. Ibid., pp. 321-322.

8. Albrow demonstrates Weber's strong dependence on Gustav Schmoller, who, in several papers in 1894 and 1898 put forward, first, an evolutionary theory about administrative forms, and second, sketched a final state of this development in terms which correspond almost detail by detail to the Weberian ideal type of bureaucracy (Albrow 1970: 52-54).

9. For Weber's description of the bureaucratic ideal type, see below, p. 55.

10. This is stressed by Sunesson (1974: 24) who goes on: "His [Weber's] theory is rather a kind of check list of phenomena which the sociologist is recommended to pay attention to."

11. Weber's enthusiasm for the parliamentary form of government was possibly more dependent on his "conviction that national greatness depended on finding able leaders than to any concern for democratic values" (Albrow 1970: 49). "As early as 1895, in his inaugural lecture, Weber had taken 'national power' as a political good of paramount importance. The extent of Weber's nationalism

and responsibility for later developments in Germany have become a matter for heated debate" (Albrow 1970: 131).

12. It is interesting to note that he tries to reconcile Karl Marx with Talcott Parsons. Despite the criticism which Berntson advances against the action theory of Parsons, the latter is used to provide the explanations of these "subjective notions which rule the explicit action of political parties" (1974: 36). To an outside observer, it would appear more natural if internal organization mechanisms were discussed and demonstrated by referring to Marxists like Trotsky, Mandel, and others. Remarkably, however, they are totally absent in Berntson's list of references.

PART II

ADMINISTRATION THEORY: RATIONALISM
AND THE SYSTEMS PERSPECTIVE

Chapter 3

"CLASSICAL" AND "MODERN"

IN ORGANIZATION THEORY

*Dad took moving pictures of us children washing dishes, so that
he could figure out how we could reduce our motions and thus
hurry through the task. Irregular jobs, such as painting the back
porch or removing a stump from the front lawn, were awarded
on a low-bid basis. Each child who wanted extra pocket money
submitted a sealed bid saying what he would do the job for.
The lowest bidder got the contract. . . .*

*Yes, at home or on the job, Dad was always the efficiency
expert. He buttoned his vest from the bottom up, instead of
from the top down, because the bottom-to-top process took him
only three seconds, while the top-to-bottom took seven. He even
used two shaving brushes to lather his face, because he found
that by so doing he could cut seventeen seconds off his shaving
time. For a while he tried shaving with two razors, but he finally
gave that up.*

*"I can save forty-four seconds," he grumbled, "but I wasted
two minutes this morning putting this bandage on my throat."*

*It wasn't the slashed throat that really bothered him. It was
the two minutes.*

*(Frank B. Gilbreth, Jr.
and Ernestine Gilbreth Carey,*
Cheaper by the Dozen.
*New York: Thomas Y. Crowell,
1972, pp. 2-3)*

The man who pushed himself and his entire family in this way was Frank G. Gilbreth. The quotation above is taken from his biography. It is a remarkably affectionate account of the man considering the fact that is is authored by two of his twelve children, Frank Gilbreth, Jr., and Ernestine Gilbreth Carey. Gilbreth was one of the pioneers of the school of rational work administration, often known as scientific management. This school of organization theory, through the use of job analyses and time-and-motion studies, attempts to establish normal times for various tasks within industrial production.[1] A colleague of Gilbreth's, Frederick W. Taylor, was responsible for the most authoritative formulation of these ideas in his book, *The Principles of Scientific Management* (1911/1969).

The picture given above of the consequences of the struggle for efficiency in the home of the Gilbreth family should be supplemented with the view of how scientific management, or Taylorism, appeared when it was employed on a larger scale.

[Taylor] looked upon the enterprise like a machine in which the different cogs and wheels were to have their specialized tasks. The worker by nature was lazy and only by supervision, stern discipline, and piece rate payment could [he] be persuaded to execute what was necessary for the functioning of the enterprise. . . . By dividing work into short cycles of just a few operations it was possible with the help of motion analysis, adjustment of the work places, and tools, to increase efficiency in manifold ways. By using the piece rate payment system, workers (who usually were not given any education) were made to carry out the monotonous work at a quick pace. It need hardly be said that the freedom of the worker in such a system was utterly restricted. The zenith (or perhaps rather the bottom level) of the development of Taylorism is the assembly line, where workers at predetermined pace repeatedly carry out a small number of operations (Karlsson 1969: 56-57).

Monotony, the piece rate system, and the strivings to make the worker an almost mechanical component of the marchine, stand as monuments to alienation and routinization in industrial work. Since the 1930s, organizational sociologists, social psychologists, and psychologists have tried to find solutions to, or rather compensatory arrangements for, those problems which are created by the extreme division of work, the piece rate system, and time and motion studies.

The so-called human relations school (Elton Mayo 1933; Roethlis-berger and Dickson 1939; Walker and Guest 1952; and others) created somewhat of a sensation within organizational sociology with its discovery that shop floor workers possessed the need for social contact and that formation of social groups was in response to this need. Gradually, it became more and more outdated to view the organization, or the industrial enterprise which was the most common object of study, like a machine which was rationally constructed and composed of parts which, if necessary, could be replaced by others. A *systems perspective* slowly emerged, i.e., a view of the organization as a living entity, striving for balance and equilibrium, continuously adjusting to forces within the system itself as well as to those in its surroundings.

The often inhuman consequences of Taylorism, the opposition by human relations school, and the organization-theoretical systems approach, have been strong forces behind the currently common rejections of the rationalistic assumptions upon which scientific management is based. Joseph A. Litterer portrays the association between rationalism and the "classical school" (Gilbreth, Taylor, Henri Fayol, and others) in the following way:

> The classical point of view holds that work or tasks can be so organized as to accomplish efficiently the objectives of the organization. An organization is viewed as a product of rational thought concerned largely with coordinating tasks through the use of legitimate authority. It is based on the fundamental and usually implicit assumption that the behavior of people is logical, rational, and within the same system of rationality as that used to formulate the organization (1969: 6).

The basis of the rational theory of organizations has largely passed into oblivion, partly because of the attacks by other theoretical schools, and partly because it never actually received any authorizative scientific support. Gilbreth and Taylor were engineers, primarily interested in exploiting their discoveries in practical manuals in order to increase the efficiency of industrial work. The "implicit assumption that the behavior of people is . . . rational" remained implicit, and was never developed into any explicit theory about organizations.

The "classical school" in organization sociology was normative in character. Because of this, it has been a favorite punching bag for organizational theoretans within the human relations and systems traditions. These theoreticians claim to be more "scientific" in their approach, describing organizations "as they actually function" rather than how they would like them to function (see pp. 121 ff.). The practical consulting ambitions of the representatives of the scientific management school,[2] however, is not a sufficient reason, in and of itself for rejecting the basic assumptions of the "classical school" in its effort to set up a goal-directed structure capable of carrying out work.

Too, it should be pointed out that human relations and systems theoreticians are also normative: they undertake to describe and explain to industrial leaders and other members of organizational executive groups the characteristics of the organization, in order that the executive can perform its tasks in a better way. And, as I shall argue more closely below, systems theory contains propositions and assumptions with clear normative purposes as well. Taylor and others often formulated their writings on organizational principles as highly concrete recommendations for the distribution of work. This was, at the time, an adequate response to the needs and demands of industrial leaders. For example, Taylor recommended to builders that their masons would be more effective if they used both hands at the same time (the left hand takes the brick, the right hand a trowelful of mortar) (Taylor 1969: 96). Today, the advice given by organizational specialists are more sophisticated. The Swedish business economists Eric Rhenman devotes his work, among other things, to explaining from where the institutional leader may get "his force, his strength, his possibilities to take responsibility and reach difficult decisions" (*God och dålig företagsledning [Good and Bad Business Management]*, 1970: 36).

The following chapters of Part II deal with the description, discussion and critique of two main currents within organizational theory. Chapters 4, 5, and 6 contain presentations of the basic assumptions of these two traditions, rationalism and the systems perspective. Chapter 7 is an illustration of the theoretical relevance and empirical usefulness of the dichotomy between mechanistic and organic structure—a dichotomy which is related, though not identical, to the distinction between the rationalistic and systems perspectives. Chapters 8 and 9 are devoted to a criticism and evaluation of the two perspectives. Both outlooks have important weaknesses, but a review of the two would appear to favor the rationalistic one. Finally, in Chapter 10 I try to develop a process model for the study of organizations. This model takes certain traits from the rationalistic perspective, but at the same time tries to supplement this by making explicit references to the material and political conditions which constitute the frame factors of organizational behavior and restrict the organization's freedom to act. This discussion is summarized in Figure 10.1, p. 176. The reading of chs. 8 and 9 is considerably facilitated by referring to this figure.

NOTES

1. The first MTM system was probably Gilbreth's invention "therbligs" (his name in reverse with slight variation): a series of standardized units of behavior like "search," "find," "select," "take," etc. The system was tested, for example, when Gilbreth had a doctor remove the tonsils of six of his children in one day, filming the operations (Gilbreth and Gilbreth Carey, Ch. 10).

2. The principles for the administrative division of work, which were established by Gulick and Urwick in their *Papers on the Science of Administration* (1937), are sometimes called administrative management. The differences between administrative management and scientific management is not great enough to require a special commentary.

Chapter 4

THEORETICAL OUTLOOKS:

Rationalism and the Systems Perspective

Introduction

In Part I of this book, I reviewed three different types of theories of bureaucracy. One of my conclusions was that Marxism lacks a theory about the inner structure of organizations, and about the relationship between this structure and the efficiency of organizations. Marxism is first and foremost a theory about external conditions, i.e., material and structural-political conditions on which organizations are dependent. If we concern ourselves with a detailed analysis of organizations, Marxist theory, as it has traditionally been formulated, does not give us many useful starting points. With Weber and Michels, however, it is another matter. As we have seen, the theories of both of these authors contain large measures of "immanent" explanations of the the actions of organizations. Also, the links backward to Weber and Michels in present-day organization theory are often very evident.

One may see Weber and Michels as representatives of two different and separate analytical schools concerned with the explanation of the inner structure and behavior of organizations. Max Weber represents a rationalistic, instrumentalistic approach. This is an approach in which the calculating and planning aspects of the actions of organizations are emphasized. Robert Michels, on the other hand, exemplifies the systems perspective of organizations, according to which oligarchic phenomena emerge because of "automatic" processes of differentiation between the "elite" and the "mass." Whereas Weber emphasizes prediction and plan, Michels emphasizes those aspects which are spontaneous and which arise "out of themselves." In this chapter, I shall briefly describe and comment on these two approaches to organization theory: rationalism and the systems perspective. A starting point for the discussion is a well-known article by Alvin W. Gouldner, "Organizational Analysis" (1959).

Gouldner on Rationalism and Systems

The growth of large, complex organizations is one of the most distinctive characteristics of modern society and something which separates it from feudal societal forms. The French philosopher Henri de Saint-Simon was one of the first to pay attention to the emergence of modern patterns of organization. He identified some of their most characteristic traits. In the future, said Saint-Simon, administration would not be practiced by force or violence. The authority of the administrator would no longer be based on ascriptive characteristics, but rather, his authority would stem from his mastering of scientific and technical knowledge. With the rise of the modern professions (doctors, lawyers, engineers, etc.), occupational loyalties would emerge and extend outside the professional's own native and local community.

There exists, according to Gouldner, a clear parallel between Saint-Simon and Weber. Both emphasize the importance of expertise and scientific knowledge for the modern organization and its administration. In addition they both thoroughly spell out the ways in which the new organizations would affect the character of modern society. The primary difference between them is that Weber, more clearly than Saint-Simon, saw that authority in organizations was not dependent only on superior technical knowledge, but also on factors of a less rational kind (e.g., charisma).

Another line of development connects Auguste Comte with modern systems theory. Gouldner notes one statement by Comte: "the final order which arises' spontaneously is always superior to that which human combination had, by anticipation, constructed." In Comte's system, the "natural" and spontaneously achieved existing order is put forward instead of a political, legal, or constitutional order which is *planned*. This idea of a natural system was later adopted and developed by Robert Michels, and even later by theoreticians within the structural-functional tradition, e.g., Talcott Parsons (Gouldner 1959: 404).

Gouldner describes the two approaches in the following way:

The rational model. The organization is viewed as an "instrument," i.e., a rationally designed means for the realization of explicit goals of a particular group of people. The organizational structure is regarded as a tool, and alterations of the organizational structure are seen as instruments for improving efficiency.

> The rational model assumes that decisions are made on the basis of a rational survey of the situation, utilizing certified knowledge with a deliberate orientation to an expressly codified legal apparatus. The focus is, therefore, on the legally prescribed structure— *i.e.*, the formally "blueprinted" patterns—since these are more largely subject to deliberate inspection and rational manipulation (Gouldner 1959: 404-405).

The rational model implies a "mechanical" perspective: "it views the organization as a structure of manipulable parts, each of which is separately modifiable with a view to enhancing the efficiency of the whole. Individual organizational elements are seen as subject to successful and planned modification, enactable by deliberate decision. The long-range development of the organization as a whole is also regarded as subject to planned control and as capable of being brought into increasing conformity with explicitly held plans and goals" (1959: 405).

Thus, modifications of the organization take place as the direct effects of the plans of a certain group (the mandator), with these modifications being made for the expressed purposes of implementing the mandator's plans. Changes are made in a deliberate manner, and the replacement or modifications of one part can be carried out without significantly affecting the other parts.

The systems perspective. Perhaps the most significant characteristic of a system is that changes in one part of it affect other parts as well. The different components of the system are dependent on each other. Changes are responses to the functional needs of the system or needs existing in the environment of the subsystem under study. According to the rational model, different parts of the organization may be changed without causing a disturbance in the other parts. According to the systems model, however, this is not possible since all parts are necessarily interdependent. Striving toward balance and survival are major characteristics of a natural system.

> The natural-system model regards the organization as a "natural whole," or system. The realization of the goals of the system as a whole is but one of several important needs to which the organization is oriented. Its component structures are seen as emergent institutions, which can be understood only in relation to the diverse needs of the total system. The organization, according to this model, strives to survive and to maintain its equilibrium, and this striving may persist even after its explicitly held goals have been successfully attained. This strain toward survival may even on occasion lead to the neglect or distortion of the organization's goals. Whatever the plans of their creators, organizations, say the natural-system theorists, become ends in themselves and possess their own distinctive need which have to be satisfied. Once established, organizations tend to generate new ends which constrain subsequent decisions and limit the manner in which the nominal group goals can be pursued.
>
> Organization structures are viewed as spontaneously and almost homeostatically maintained. Changes in organizational patterns are considered the results of cumulative, unplanned, adaptive responses to threats to the equilibrium of the system as a whole. Responses to problems are thought of as taking the form of crescively developed defense mechanisms and as being importantly shaped by shared values which are deeply internalized in the members. The empirical focus is thus directed to the spontaneously emergent and normatively sanctioned structures in the organization. . . .
>
> The natural-system model is typical based upon an underlying "organismic" model which stresses the interdependence of the component parts. Planned changes are therefore expected to have ramifying consequences for the whole organizational system. . . . Long-range organizational development is . . . regarded as an evolution, conforming to "natural laws" rather than to the planner's designs (Gouldner 1959: 405-406).

The distinction between rationalism and the systems perspective is of utmost importance within modern organizational theory. As we shall find, the two philosophical traditions are reflected in a great variety of theoretical contributions by well-known social science writers, some of whom are discussed in the following sections.

Open and Closed Systems: Organizational Balance and Survival

James D. Thompson (1967) has taken up Gouldner's distinction for further development. Thompson draws a parallel between, on the one hand, the rational model and the vision of a closed system, and on the other hand, what Gouldner calls the natural-systems model and the idea of an open system. As exponents of the "closed" tradition he identifies Taylor and the scientific management school, Gulick and Urwick and their theory of administrative management, and Weber's model of bureaucracy (1967: 4-6). Representatives of the "open" tradition are, e.g., Roethlisberger and Dickson; Chester I. Barnard; Herbert Simon; and Philip Selznick.

Thompson strongly stresses the character of the rational model as being a theory for planning and control of organizations. To his mind, it is primarily designed as a theory of efficiency and not as a theory of how organizations actually function.

> It seems clear that the rational-model approach uses a closed-system strategy. . . . All resources are appropriate resources, and their allocation fits a master plan. All action is appropriate action, and its outcomes are predictable.

> It is no accident that much of the literature on the management or administration of complex organizations centers on the concepts of *planning* or *controlling*. Nor is it any accident that such views are dismissed by those using the open-system strategy (1967: 6).

Concerning the open-systems model, Thompson directs our attention to one feature that forms an important part of organizational systems theories: the assumption that the equilibrium of the system is maintained through a balance between the contributions given by the participants of the organization and the rewards received by them.

> Approached as a natural system, the complex organization is a set of interdependent parts which together make up a whole because each contributes something and receives something from the whole, which in turn is interdependent with some larger

environment. Survival of the system is taken to be the goal, and the parts and their relationships presumably are determined through evolutionary processes. Dysfunctions are conceivable, but it is assumed that an offending part will adjust to produce a net positive contribution or be disengaged, or else the system will degenerate (1967: 6-7).

Rationalism and the Systems Perspective: Some Related Theories

The two perspectives stress different aspects of the inner structure of organizations. In this section, I shall review some conceptual dichotomies and distinctions presented by other authors which should be of particular interest for our discussions here.

BURNS AND STALKER ON MECHANISTIC AND ORGANIC SYSTEMS

Burns and Stalker in their book, *The Management of Innovation* (1961) deal with the conditions for renewal and change in organizations. Their major thesis is that the adequacy of a particular organizational structure is contingent on the conditions under which the system works. They perceive two opposite types of administrative systems, namely (a) the mechanistic and (b) the organic.

The mechanistic system is best suited for stable conditions, i.e., when the organization is not subject to many pressures toward change. The organic form of organization, however, is more adequate when the environment of the organization is unstable and varying. For example, the organic form is better adapted to tasks which cannot be easily distributed between different positions in the organization. Thus, the major formula is that a stable environment allows a rigid organizational structure, whereas a changing environment requires a structure which is loose and adaptable. The major traits of the mechanistic vis-à-vis the organic structural type are presented in the following sketch.

A *mechanistic system* is characterized by

(a) the specialized differentiation of functional tasks into which the problems and tasks facing the concern as a whole are broken down;

(b) the abstract nature of each individual task, which is pursued with techniques and purpose more or less distinct from those of the concern as a whole; i.e., the functionaries tend to pursue the technical improvement of means, rather than the accomplishment of the ends of the concern;

(c) the reconciliation, for each level in the hierarchy, of these distinct performances by the immediate superiors, who are also, in turn, responsible for seeing that each is relevant in his own special part of the main task;

(d) the precise definition of rights and obligations and technical methods attached to each functional role;

(e) the translation of rights, obligations, and methods into the responsibilities of a functional position;

(f) hierarchic structure of control, authority, and communication;

(g) a reinforcement of the hierarchic structure by the location of knowledge of actualities exclusively at the top of the hierarchy, where the final reconciliation of distinct tasks and assessment of relevance is made;

(h) a tendency for interaction between members of the concern to be vertical, i.e., between superior and subordinate;

(i) a tendency for operations and working behavior to be governed by the instructions and decisions issued by superiors;

(j) insistence on loyalty to the concern and obedience to superiors as a condition of membership;

(k) a greater importance and prestige attaching to internal (local) than to general (cosmopolitan) knowledge, experience, and skill.

An *organic system* is characterized by

(a) the contributive nature of special knowledge and experience to the common task of the concern;

(b) the "realistic" nature of the individual task, which is seen as set by the total situation of the concern;

(c) the adjustment and continual redefinition of individual tasks through interaction with others;

(d) the shedding of "responsibility" as a limited field of rights, obligations, and methods. (Problems may not be posted upwards, downwards or sideways as being someone else's responsibility);

(e) the spread of commitment to the concern beyond any technical definition;

(f) a network structure of control, authority, and communication. . . .

(g) omniscience no longer imputed to the head of the concern; knowledge about the technical or commercial nature of the here and now task may be located anywhere in the network; . . .

(h) a lateral rather than a vertical direction of communication through the organization, communication between people of different rank, also, resembling consultation rather than command;

(i) a content of communication which consists of information and advice rather than instructions and decisions;

(j) commitment to the concern's tasks and to the "technological ethos" of material progress and expansion is more highly valued than loyalty and obedience;

(k) importance and prestige attached to affiliations and expertise valid in the industrial and commercial milieux external to the firm. (Burns and Stalker 1961: 120-122)

The more "floating" character of the organic form does not mean that the organization is completely unstratified. The actors have a more or less valued position. Their performance, however, is evaluated primarily on the basis of demonstrated expert knowledge. The more experienced people will often assume leadership, but it is a fundamental assumption of an organic system that the one who is best informed and has the most relevant knowledge should become the leader.

The characteristic of the organic type of being a somewhat more open system is demonstrated by items (j) and (k), which stress that the loyalties of the positions extend further than is the case in a mechanistic system. The organic model is also based more on mutual relationships, consultation, and continuous inner change. Participants are governed more by referring to long-range programs and aims rather than through detailed instructions or strict adherence to their contractual relationship with the organization. A relative absence of hierarchy, division of tasks, centralized information, and strict definitions of positions differentiate the organic model from the mechanistic.

Demonstration cases of the two organizational models are not difficult to find. The military organization or the assemblyline car factory exemplify the mechanistic variant; a scientific institution, a research department of a company, or a public relations office exemplify the organic.

Burns and Stalker emphasize that their conceptual dichotomy is not only a theoretical construction. The concepts are not "merely interpretations offered by observers of different schools," but are forms of organization which "exist objectively" (1961: 119). This approach can be contrasted to Gouldner's, which contends that the rationalist type of theory and the systems perspective represent different *theoretical ideal types* (Gouldner 1959: 406-407).

As I shall further argue below (Ch. 7), the issue about different *empirical structures* of the organization should not be mixed with the question of advantages of drawbacks of particular *organizational theories*. Burns and Stalker's approach implies that the two types of structural models are more or less suitable solutions to particular organizational problems, with the choice between a mechanistic and organic solution depending on environmental conditions. In contrast to the distinction between mechanistic and organic structures, the rationalist perspective and the systems perspective represent theoretical points of departure for observing the organization as a totality. This total perspective includes, but is not the same as, the views of what is an adequate (or inadequate) inner structure in a particular situation.

ARGYRIS, LIKERT, PERROW, AND OTHERS

Conceptions about the latent conflict between a mechanistic structure and a humanistic development—an optimistic and dealienating view of man—are very common in the organizational-sociological literature. For example, Chris Argyris states that there exists a contradiction between properties of the individual and certain organizational characteristics. According to him the development of the individual is characterized by an increasing motivation to take initiatives, to learn and develop, to take on still greater responsibility, and to make more and more encompassing decisions. When the individual is fit into a mechanistic organization, however, he becomes the object of pressures in the opposite direction, i.e., pressures to subordinate himself, to carry out routine and monotonous tasks, to take on very limited responsibility, and to make few, if any, important decisions (Argyris 1967). Thus, a major line of thought in Argyris' work is that the organic type of organization should be sought after when "decisions in which maximum individual productivity and maximum feelings of responsibility and commitment are desired—for example, decisions regarding promotion, salaries, or the acceptance of a departmental production objective" (1964: 210). In other words, the organic type of organization is better able to produce harmony between individual characteristics and organizational demands. Within the organic type of organization which is made up of "essential properties," the individual has greater possibilities of achieving "positive mental health" (1964: 160 ff.). ("Essential properties" means, briefly, that the organization approaches organic characteristics, i.e., develops interrelations between different parts, achieves goals which are related to the whole system rather than parts of the system, and maintains balance and equilibrium. 1964: 119 ff.).

Rensis Likert, in his book, *New Patterns of Management* (1961), distinguishes an authoritarian form of organization from one where the individual participates and cooperates. Authoritarian organizational forms can vary from being directly exploitative to benignly authoritarian. In the participate forms, decisions are made by the total organization. The authoritarian form is characterized by one-sided control, whereas the participative one has a more collectively distributed control (1961: 423 ff.).

Other authors who present dichotomous pictures of organization via the use of concepts which emphasize "rigid" as opposed to "loose" structures (or "closed" versus "open" structure) are McGregor (1960), Bennis (1959), Barnes (1960), and Litwak (1961). For example, McGregor contrasts an "open" and more philantropic theory of management ("theory Y") to a theory which is more "closed" and authoritarian ("theory X"). Bennis describes the organic organization as "problem-solving," Barnes uses the concept "open system," and Litwak bases his discussion on the term "human relations."

Of particular interest in this connection is an article by Charles Perrow (1967). Perrow suggests that organizations should be classified with regard to what type of technology they use, and by what types of decisions are required by production. According to Perrow, it is especially important to distinguish organizations with routine production from those with nonroutine production. In routine production, the organization encounters few situations which present unusual or abnormal demands; it has to master few exceptional cases or particular circumstances, and it can draw upon well-established, standardized logical and analytical methods for solving problems. In nonroutine production, the situation is the reverse. The organization encounters a multitude of previously unknown problems and does not have recourse to established problem-solving routines. A good example of the latter case is the space industry, and of the former, steel production (1967: 195-196). A more mechanistic structure is to be expected in steel production than in the space industry.

Chapter 5

RATIONALISM AND MEANS-ENDS

ANALYSIS

Introduction

In the previous chapter, I outlined certain traits which separate the rationalistic perspective of organizations from the systems perspective. Additionally, I pointed to how the differentiation of a rationalism and systems perspective is related to a variety of other well-known organizational-theoretical approaches. In this chapter, I shall go further into the basic assumptions of the rationalist theory and provide some examples of rationalistic analysis.

The rationalist approach has two basic characteristics. First, the actions of organizations are seen as a *function of goals,* which are set up by some individual or group of individuals (the organization's mandator). Second, it is assumed that the person or persons who are able to implement the goals on a day-to-day basis are capable of carrying out an *inventory of different alternative ways of reaching the organization goals,* and that the individual is able to choose an adequate means for performing the chosen strategy in the most economical fashion ("economy" construed broadly).

The rationalistic model of analysis is interesting not only from a social-scientific viewpoint, but also from the perspective of practical application. In Swedish government administration today, the rationalistic model of planning and control is widely esteemed and probably will become even more so in the future. The parliamentary commission on budgeting (*SOU* 1967: 11-13) blueprinted the basic guidelines for the organization, planning, and evaluation of the work of government offices. This committee's model created a considerable impact after its presentation. In this chapter, we shall look at two examples of the application of the means-ends analysis sketched out by the budgeting commission. We shall focus first on the recommendations by the Swedish National Audit Bureau (NAB) for the planning and evaluation of work within the public sector, and second, on the model put forward by the parliamentary commission on social problems (*SOU* 1974: 39).

The Anatomy of the Decision Process

GOAL-RATIONALITY AND VALUE-RATIONALITY

Social action, according to Max Weber (1968: 24) is goal-rational or instrumentally rational (*zweckrational*) when it is based on the expectation of the actions of other people and objects in the environment. The actor uses these expectations as "conditions" or "means" in order to achieve his own consciously pursued goals. According to the model of goal-rational behavior, the individual strives to evaluate in one composite calculus the goals, means, and possible secondary consequences of his action. This means that the individual consciously and deliberately surveys alternative ways of reaching his goal, that he relates the goal to the secondary consequences, and that he tries to estimate the relative importance of different possible goals (Weber 1968: 26). Goal-rational behavior differs from value-rational (*wertrational*) action, the latter being determined by "a conscious belief in the value for its own sake of some ethical, aesthetic, religious, or other form of behavior, *independently* of its prospects of success" (Weber 1968: 24-25; my emphasis).

The bureaucratic ideal type, sketched out by Weber and subject to much sociological controversy, can be seen as a survey of the organizational and administrative arrangements which are best suited to achieve full goal-rationality in organized action (see above, p. 55). The bureaucratic ideal type is a theoretical construction, a kind of measuring device against which one can compare different empirical cases.

There is a multitude of misunderstandings associated with the bureaucratic ideal type. In American organizational sociology, considerable effort has been devoted to the task of showing or implying that the bureaucratic organization is not optimally effective. The most well-known analysis of this kind is Robert K. Merton's article, "Bureaucratic structure and personality" (1957). A similar thesis is advanced by the Frenchman Michel Crozier in his book, *The Bureaucratic Phenomenon* (1964). Merton points out, among other things, that the official in an administrative system often develops a behavior in which discipline becomes an immediate value, with the original goals of the organization tending to be displaced and subordinated to his loyalty to rules ("an instrumental value becomes a terminal value"; 1957: 199). Furthermore, the official, because of his concentration on special areas of competence, may develop what Veblen calls "trained incapacity," i.e., an condition in which the official's expert knowledge functions as an obstacle to flexibility and creativity.

In his description of the bureaucratic type of organization, Merton emphasizes the dysfunctions of bureaucracy, in contrast to the positive aspects brought forward by Weber, or rather, the positive aspects which Weber *seems* to have brought forward. Merton presents the bureaucratic ideal type as if Weber had given it only positive connotations. According to Merton, Weber's analysis implies that "the positive attainments and functions of bureaucratic organization are emphasized and the internal stresses and strains of such structures are almost wholly neglected" (1957: 197). In a similar way, Crozier emphasizes that a bureaucratic organization has several negative effects, the significant characteristic of bureaucracy being a tendency toward inability to adjust adequately to changes in the environment of the organization (1964: 187 f.).

The contributions of Merton and Crozier are excellent pieces of sociological analysis and contain many important arguments. However, I find it difficult to see them as valid criticisms of Weber. Weber did not maintain that the bureaucratic organization necessarily is effective because of hierarchy, distribution of labor, universalism, etc., but, and this is an important distinction, that an organization with these characteristics is "capable" of reaching maximum possible efficiency (Weber 1968: 223). This capacity of the bureaucratic form of organization is associated with its technical characteristics, and in these technical characteristics it is, according to Weber, superior to any other form of organization (1968: 223). As I have tried to show in the first part of this book, Weber emphasizes in many places the need for bureaucracy to be subordinate to its master. The list of German words which was used to characterize the Weberian ideal type in Chapter 1 ("Präzision, Schnelligkeit, Eindeutigkeit," ... etc.) also included the important term "straffe Unterordnung" (strict subordination). The views advanced in Part I of this book imply that the technical efficiency of the bureaucratic ideal type needs to be related to the purposes and goals which the organization is set up to accomplish. Thus, in certain respects, it seems pointless for Merton to object to Weber on the basis that the bureaucratic form of organization has certain dysfunctions which show themselves empirically as tendencies toward rigidity, displacement of goals, etc. As I have pointed out, Weber himself stressed these tendencies of the bureaucratic apparatus (note, for example, his analysis of Prussia after Bismarck) and he conceived of such characteristics precisely as dysfunctions, as deviations from the ideal type sketched by him (cf. Lindskoug 1974).

THE ELEMENTS OF RATIONAL DECISION-MAKING

Herbert A. Simon, in his book *Administrative Behavior* (1947; quotations below from the second edition, 1957), developed a theory about the decision process in administrative systems. The book contains a detailed treatment of the anatomy of rational decision-making, a discussion which takes place within a more general organizational-sociological framework of a systems character. One might say that Simon has separated from Weber's treatment of the bureaucratic form of organization that special part which deals with the logic of rational decision-making. The historical aspect of goal-rational behavior are totally missing in Simon's book, which concentrates, rather, on the technicalities in the process of establishing goals and subgoals and choosing adequate means of action.

What is a decision? A complex decision (and the decision processes of organizations are complex) "is like a great river, drawing from its many tributaries the innumerable component premises of which it is constituted" (1957: xii). Many individuals and units of organization contribute to every decision. These contributions may be viewed as the preconditions for the final composite decision ("the river") and therefore, according to Simon, it becomes meaningless to put the question, "Who really makes the decision?" (1957: xii).

Organizational decision-making is a kind of compromise between rational, goal-oriented behavior and nonrational action. Simon suggests

that a central field of administrative theory is "the boundary between
the rational and the nonrational aspects of human social behavior"
(1957: xxiv). An organization, in Simon's perspective, is a structure
which provides the framework for the decisions. The organization sup-
plies every member of the group with the information, preconditions
and goals on which to base his decisions. In addition, it defines the
space of action for other people in the organization to whom the
decision-maker has to relate.

The conflict between the rational and the nonrational in human
behavior means that administrative theory has to take into account the
fact that the behavior of human beings can never be at an optimum.
According to Simon, people act in order to achieve satisfying solutions
since they do not have the ability to reach the best solutions by absolute standards. "While economic man maximizes—selects the best alternatives from among all those available to him, his cousin, whom we
shall call administrative man, satisfices—looks for a course of action
that is satisfactory or 'good enough'" (Simon 1957: xxiv).

An alternative is *optimal* if: (1) there exists a set of criteria that
permits all alternatives to be compared, and (2) the alternative
in question is preferred by these criteria, to all other alternatives.
An alternative is *satisfactory* if: (1) there exists a set of criteria
that describes minimally satisfactory alternatives, and (2) the alternative in question meets or exceeds all these criteria (March
and Simon 1958: 140).

Note the extremely strong demands which are put on the decision
process in the optimum case. In principle, all known alternatives should
be possible to compare, after which the *best* alternative is chosen. In
the case of satisfying solutions, it is enough that *some* alternative corresponding to certain minimum criteria is chosen. The difference between
the two ways of action may be illustrated with the situation of search-
ing through a haystack to find the *most sharp-pointed* needle hidden in
the haystack, in comparison with the situation of finding a needle
which is *sharp-pointed enough* (1953: 141).

Let us look closer at the meaning of Simon's concept "decision
process." A decision process may be defined as a choice among alternatives which are perceived as adequate means for achieving pursued
goals. These goals, however, in themselves are means for reaching more
final purposes, or ultimate goals. (On ultimate goals, see Langefors
1971. The term refers to the ultimate aims of the organization, or "the

reason that the activity, or the system, is kept running." Below the ultimate goals are goals of lower priority. These subgoals should ideally be consistent with the ultimate goals. "Thus, one has to have some conception of which ultimate goals one wants to pursue in order to judge the efficiency of the subgoals, this being necessary also in order to allow for estimations of total efficiency" (Langefors 1971 : 22).

Goals are founded on *values*. Simon explicitly (1957: 45-46) accepts logical empiricism and its emphasis on the distinction between propositions of fact and propositions of value. Propositions of fact can be tested by empirical observation, whereas propositions of value have "imperative quality," i.e., they select a certain future condition at the cost of one or several others. Because decisions contain value as well as factual statements, they cannot be objectively described as correct or incorrect.

The decision process has to start with some value premise which is taken as given. According to Simon, this "ethical premise" is represented in organizations by the description of organizational objectives (Simon 1957: 50). The objective has to be described in such concrete terms that it is possible to determine to what degree the goals have been implemented as a result of organizational action.

In order to achieve a certain goal, one will usually employ a variety of different strategies. The achievement of a goal, therefore, demands a choice between alternative strategies. In the evaluation of strategies, all those consequences which follow from each alternative should be judged. "Consequences," according to this optimum model, is a term comprising not only those outcomes which were predicted from the beginning, but also those effects which were not originally predicted.

After establishing the goal, the decision may be described as a process of four steps: (1) Make an inventory of all alternative strategies (A_i); (2) establish which consequences (c_{ij}) will follow from every A_i; (3) carry out evaluations (V_{ij}) of the consequences taking into account the established goals; (4) Choose a strategy (i.e., make a decision) (Simon 1957: 67).

The "decision tree" (Figure 5.1) illustrates the process:

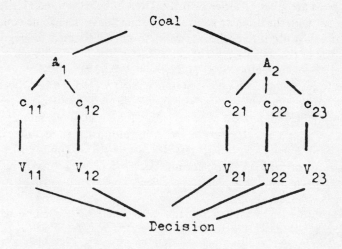

Figure 5.1

NOTE: For similar models of the decision process, see, e.g., Hedberg et al. (1971: 63) and Rhenman (1968: 43).

Applications of Means-Ends Theory

In his book, *Sweden: Prototype of Modern Society* (1970), Richard F. Tomasson writes:

> Swedes believe that institutions can and should be restructured to accomplish certain agreed-upon ends. This is true in spite of the fact that the traditional component in many Swedish institutions is great, particularly in the government, the universities, and the legal system. . . . Contemporary Sweden abounds in examples of change in the most fundamental institutions. . . . The radical restructuring of the school system to make it more egalitarian is one example. The radical revision of the constitution to bring it in accord with contemporary practice is another example. . . . Even sex roles and the relations between the sexes are believed to be amenable to change through changing educational and economic institutions (pp. 274-275).

The emphasis on empiricism and rationality, which Tomasson sees as dominant values in Swedish society, is well exhibited by the Swedish parliamentary reports (*Statens Offentliga Utredningar,* or briefly *SOU*). Partly because they recruit members from a broad spectrum of political parties at an early stage in their work, the parliamentary committees tend to emphasize compromise rather than ideological conflict. This is also due to the fact that the committees are anxious to seek the co-operation of experts from different fields and of different persuasions, in order to insure maximum objectivity. Their reports, therefore, "tend to be factual, filled with statistics, and parsimonious in the use of generalizations and assumptions." (Tomasson 1970: 274). This becomes especially clear if the Swedish reports are compared to the British government reports. "The Swedish reports take little for granted, whereas the British reports are replete with ideological assumptions and general beliefs" (p. 274).

The two examples of Swedish parliamentary reports, given below, well illustrate the "secular rationalism" and the "instrumental attitude toward institutions" which Tomasson has found to be characteristic of Swedish society. The first example concerns the very methods by which institutions can be changed and checked. The second illustrates how the rational approach is employed for overseeing procedures in social welfare and social work.

EXAMPLE 1: PROGRAM BUDGETING AND EFFECTIVENESS AUDITING

Several years of experiments with and evaluations of so-called program budgeting have been carried out within the Swedish state administration. The theory and arguments for program budgeting are stated in the report of the parliamentary commission on budgeting (*SOU* 1967: 11-13). Briefly, program budgeting may be defined as a

> system of planning, direction, and control of the activity of a government office for the purpose of increasing efficiency. It is presupposed that the tasks of the office (*goals*) are to be carried out by goal-directed programs, that adequate funding is provided for each program, that planning and budgeting take place on the basis of different alternatives, that the government office makes use of internal budgeting and cost accounting, and that the performance and effect of government action are evaluated against these costs (RRV 1970: 212).

It is easy to see the parallel between this definition and the ideal model of rational planning which has been discussed above. In order to achieve an established goal, the government office is supposed to screen various action alternatives (and presumably also to study the different consequences of each alternative), to evaluate these alternatives with regard to costs and to compare the results of a certain strategy with its costs, once that strategy has been chosen and carried out. Instead of controlling each specific expense account of each public organization, which was the previous practice, the state now attempts to supervise the public sector by controlling the *goal-achievement* of state offices.

A professor of economics expresses one of the basic theses of the program budgeting methodology in the following way:

> To indicate the goals, to judge how well they have been achieved, and preferably also to measure them, seems . . . necessary in order to achieve efficiency as well in the top level of government administration as within government bureaus. . . . [According to the theory of program budgeting] the actions taken by government authorities [should] . . . be made in a more goal-directed fashion. . . . On the part of government authorities, the concentration on goals should contribute to making activity more effectively directed along the lines preferred by the authorities; thereby it is possible to better guarantee that detailed decisions are made exclusively by the public employees themselves (Lars Werin in RRV 1973).

Thus, according to Werin, the rationalist model as applied to Swedish state administration becomes not only a means of insuring that the intended effects of public activity are achieved; program budgeting also contributes to a greater local self-determination and represents a guarantee that "detailed decisions are made by the public employees themselves." Economic support is no longer given to different posts in the total budget of a bureau but a special budget is established for every particular program. Thus, the *effectiveness* (I shall return to this concept in Chapter 8) of a bureau is measured by the degree to which it achieves the indicated goal and by measuring the costs of the activity. As indicated by Simon, it is obvious that great attention has to be paid to the problem of formulating goals which are concrete enough to make it possible to establish whether they have been achieved or not (see further pp. 145f. below). Operational planning, i.e., the indication of goals for operations and the application of various strategies to achieve these goals, makes possible the control of efficiency in a government bureau. This control activity is called *effectiveness auditing* (förvaltningsrevision). Figures 5.2 and 5.3 lay out the major elements of effectiveness auditing.

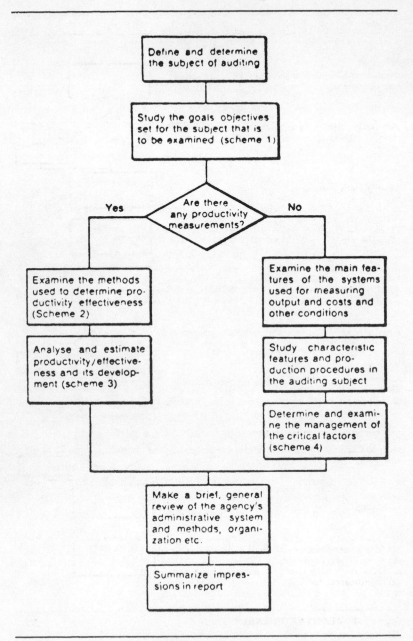

Figure 5.2: GENERAL FLOW CHART FOR THE WORK OF AUDITING
Source: Swedish National Audit Bureau (RRV 1971: 78).

Study and analyse the goals given for the activity being inspected.

Are these sufficiently accurate to be used in planning, directing and controlling? — if not, make closer examination and note.

No

Yes

Study means-end chain.

Study how the main goal is broken down into subgoals, etc.

How are the subgoals, etc., presented? In written plane of operations, job descriptions, etc.?

Are the formally presented subgoals consistent with the main goal and other goals? — If not, make closer examination and note.

No

Yes

Investigate if there are any so-called informal goals. If so, what are they?

Do informal goals happen to be inconsistent with the main goals? — If not, make close examination and note.

No

Yes

How are the goals within the agency determined? How often are they adjusted?

Summarize impressions of the investigation. State any deficiencies observed. State cause of confirmed shortcomings or at least probable cause. State if defective goal accuracy is of critical significance for the effectiveness of the activity.

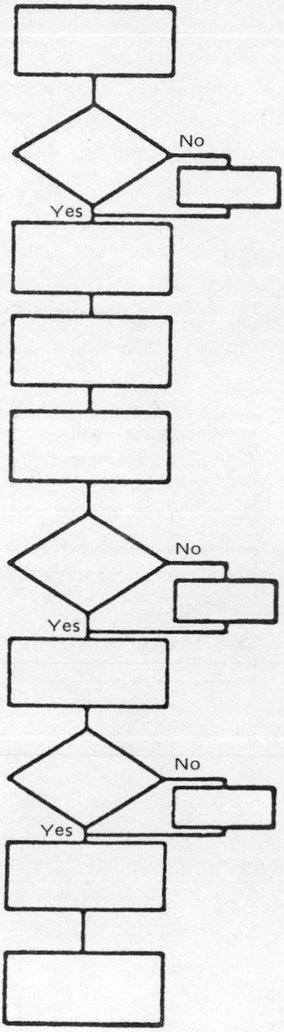

Figure 5.3: MEANS-ENDS ANALYSIS
Source: Swedish National Audit Bureau (RRV 1971: 82).

Figure 5.2 contains the general flow chart for the auditing tasks, and Figure 5.3 indicates the content of goal analysis (box no. 2 in Figure 5.2). In particular, the latter diagram clearly shows how the major principles of rationalism are implemented into detailed recommendations, applicable to each step in the hierarchy of goals and means.

The application of new techniques for means-ends analysis represents a pressure on public organizations to make their own planning coherent with the expectations of the auditing institutions. To a certain extent, then, the principles of evaluation will function as an instrument for directing operations within the organizations under scrutiny. Thus, one may expect that rationalistic means and techniques will be applied more and more as a basis for planning by the state authorities and will gradually become more accepted as a model of long-term state surveying activity. The parliamentary commission on social problems and social legislation (*SOU* 1974: 39-40) is an example of the latter.

EXAMPLE 2: THE SURVEY OF SOCIAL
LEGISLATION, 1974

The social legislation survey states that the formulation of precise goals is a precondition for decision-making regarding social service organizations, the relation of social services to other societal areas, and for the cooperation between the social service authorities and other organizations. In addition, explicit goals are needed for the development of working methods, the legislative specification of social service tasks, etc. and, most importantly, to insure that social service activity can be made subject to follow-ups and evaluation of results (*SOU* 1974: 39, pp. 157 f.).

The goals, therefore, become both the starting point and the end point of the activities within social care, social treatment and social planning. The scheme of principles for the solution of social problems, sketched out by the committee, is also designed to function as a guideline for the individual social worker and for his way of making decisions when confronted with the various problems. The committee argues that the sketch for the solution of social problems (shown in Figure 5.4) is applicable to all three areas of social service, namely, (a) individual and family treatment, (b) community work, and (c) social planning (*SOU* 1974: 39, pp. 355-356).

The sketch contains five steps and starts with a social worker together with a client trying to describe the current situation for the client, in order to see what problems it may contain (problem formu-

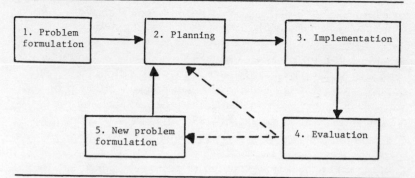

Figure 5.4
Source: **SOU** 1974: 39, p. 356.

lation). One tries to answer the questions, "Which causes lie behind the client's present situation? To what extent can the client himself affect this situation?"

The second step (planning) is the formulation of goals, analysis of action alternatives, and evaluation of the effects and causes of these alternatives. With regard to *goals,* the committee states that the general goals that have been indicated and commented on in the committee report, i.e., democracy, equality and security, should function as "targets" for the social worker (*SOU* 1974: 39, p. 357). For natural reasons, it is difficult to see how these goals are to be implemented in each specific case. Treatment, therefore, often has to be aimed at more short-sighted goals, "subtargets." After the goals have been established, the action alternatives are clarified. In this stage, the social worker tries to answer the question regarding which social services can be beneficially utilized in the case under consideration. Finally, within this step, the action alternatives are evaluated. Attempts are made to determine what effects the implemented actions may have on the client's situation and what are the costs of each alternative action. "It is . . . important that all costs are taken into consideration. . . . On the other hand, it cannot be required that every social worker make a complete review of resource assets and costs" (p. 357).

Before leaving box number 2, a decision should have been made, by comparing the expected effects of each action alternative with the resources required to implement it. It may then happen that

none of [the action alternatives] offers a satisfactory solution with regard to the established goal, or that the costs of achieving the goal appear too high. If so, the goal should be re-evaluated. With regard to a new goal, one performs a new analysis of the available action alternatives, etc. (*SOU* 1974: 39, p. 357).

Once a plan for treatment has been worked out, we then enter the third step of the means-end scheme and carry out the action program decided upon. Assuming that the action program can be performed without too many problems (if not, the program should be modified), we can then move to the fourth step, i.e., the evaluation of the performed work. This evaluation should contain the following:

> First, continuous documentation of the actions taken and the changes which are achieved in the life conditions of the client or the group . . . and of the results which have been achieved in relationship to the established goals. Second, an analysis with the purpose of providing a basis for possible modifications of social service operations (*SOU* 1974: 39, p. 358).

Hopefully, this evaluation process will provide experience such that a new problem area can be formulated, and thereafter the process starts anew, from box number 2, with new planning, implementation, etc.

Chapter 6

THE SYSTEMS PERSPECTIVE:

Some Basic Characteristics

Systems Theory and Structural-Functionalism

Looking at organizational theory today, we find it surprisingly unaffected by the sometimes violent critical discussions about the functionalist school which have been going on in sociology for the last twenty years. The systems perspective, which takes many of its essential traits from functionalism, has strongly dominated organizational sociology and has developed under the influence of writers such as Chester I. Barnard, Herbert A. Simon, James G. March, D. Katz and R. L. Kahn, and Amital Etzioni.

Structural-functionalism emphasizes the idea that society has a stable character and is made up of a well-integrated structure of elements. To the structural-functionalist, the *structure* of the social system is founded on a consensus between the members on values and norms, and further, the different elements of society fulfill *functions* which contribute to the maintenance of the system. The system's survival, its equilibrium, and the balanced relationship between its various parts are three essential components of both functionalist sociological theory and the systems variant of organizational sociology. Two Norwegian organizational researchers, H. M. Blegen and B. Nyléhn, say in the introduction of their book *Organisasjonsteori* (1969):

> When we study organizations, it is fruitful to look upon the world as composed of systems. The systems theory, which we take as our point of departure, is still not a unified discipline. It represents today a very incomplete construction which can be only partially described, and at that, only in an imprecise and qualitative way. Still, the *idea* which is the basis of this theory is acknowledged by scientists from a large variety of professional fields, a model of the world where everything is contingent upon everything—"wheels within wheels within wheels"—where the mutual relations and the reciprocal communication between systems, subsystems, and superordinate systems are the fundamental characteristics (p. 6).

The limitations of space do not allow a treatment of general systems theory as presented by Wiener, von Bertalanffy, Ashby, and others. Good introductory discussions on general systems theory may be found in Hall and Hagen (1956); and Emery (1969). I will limit myself to a few comments on the functionalist tradition within sociology, comments which are of importance for the discussion to follow.

Within sociology, functionalist ideas have had their most prominent spokesman in Talcott Parsons. The social system is described by Parsons as a number of individuals in mutual interrelationships with one another. Individuals cooperate because of their common motivation to achieve "optimum need gratification." Their expectation is that their interaction with other individuals within the system carries greater need gratification for them than would result from their own individual activity or their activity in other systems. Thus, the basis for their participation in the system is their expectation that a positive individual exchange balance will result. (Parsons 1951: 5-6, and Chs. II and III).

The notion of a positive balance of exchange as lying behind the motivation of individuals to participate in the organization (which, in its turn, is a precondition for the continued existence of the system) is a cornerstone in the theories of, among others, Simon (1957); March and Simon (1958); Ramström (1963); and Rhenman (several works, see, e.g., 1968; see below, pp. 164-162 and quotation from Thompson, above pp. 95-96). As I will argue more specifically below, the idea of exchange balance also represents one of the major problems of the systems theory tradition in organizational sociology.

The fundamental mechanism for the integration and stabilization of social systems is *institutionalization*. Institutional patterns are patterns of expectations of "culturally adequate behavior," expectations directed towards the role occupants of the system. Briefly, institutionalization is that process by which the adequate behavior of each individual in the system is insured, i.e., the process by which a certain way of acting becomes accepted by them as a positive value. The result of effective institutionalization is that each individual will accept the priority of collective interests over his own particularistic interests. "Institutionalization" appears as an important concept in the writings of Philip Selznick, and also forms a dominant part of the theories which in Sweden have been presented by the business economists Eric Rhenman and Dick Ramström (see below, pp. 120 ff.).

On Stakeholders

A key concept within the systems theory variant of organizational sociology is that of the "stakeholder" (*intressent,* or "participant" in March and Simon 1958: 89-90). The organization is perceived as a kind of market for various groups of stakeholders, i.e., different parties which find that they may have something to win by cooperating with the organization. In turn, the equilibrium of the organization is dependent on an undisturbed relationship between the organization and its different stakeholders. The organization as a system is contingent upon this exchange with its environment; the character of the exchange varies with the different needs of the organization, and consequently, the set of stakeholders also differs from time to time and between organizations. Therefore, definition of a stakeholder must necessarily be somewhat arbitrary. The most important stakeholders in a commerical organization are the employees, investors, suppliers, distributors, and consumers (March and Simon 1958: 89).

The pluralistic image of stakeholders or "participants," which has been developed within the systems theory tradition primarily by March and Simon, has become widely popular in Sweden, e.g., through the work of Eric Rhenman. Some of the organizational theorists who explicitly adopt the picture of the organization by Rhenman, following March and Simon, are Ramström (1963: 23), Mabon (1971: 64 ff.), Norrbom (1971: 78), Asplund (1973: 104), and Hedberg et al. (1971: 13). The stakeholders of the organization are those individuals or groups who are dependent on the enterprise for the implementation of

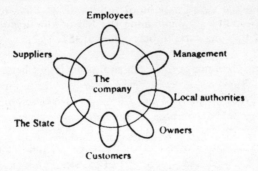

Figure 6.1
Source: Rhenman 1968: 25.

their own personal needs, and upon whom the enterprise is dependent for its continued existence.

In contrast to the basic ideas of the rationalistic tradition, the systems perspective does not see the organization primarily as an instrument for the realization of the mandator's goals. Rather, the organization is perceived as a structure which responds to, and adjusts itself to, a multitude of demands from various stakeholders, and which tries to maintain balance by reconciling these demands. The organization's management acquires a kind of mediator role, i.e., a role of weighing the demands from different stakeholders against each other. One can contrast this role description to that forwarded by the rationalistic tradition, in which the organizational management is seen more as the "extended arm" of the mandator.

The image of a set of stakeholders and the other primary components of the systems view of organizations, i.e., requirements for the system's survival and the balance between rewards and contributions, clearly emerges from the short and concise summary made by Herbert A. Simon in his chapter, "The Organizational Balance" in his book, *Administrative Behavior* (1957).

The organization has been described in this chapter as a system in equilibrium, which receives contributions in the form of money or effort, and offers inducements in return for these contributions. These inducements include the organizational goal itself, conservation and growth of the organization, and incentives unrelated to these two.

The organization equilibrium is maintained by the control group, whose personal values may be of various kinds, but who assume the responsibility of maintaining the life of the organization in order that they may attain these values (1957: 122).

To a large extent, Simon speaks here as an apostle of Chester I. Barnard, whose book, *The Functions of the Executive*, which appeared at the end of the 1930s, is perhaps the first comprehensive employment of systems theory for the purpose of enterprise government. Barnard, for example, states the following: "The survival of an organization depends upon the maintenance of an equilibrium of complex character in a continuously fluctuating environment of physical, biological, and social materials, elements, and forces, which calls for readjustment of processes internal to the organization" (1968: 6). Simon's systems perspective of the organization as a structure which directs and regulates individual decisions for the benefit of the totality is fully developed in Barnard's work as well. According to Barnard, the organization establishes limits to the individual's freedom of choice (1968: 14). Furthermore, Simon's discussion on the reward/contribution balance has a direct forerunner in Barnard's discussion (1968: 140, 153). (For some further comments on the similarities between Barnard and Simon, see Krupp 1961: 91 ff.).

Balance and Exchange

The criteria of balance and exchange are formulated by March and Simon in their very influential book, *Organizations* (1958) in the following way:

(1) An organization is a system of interrelated social behaviors of a number of persons whom we shall call the *participants* in the organization.

(2) Each participant and each group of participants receives *from* the organization *inducements* in return for which he makes *to* the organization *contributions*.

(3) Each participant will continue his participation in an organization only so long as the inducements offered him are as great or greater (measured in terms of *his* values and in terms of the alternatives open to him) than the contributions he is asked to make.

(4) The contributions provided by the various groups of participants are the source from which the organization manufactures the inducements offered to participants.

(5) Hence, an organization is "solvent"—and will continue in existence—only so long as the contributions are sufficient to provide inducements in large enough measure to draw forth these contributions (1958: 84).

Thus, "equilibrium because of a positive balance of exchange for the participants" can be viewed as the basic summary thesis of the systems perspective within organizational sociology. Or, as Emery and Trist say in a much-quoted article titled "Sociotechnical systems": "The continued existence of any enterprise presupposes some regular commerce in products or services with other enterprises, institutions and persons in its external social environment. If it is going to be useful to speak of steady states in an enterprise, they must be states in which this commerce is going on" (1969: 282-283).

Institutionalization

Institutionalization is a key concept within both functionalism and systems theory. The term refers to those processes and methods by which the organization inculcates a set of strategic values in the individuals who work in the organization. But how, more specifically, does the organization create consent around these values? This issue has been discussed by Philip Selznick who argues in his book *Leadership in Administration* (1957), for the importance of leadership for creating value homogeneity within the organization.

According to Selznick, institutionalization means "to *infuse with value* beyond the technical requirements of the task at hand. . . . From the standpoint of the committed person, the organization is changed from an expendable tool into a valued source of personal satisfaction" (1957: 17). Selznick emphasizes the importance of developing an *administrative ideology,* an official philosophy which is helpful in establishing a homogeneous staff in the organization and in guaranteeing continuity in the work of the leading group. "A well-formulated doctrine is remarkably handy for boosting internal morale, communicating the bases for decisions, and rebuffing outside claims and criticisms" (1957: 14).

Second, Selznick speaks of the importance of controlling the *creation and defense of elites.* It is a practical problem of great importance for organizations to form elite groups. "Specialized academies, selective recruiting, and many other devices help to build up the self-consciousness and the confidence of present and potential leaders. However, . . . counter-pressures work to break down the insulation of these elites and to warp their self-confidence. A problem of institutional leadership, as of statesmanship generally, is to see that elites do exist and function while inhibiting their tendency to become sealed off and to be more concerned with their own fate than with that of the enterprise as a whole" (1957: 14). The importance of uniform values in the organic type of organization can hardly get a more eloquent spokesman than Selznick: "The art of the creative leader is the art of institution-building, the reworking of human and technological materials to fashion an organism that embodies new and enduring values" (1957: 152-153).

It is not goal-rationality, but rather, value-rationality which dominates Selznick's description of the organization. One could say that Selznick's perspective on organizations, in contrast to Weber's, emphasizes the organization as an ideological and normative habitat for the individual. In such a perspective, the charismatic and policy-directed characteristics of leadership are made to dominate over the instrumental aspects, with the final result being a kind of manual for managers eager to build empires and institutions around a set of values which they consider necessary to promote and to conserve.

The Systems Perspective and Organizational Goals

The conception of an organization as a system, existing to fulfill the needs of certain stakeholders and constantly adjusting to environmental pressures and forces within the system itself, itself scepticism of any analysis of organizations in terms of goals. One of the most influential theoretical books on organizations appearing in the 1960s, Katz and Kahn's *The Social Psychology of Organizations* (1966) strongly attacks the rationalistic approach and argues for the superiority of systems theory in the study of organizations. According to Katz and Kahn, the goals which have been laid down by the founders or initiators of the organization, as well as the goals which are regarded as important of the present leaders of the organization, cannot be used as the basis for a theory of organizations. The authors do accept that it would be wrong to discount the goals that organizations have deliberately built into the "social contracts" on which they are formed. However, and this is their main theme, such goals are often deceptive. Goal descriptions may idealize, explain away, hide, or even leave out certain essential aspects of organizational behavior. Which, then, are these essential aspects? The following quotation from Katz and Kahn shows where they think the answer can be found.

> The organization as a system has an output, a product or an outcome, but his is not necessarily identical with the individual purposes of group members. Though the founders of the organization and its key members do think in teleological terms about organizational objectives, we should not accept such practical thinking, useful as it may be, in place of a theoretical set of constructs for purposes of scientific analysis. Social science, too frequently in the past, has been misled by such short-cuts and has equated popular phenomenology with scientific explanation (1966: 15-16).

Thus, the systems-theoretical approach fulfills the requirements of being scientific, whereas rationalism does not. Assumptions concerning organizational goals "scarcely provide an adequate basis for the study of organizations and at times can be misleading and even fallacious" (1966: 14). According to the opinion of Katz and Kahn, systems theory in these respects differs favorably from what they call "common sense approaches" (p. 14).

Not all authors within the systems tradition are as critical of "common sense approaches" as Katz and Kahn, but I believe it is fair to say that systems theories are strongly ambivalent when confronted by the concept of goals or objectives. True, they often acknowledge that it is possible to distinguish a multitude of different goals within an organization. This acknowledgement, however, is usually accompanied by a denial that the organization has a superordinate or dominating goal. At the most, "goals" are treated as something which is associated with the various components of the organization (individuals, offices, departments, etc.), and quite often, there is a noted reluctance toward the idea that the leadership of an organization or a company may have more dominating goals than other groups within the organization. The systems-theoretical school emphasizes that even though goals may exist within the organization, the *action* of the organization need not be directly related to these goals. The difference between the rationalistic school and the systems perspective may best be explained in the following manner: In rationalistic theory, goals represent an independent variable, and the organizational structure a dependent variable; in the systems-theoretical school, both goals and structure are responses to functional needs within the organization and in the surrounding supersystem, and because of this, are dependent variables. The latter position implies that a good explanation or prediction of organizational behavior cannot be achieved as a result of research which primarily focusses on the organization's goals. Let us look somewhat closer into this problem.

Etzioni (1964: 5) stresses that goals supply *orientations* for organizations. They depict a future condition, lay down directions for organizational activity, represent a source of legitimacy, and function as a model against which one may gauge the efficiency of the organization. Almost all organizations have a formal body for setting goals and for reformulating them (1964: 7). Etzioni also admits that organizations usually have some stakeholder or power-group which has the ultimate command of the organization (1964: 10, 12).

As Etzioni argues, these factors, however, are not an adequate basis for a scientific study of organizations. It is true, he says, that organizations have goals. However, they also have needs which arise from their day-to-day activities, and thus are tempted to satisfy their current needs at the cost of the original goals. Organizations often abandon their initial goals. Sometimes they also replace their primary goals with other goals, a process frequently associated with a bid for power by various professional groups (1964: 5, 9-12). Thus, during their daily operations, new goals and purposes arise which often clash with the original goals. (The discussion has a parallel in Perrow's distinction between official and operative goals, see pp. 181-182.)

Etzioni puts forward another objection to the study of organizational goals. He argues that such studies can easily achieve the character of "social criticism" and in the process become less scientific. Since organizations rarely reach their goals, they can be too easily construed as inefficient. Therefore, organizations should not be compared with their ideals as formulated in their goals but with each other. (1964: 16-17). (Etzioni overlooks the fact that organizations often have goals below the ideal or ultimate level, goals which are considerably more concrete and specific and which, better than the ultimate goals, may be used for a survey of organizational effectiveness. See p. 143 of this book.)

Etzioni finds the systems model more satisfactory to the scientific study of organizations. The systems perspective deals with the specification of those relations that have to exist in the organization in order for it to operate effectively (1964: 17). Effectiveness involves not only the achievement of goals but also of so-called "non-goal activities," an example being the increasing of employee motivation.

A similar viewpoint is put forward by Silverman (1970). He emphasizes that the possible advantage of classifying organizations in terms of goals is that the concept of goal offers a point of reference against which one may judge the system's "health" (p. 9). The problem, however, is that an organization can rarely be characterized as having any goal, thus rendering this approach as generally unfeasible. According to Silverman, it is legitimate to conceive of an organization as having a goal only in the case "where there is an ongoing consensus between the members of the organization about the purposes of their interaction" (1970: 9).

"Does the organization behave? Can 'it' desire?" are questions put forward by Chris Argyris in his book, *Integrating the Individual and the Organization* (1964). These questions are used as a prelude to his discussion of organizational goals. In Argyris' opinion, organizations have goals. However, these goals are not formulated by any mandator or dominating group of stakeholders, but constitute reactions to several complex processes. "When we say that 'it' is doing something or other we are summarizing a complex state of affairs within the organism in question. In psychology we learn that when we say 'he is perceiving' or 'he is learning to read,' we are summarizing an extremely complex set of interrelated activities not as yet fully understood. The same is true for the group and the organization" (1964: 155). The organization is characterized by three forms of activity: (1) achieving objectives, (2) maintaining the internal system, and (3) adapting to the external environment (1964, p. 120). According to Argyris, these "core activities" may be found in all organizations.

How does Argyris characterize the process of goal achievement? Goal-setting activities "are part of the problem-solving process." Again, what is this? Problem-solution exists in order to "help the organization overcome the forces toward organizational ineffectiveness" (1964: 145). What is a "problem?" A "problem" may be defined as an external or internal stimulus "that creates a chain reaction of complex events inside the system and upsets the existing steady state of the system" (1964: 137).

Goals and goal-setting are directly linked to organizational problem-solving, a process which is activated as a result of disturbances which affect the system from the inside or from the outside. The implications of Argyris' discussion are the same as those of Katz and Kahn's: goals are treated as a dependent variable, an effect of "complex processes within the system," and thereby, cannot be conceived of as either the starting point for, or cause of, organizational action.

Simon (1957) presents a comparatively goal-directed variant of modern organizational systems theory. For example, he emphasizes that "most organizations are oriented around some goal or objective which provides the purpose toward which the organization's decisions and activities are directed" (p. 112). However, at the same time he views the organization as a "natural system." In his conception of organizational goals, he approaches the notion that the organizational goal structure is a complex expression of the multitude of goals which are presented by the various participants. At a certain point, this goal structure emerges as a compromise between the interest of the different "potential participants." The organizational goal makes up a kind of least common denominator around which the different groups of participants can be joined. If the organizational goal is not acceptable to a certain individual group, that group will end its cooperation with the organization (1957: 115).

Chapter 7

MECHANISTIC AND ORGANIC

STRUCTURES

The rationalistic perspective stresses the role of organizations as instruments for certain goals and objectives, determined by some individual or group. It emphasizes the importance of the organization as a resource, and maintains that it should be studied as a goal-directed structure. How the organization is constructed, and how the relations between its different parts (positions, sections, departments, etc.) are formed, is determined by the "blueprint" which is drawn up by the organization's "architect" (the mandator). This blueprint allows for the different parts of the organization to be manipulated independently of each other. The rationalistic perspective maintains, as has been previously pointed out, that certain parts may be modified or eliminated without necessarily causing serious consequences for other parts. Modification or elimination processes are primarily means for better meeting the demands of the *plan,* and are not primarily measures for preserving equilibrium (a concept of little relevance to the rationalistic approach).

The *mechanistic type of organization,* which is clearly related to the rationalistic perspective, is characterized by a carefully planned division of labor, a hierarchical authority structure, and centralized information and instruction.

The systems perspective maintains that the achievement of goals is only one of the organization's functions. Other important functions are the integration and adjustment of the organization to the environment. Organizational goals are usually complex and are the products of the needs and demands of a multitude of stakeholders. The organization is conceived of as an institution being at the service of all its stakeholders, an institution living under the pressure of, and having to adjust to, environmental influences. The *organic type of organization,* which is the structural complement of the systems perspective, is characterized by a loose rather than fixed structure, and by a great adjustability and readiness to act. The tasks of the individuals, as Burns and Stalker emphasize, are "realistic" and seen "as set by the total situation of the concern." Their coordination is primarily achieved by norms expressing the expectation that they all work for the common purpose of the organization. In contrast to the mechanistic type, the role of the organization as "center" is less emphasized, and it is pointed out that information relevant for decisions may be found at different levels and in different segments of the organization. Similarly, action initiatives can originate at any level in the organization.

It is a remarkable fact that the different perspectives on organizations are so interwoven with recommendations concerning the "best structure." The systems perspective emphasizes that organizations can be conceived of as "open systems." Usually accompanying this viewpoint is the normative thesis that organizations should be given systems characteristics, i.e., an organic "loose" structure, the coordination and balance of which should be preserved (which leads the proponents of this perspective to pay great attention to theories of motivation). The rationalistic perspective, on the other hand, emphasizes that organizations can be conceived of as instruments of goal-directed action. Connected with this viewpoint is usually the idea that the organization should be given "machine" properties, i.e., the character of a goal-directed administrative apparatus, carefully regulated.

Examples of the above are easily found. "The machine perspective" in organizational sociology is primarily represented by the Scientific Management tradition, put forward chiefly by Taylor, Fayol, and Gilbreth. This perspective emphasizes task specialization and attempts to utilize the human organism in production in the most efficient way (often as a complement to the machine). Its normative character is evident. The contrasting perspective, i.e., the systems tradition, has a less normative appearance (which is the reason that Ramström [1964: 13] characterizes it purpose as "describing and explaining the actual behavior of organizations," and why Mabon states that with Simon's *Administrative Behavior* "the old, normative days" are over [1971: 56].) But consider, for example, the following quotation from two of the most prominent spokesmen of organizational systems analysis:

> Human organizations have unique properties . . . which distinguish them from other categories of open systems. Perhaps the most basic of these unique properties is *the absence of structure* in the usual sense of the term—an identifiable, enduring, physical anatomy which is observable at rest as in motion, and which in motion generates and performs those activities which comprise the systemic function. . . . The fact that organizational structure is created and maintained only as the members of the organization interact in an ordered way suggests a high degree of openness, *a persistent and inherent vulnerability to forces in the organizational environment*. . . . Much of the theorizing and empirical work about organizations has assumed explicitly or implicitly a closed system, in which the inputs into the system are regarded as constants. The open-system approach reminds us that *organizational inputs are neither constant nor guaranteed*. In particular, the organization lives only so long as people are induced to be members and to perform as such (Karz and Kahn 1966: 453-454; italics mine).

This quotation clearly shows the implicit assumptions of the systems perspective, propositions which are usually not subject to questioning. First, it is postulated that "structure" or "anatomy" is missing (an extreme emphasis of the systems assumption of "loose structure"); second, that organizations always (note the word) are vulnerable to "forces in the organizational environment"; and third, that inputs into the organization (i.e., broadly defined as the preconditions for its activity, e.g., people and material) may not be regarded as constants.

All this appears highly reasonable, especially when contrasted with the fairly unflexible and static perspective of the scientific management tradition. But are there not also important theoretical limitations built into Katz and Kahn's discussion?

The three statements above require the following commentary. First, it can be argued that the organizational structure need not be *either* rigid (scientific management) *or* loose (systems perspective) but may vary depending on, e.g., environmental conditions. Second, organizations may vary in the degree to which they are vulnerable to, and subject to, forces in their environment. Third, inputs may vary in their degree of stability and predictability. Granted, this is expressed also by

Katz and Kahn, but in a very extreme fashion. It is quite conceivable that the organization's mandator and/or leaders in certain situations make the most correct analysis by seeing inputs as constants. In any case, the striving by the organization's leadership is often to create this constant situation, e.g., by guaranteeing continuous supply of raw materials and semimanufactured products by vertical integration, or by insuring a constant supply of labor force by achieving monopoly of the labor market. Thompson (1967: 21) deals with this under the term "standardization of inputs."

Sherman Krupp (1961: 38ff.) has made an exposé of the normative elements in theories of equilibrating systems (such as the one suggested by Katz and Kahn). He distinguishes between four types of biases which may occur in this type of analysis. (1) Normative elements frame the problems that are to be considered: e.g., managerial needs may determine the questions that are asked ("bias of scope and orientation"). (2) Some variables may appear not to be meaningful to equilibrium, and are therefore excluded (e.g., unions did not seem important to the earlier human relations researchers; "bias of omission"). (3) The values on the variables selected may become excessively narrowed, e.g., dissatisfaction may be included, but wildcat strikes may remain unexplained ("bias of shortsightedness"). (4) The variables included may have the capability of achieving certain desired values, but this is overlooked. "Sights for improvement are set at a level far lower than may be, in fact, achievable. . . . For example . . . employee control is not regarded as compatible with efficiency and harmony when , in fact, it may be" ("bias of conservatism").

Thus, the claims by organizational systems theory to be less "normative" than earlier, rationalistic approaches can be disputed on the ground that systems theory itself is affected by biases of selection, relevance, and scope. Furthermore, it can be seriously questioned whether it is at all possible to establish theoretical systems uncontaminated by normative expectations concerning content and types of predictions. *Some* selection of variables, and *some* specification of their values must always be done, and these procedures can not be completely isolated from the goals and aspirations of the system-constructor.

It is tempting to see the rationalistic perspective and the systems view as two opposing types of inductive generalizations, as contrasting theories which have been developed on the basis of observations of organizational types at the extremes of the mechanistic/organic continuum. A problem with the inductive way of reasoning is that one may overlook certain possible empirical cases and consequently draw conclusions which are not generally valid. I believe that both the rationalistic and systems perspectives are examples of such unjustified generalizations. Both perspectives may be said to be "wrong" in the sense that they base their theses on insufficient facts. Or, in other words, there is a lack of fit between the *observations* of organizational structure and the *theories* which are constructed to interpret this structure as well as the organization's objectives and functions. As we shall see below, the observations often note a high degree of variation on a continuum from "rigid" to "loose" structure, whereas the theories emphasize that *one or the other* form is to be preferred. Burns and Stalker comment on this by saying that "there is no one optimum type of management system" and by objecting to the common assumption that "mechanistic systems should be superseded by organic in conditions of stability" (1961: 125). A considerable problem for organizational sociology seems to be to construct theories which take careful notice of variations in structure and attempt to explain the causes of these variations. In all probability, these explanations have to be based on both observations of rational processes and on observations of environmental influences. With regard to the latter, the possible merits of the open-systems theory should be evaluated. I shall return to this problem in Chs. 8 and 9.

Some Empirical Studies

Perrow (1967) regards organizations primarily as systems for carrying out work and for employing certain techniques to change certain kinds of raw materials in a desired direction. Perrow suggests that organizations should be classified according to type of technology. As we have seen (above, p. 100), he stresses that the degree to which the organization is forced to make routine and "exceptional" decisions has consequences for a number of relations within the system. Organizations with a routine decision-making pattern are characterized by a mechanistic rather than an organic structure, whereas organizations confronted by repeated exceptional cases and which are forced to undertake continuous modifications are of a more "organic" type. This is a reasonable assumption, and as we shall see in the continuation of this chapter, it is also an assumption which gains support from a variety of empirical research results.

TECHNOLOGY AND ORGANIZATION STRUCTURE

In the 1950s, Joan Woodward studied one hundred commodity-producing enterprises of different sizes in Essex, England. Among other things, the research purpose was to investigate the conditions for their possible commercial success or failure. The information collected about these enterprises concerned, e.g., descriptions of their fabrication processes and methods, data on organizational forms and routines, and data on their relative position on the market (1965: 10ff.). After several attempts to establish a classification of these enterprises, Woodward found that the most fruitful basis for a typology was to group the enterprises according to their production methods. She found that the organizations could be classified on a scale measuring their degree of technical complexity. At the lower end of this scale were enterprises involved in unit and small-batch production (production of articles on special request by customers, production of prototypes, fabrication of complex equipments). In the middle were enterpriese of large-batch and mass production (few products in long series, e.g. production on assembly lines). At the upper end of this scale of technical complexity were enterprises for process production (production of chemicals, liquids, gases and crystalline substances).

Woodward found that the enterprises in the different categories could be clearly distinguished with regard to inner structure. A positive correlation was found between a high degree of technical complexity and, for example, the number of authority levels, proportion of foremen, and proportion of staff (1965: 51-60).

Of more interest for our purposes, however, are those similarities which were found between enterprises at the two extreme ends of the continuum. Single-unit and process enterprises were quite similar to each other, and differed from the mass-production enterprises, in the following way:

> Clear-cut definition of duties and responsibilities was characteristic of firms in the middle ranges, while flexible organization with a high degree of delegation of authority and of the responsibility for decision-making, and with permissive and participating management was characteristic of firms at the extremes. There was less "organization consciousness" at the extremes; it was the firms in the middle ranges which found it easier to produce organization charts (1965: 64).

The enterprises at the extreme ends of the continuum were also characterized by smaller work-groups, less severe control of the production process, and less formalized communication (e.g., these enterprises more often used informal rather than written communication).

Let us return for a moment to Burns' and Stalker's dichotomy. As we have seen, the mechanistic type was represented by a high degree of specialization of tasks, a hierarchical structure with control from the top, precise definitions of rights and obligations, and a careful direction of the work of subordinates through instructions and decisions from the top. The organic structure, on the other hand, was seen as less hierarchic and functionally divided, less governed by detailed orders, less regulated and more directed to consultation and horizontal communication. There is a striking parallel between this dichotomy and Woodward's descriptive contrast between enterprises at the extreme ends of the continuum and enterprises located at the center. It is hardly surprising that Woodward also explicitly uses Burns and Stalker's terms in her description. Thus she says that "there was a tendency for organic management systems to predominate in the production categories at the extremes of the technical scale, while mechanistic systems predominated in the middle ranges" (1965: 64).

How are these results by Woodward to be explained? Why do, for example, unit-production enterprises tend to have an organic structure, whereas mass-production enterprises tend toward a more mechanistic structure? One obvious explanation, taken from Perrow, is that the former kind of organization is characterized by insecurity and nonpredictability to a greater degree than that of the latter. They are continuously forced to master new and insecure situations, and a hierarchical, top-directed, and strongly regulated organization is therefore less feasible. Continuously renewed and changing tasks require them to be flexible and to give maximum freedom for innovation, problem discussion, and intensive internal relations (cf., Perrow 1967: 207).

The mass-production enterprises, however, are able to plan for a longer time span. Their product assortment is determined for long periods to come, and they have usually made big investments in expensive and complicated tools, e.g., assembly lines. In contrast to the other two enterprise types, their calculations involve relatively constant input factors. As long as production remains unchanged, there are usually no particularly strong reasons to change the structure of the enterprise. Therefore, one may try to increase efficiency of production by breaking down tasks into short repetitive cycles. Innovation and initiatives from all employees are less important, since the product is centrally decided upon and since the processes for its manufacture also have to be changed by central directives and centrally determined production schemes.

How, then, can one explain that the process enterprises, according to Woodward, are also of an organic kind? Process production means that the employees are less tied to particular production cycles, and that the tasks are not strongly fractionalized. Instead, it often consists of supervision of automatic sequences. The need for detailed regulation is thereby eliminated, since regulation is built into the production process itself. This allows for greater freedom for the individual worker, better possibilities of contact and communication while also decreasing the need for detailed work instructions.[1]

EXTERNAL RELATIONS AND INNER STRUCTURE

Michael Aiken and Jerald Hage have studied the internal consequences of external relations for a quite different type of organization, i.e., organizations in the health care sector in the USA. They have investigated the extent to which the existence of so-called joint programs (projects involving the cooperation of several organizations) co-vary with the internal structural characteristics of these organizations. They found a correlation between a high degree of external contacts for an organization and a high degree of internal communication (measured, e.g., by the number of internal meetings and conferences). External contact also correlated with a tendency to greater decentralization of decision-making and greater work autonomy among the personnel (1968: 924, 928). These correlations appeared to hold even after the elimination of the possible effects of size.

Aiken and Hage's data are fairly scanty since they are valid for only sixteen organizations. However, they represent an interesting parallel to Woodward's investigations by showing that in these organizations, a multitude of demands from the environment (cf., Woodward's single-unit enterprises) seems to correlate with a tendency toward organic rather than mechanistic characteristics. Burns and Stalker, as well as Perrow, explicitly point out that the organic rather than the mechanistic structure is more feasible for organizations that have a rapidly changing environment.

In a study of forty-three Canadian industrial organizations, Harvey (1968) following Woodward, investigated the connection between technology and inner structure and found largely the same results. Just as in Woodward's case, he discovered that a low predictability of the organization's external relations was related to the development of an organic-type inner structure.

The point raised in what has been said above is that the inner structure of organizations varies depending on which tasks they have, which technology they apply, and more generally formulated, which demands are directed towards them from other organizations and power centers.

If one recognizes the existence of this variation, a logical complement is to question, as Burns and Stalker do, the possibility of establishing a "one best theory" of structure as a normative model for organizations. The structure of organizations and the best way to administer them cannot be determined a priori. According to this perspective, they are functions of those tasks which the organizations have established in order to implement their goals.

The success of a military organization greatly depends on its ability to strike forcefully and quickly and with good coordination. This is independent of whether the organization is a professional army or a guerilla force. On the opposite pole, one may consider a scientific institution. The structure of such an institution can be considerably looser since its tasks do not require quick, coordinated action, and since long-term innovation and creativity are emphasized instead of rapid action.

Argyris (1964) puts forward the general thesis that the "essential properties" of organizations are related to organic rather than mechanistic principles. However, he also points out that, in certain cases, an organization of the mechanistic type (pyramidal structure) may be superior to other forms, i.e., when time is of the essence, when the decision to be taken is of a routine character, when the decision does not strongly affect the organization's pattern of power and rewards, when "the number of people to be influenced is high relative to the space or time available to bring them together," and when the individual participants "prefer to remain apathetic and non-involved, and dislike the organization so intently that they are constantly striving to harm it" (1964: 199-200). Thus, according to Argyris, there may be reasons that organizations must *change* between different kinds of structure in order to cope with different kinds of decisions (1964: 211). The rationalistic approach and the systems perspective should not be regarded as general organization theories which are mutually exclusive, but rather as complementary constructs based on observations at the extreme ends of the mechanistic-organic continuum. (Cf., Edmund Dahlström's analysis of integrationist vis-à-vis conflict theories (1971: 38f.) where he emphasizes that these two perspectives *to different degrees* are applicable to different societies.) The strongly dominating role of the systems perspective in current administration theory may thus already be questioned on this ground. Some more arguments relevant to this are discussed in Ch. 9.

NOTE

1. Cf. the discussion by Gardell and Dahlström concerning the consequences of the development from medium to high degrees of mechanization of industry, i.e., in the direction towards process production. They say that "this development carries the promise of quite different conditions for work engagement and positive job evaluations than what is the case during the phase from low to medium degree of mechanization. We have especially emphasized the increased integration between different hierarchical levels which puts still greater demands on cooperation and communication. . . . The highly mechanized work situation thus appears to open up greater possibilities for satisfying the self-esteem and status of individuals" (1966: 159).

Chapter 8

THE RATIONALISTIC PERSPECTIVE:

Problems and Shortcomings

Introduction

As the spokesmen of the systems perspective often argue, there are more essential aspects to an organization than its goal-achieving activities. For example, Argyris stresses that besides goal-achievement, the organization has to fulfill certain requirements of integration (preservation has of the inner system) and adaptation (adjustment to the environment). With regard to both of these points, one may argue that the rationalistic perspective is insufficient. It calls attention to questions concerning the suitability and success of the organization as an instrument for its mandator. If one regards the organization as a means for carrying out work, this viewpoint is of central importance. However, it is clear that this far from exhausts the problems relevant to organizational life. In this chapter I shall try to cover some of the limitations of the rationalistic perspective. The discussion will contain comments on, (a) the limits of implementing the means-end scheme that are derived from the outer conditions for organizational activity, (b) the difference between this type of rationality limitation and those limitations which have been discussed by Simon, (c) some viewpoints concerning an analysis of the informal system carried out by the human relations school, and finally, (d) certain problems relating to the application of the means-ends scheme.

The Limits of Rationality

EXTERNAL FORCES

Organizational analysis of the rationalistic type takes its point of departure from the notion that the organization is a product of the plans of an acting subject. The emphasis on goal factors (transformed into recommendations for action through the means-ends scheme) is at one and the same time the strength and weakness of rationalistic theory. The strength lies in its continuous insistence that organizations be regarded as the instruments for implementation of certain objectives. That is, rationalistic theory emphasizes the notion that some actor, here generally labeled the mandator, has a particular interest in the organization's work, and that this actor accordingly can be expected to maintain in different ways his superiority over the organization.

The weaknesses in rationalistic theory stem from its inattentiveness to factors which may limit the space for rational choice and planning. It is impossible to conceive of an organization completely without rationalistic components. At the same time, however, it is necessary to realize that rational action is limited by certain frame factors or conditions which delimit the space within which action may take place, and which provide the material and economic base for action.

Organizational theory can be subjectivistic only within the field indicated by these factors. How large this field is in reality is a question of much debate, and is subject to many arguments of a more or less materialistic-deterministic kind. Sunesson (1974: 71) strongly stresses his objections to "all forms of organization-theoretical voluntarism and idealism," and carries his criticism so far that one gets the impression that organizational action is determined almost completely by material factors and/or relations to the state. Berntson (1974), who also argues from an historical-materialistic point of departure, is considerably less categorical when he says that "the action motives of actors, their subjective orientation plays a definite role" within the framework of "external objective conditions" (p. 35). In general, I agree with Berntson.

Three important classes of conditions limiting subjective rationality are (1) economic, (2) technological, and (3) political frame factors. Economic factors have to do with the availability of land, capital, and labor to the organization; technological factors derive from the development of the productive forces, i.e., the efficiency of machines, means of communication, etc., which are necessary for the daily tasks of the organization; political factors concern the organization's relationship with, and dependence on, the state and other dominating power groups (a dependency which is often codified in laws and statutes; see above, p. 30). At the same time that one stresses the importance of incorporating rationalistic assumptions into general organization theory, one has to emphasize the necessity for explicitly taking into account those limitations which stem from the aforementioned frame factors and which circumscribe the goal rationality of actors.

LIMITS OF HUMAN RATIONALITY

A quite different type of rationalistic limitation is emphasized by Herbert A. Simon. In contrast to those frameworks of rational action which are sketched out by Marxist theory (based on assumptions about *society*), Simon stresses those limits for complete rationality which are inherent in the *individual*. When Simon talks about the "limits of rationality," he does not primarily refer to factors which limit the freedom of action for the *organization* but for the organization *member*. (The term "member" is Simon's. On the problems of applying it in organizational theory, see below, pp. 167-169).

The knowledge which the individual possesses or is able to acquire is by necessity always fragmentary. It is against this background that the organization becomes important: "One function that organization performs is to place the organization members in a psychological environment that will adapt their decisions to the organization objectives, and will provide them with the information needed to make decisions correctly" (1957: 79).

Left to himself, man is weak and incapable of reaching "correct" decisions, says Simon. He needs the support of the organization, which carries out distribution of tasks, decides on how tasks are to be carried out, transmits decisions through its ranks "by establishing systems of authority and influence," and educates and indoctrinates "its members." Through these processes, the organization "injects into the very nervous system of the organization members the criteria of decision that the organization wishes to employ" (1957: 103). These citations illustrate that the foundation of Simon's perspective on man is *irrationalism*, rather than rationalism. The organization is perceived of as a means not primarily for overcoming material and structural obstacles to action, but for counteracting tendencies inherent in the individual organizational member which undermine his possibilities of reaching "correct" decisions.

CONCEPTIONS OF MAN: ON "PRAXIS"

Herbert McClosky has pointed out the links between the irrational concept of man and conservative thinking. According to him, the conservative thinking emphasizes the unpredictability of human action and its tendencies to anarchy. A conservative person is apt to stress the need for strengthening social institutions, law and order. "Order, authority, and community are the primary defense against the impulse of violence and anarchy" (McClosky 1958). Simon's idea of the limitations of rational behavior inherent in the individual offers an excellent motive for defending the role of authority within organizations. If the individual cannot be expected to reach completely rational decisions, he is supplied with the means for this by the organization. The latter is expected to be more rational than the individual organizational member. According to Simon, the behavior pattern of the subordinate is governed by the decision criterion to "follow that behavior alternative which is selected for me by the superior" (1957: 126).

It may be interesting to contrast the perspective of man as exhibited by Simon with conceptions represented by humanistic Marxism. According to the latter, the subject is treated as an "active, creative, consciously acting individual" (Israel 1972: 44). Man is seen as possessing an active, expansive mind. Practical activity, "praxis," is an important condition for achieving and expanding his knowledge (cf., Israel 1971: 84ff.)

The rationalistic undertone in Marxism is also well illustrated by the following well-known quotation from *Capital*:

> A spider conducts operations which resemble those of the weaver, and a bee would put many a human architect to shame by the construction of the honeycomb cells. But what distinguishes the worst architect from the best of the bees is that the architect builds the cell in his mind before he constructs it in wax. At the end of every labour process, a result emerges which had already been conceived by the worker at the beginning, hence already existed ideally (1976: 284).

In sum, one may argue that Marxism's concept of man and the rationalistic approach to organizations are quite compatible if one explicitly takes into consideration those material conditions which delimit and circumscribe man's actions (cf., Sjoberg and Nett 1968: 62-63). The process model developed below (Ch. 10) combines elements of rationalistic theory with assumptions concerning the material limits to rationality.

The Informal System

An obvious and justified point of critique against rationalistic theory is its inattention to most informal group formations which emerge within organizations. That is, groups which arise outside the blueprint drawn up by the organizational mandator are not adequately discussed within rationalistic theory. Proponents of scientific management ideas concentrate their observations on the formal organization, and attempt to make it as perfect as possible. The correct distribution of work and central coordination were to Taylor the keys to good organization and high productivity. If the workers made agreements among themselves with the purpose of reducing work pace, this was a disturbance in the smoothness of production which Taylor simply could not accept. "It should be plain to all men . . . that this deliberate loafing is almost criminal," he growls (1969: 96).

The first important break with the scientific management ideology and its emphasis on the formal principles of job distribution came with Roethlisberger's and Dickson's Western Electric studies. Because of their research contributions, organizations increasingly came to be described as social systems in which the informal relations of the employees— their feelings, their values, their early history, and relations to groups outside of the organization (e.g., their families)—became important analytical components. "There is something more to the social organization than what has been formally recognized," wrote Roethlisberger and Dickson. "The blueprint plans of the company show the functional relations between working units, but they do not express the distinctions of social distance, movement, or equilibrium previously described." And: "Man is not merely—in fact is very seldom—motivated by factors pertaining strictly to facts or logic" (1969: 54-55). One conclusion that has been drawn from this study, and which has stimulated further research, is that informal organization, if correctly utilized, can be employed to support the goals of the enterprise. Conversely, if employees have goals of their own which are contradictory to those of the enterprise, coordination and communication are obstructed (1969: 57).

Since the publication of *Management and the Worker* (1939), a vast number of analyses have focussed on the human relations aspect of organizations. It is not an overstatement to say that the human relations tradition has dominated, for example, Swedish sociological research on enterprises and organizations during the 1940s and 1950s; see, for example, Boalt (1954); Boalt and Westerlund (1953); Lundquist (1957); Segerstedt and Lundquist (1952); and Dahlström (1956).

The human relations approach has primarily been used for the research analysis of the lower levels of the enterprise. Roethlisberger and Dickson distinguish between, on the one hand, the logic of cost and efficiency, which is said to characterize the enterprise leadership, and, on the other, the logic of sentiment which governs the employees. As Gouldner stresses, the goal-oriented strivings of the employees tend to be seen as not rational in themselves, but "as a façade for their own underlying non-rational needs" (1959: 407). Like Simon's approach, the analysis of Roethlisberger and Dickson emphasizes that employees within an organization should be treated primarily as nonrational actors.

The Application of Means-Ends Analysis: Some Problems

The practical employment of a means-ends analysis is complicated by several factors. A short recapitulation will make this clear. (1) The means-ends method is based on the supposition that it is possible to construct a coherent means-ends hierarchy in which super- and subordinate goals are logically connected with each other. In actual practice, these demands are seldom completely fulfilled. (2) On all goal levels, implementation requires that the goals be so well specified that they can be transformed into programs for action (i.e., operationalized) without too much difficulty. This puts high demands on the persons responsible for planning, and failures in this respect can lead to discontent and criticism from those who are to carry out the program. (3) Finally, there is considerable risk that "efficiency" will be too narrowly defined with the result that short-sighted productivity goals are emphasized at the cost of more wide-ranging objectives. I shall comment on some of the problems connected with these three points in the continuation of this chapter.

"ORGANIZATIONS DO NOT REACH THEIR GOALS"

It is almost trivial to point out that decision-making in real situations often looks quite different from what is designed in rationalistic blueprint. Simon's observations concerning the difficulty of achieving a complete overview of the goals and action alternatives can hardly be questioned. Individuals satisfy instead of optimize. That is, they choose between available acceptable alternatives rather than look for what is best by absolute standards.

When Etzioni (1964: 16-17) maintains that organizations rarely reach their goals, he seems to take his point of departure from an optimalization model. It is true that organizations often do not reach their ultimate goals, but this does not mean that the organization does not *approach* these goals. To take just one example, the Swedish trade union movement in its program of 1886 defined its goals as "protecting the workers against the repression and despotism of employers, and step by step to guarantee all members of society complete human and citizen rights" (Gunnarsson 1965: 62). It can be disputed to what extent this goal has been reached. But it can hardly be disputed that the success of the organization at least partly can be measured by studying how different subgoals, which are related to the more ultimate ones, have been reached. Many of the necessary steps or subgoals specified by the program have been achieved. For example, the reduction of working hours, general health insurance, old-age pensions, general and equal voting rights, progressive income tax, and general basic education. Although superordinate goals are often vague, they can still be essential components in the formulation of organizational aspirations.

It can be somewhat pointless to criticize an organization for not achieving its superordinate goals. Yet it is a reasonable request that lower goal-levels can clarify the general purposes and that the lower-level goals are specific enough to allow controls of whether they have been carried out (e.g., the subgoal, "eight-hour working day").

INCREMENTALISM AND "MIXED SCANNING"

A problem in the application of a rationalistic method of decision-making is that it requires a certain unanimity about the goals. As the proponents of the systems perspective and the human relations school are quick to point out, there are often a great number of goals within an organization, goals which are frequently in conflict with one another. Incrementalism, a term used by C. E. Lindblom, is a concept of planning which tries to take into account the existence of such differences between goals, and at the same time, attempts to incorporate Simon's thesis about the limitations of individual rationality. According to Lindblom, decisions are reached by a process of negotiation between different actors, a process where the selection of goals and the analysis of the required action needed to implement these goals are not clearly separated. In the incrementalistic decision process, the aim is not primarily to go through all possible solutions to a problem, but rather, to reach an "acceptable" policy. The criterion of such a policy is that the different participants in the decision process are in basic agreement about the goals (although not necessarily about the best way to reach them). Mutual and gradual adjustment between actors is a basic sign of incrementalism. This adjustment is seen as a function of, partly, the inherent limitations of the rationality of the decision-maker himself, and partly, the pluralistic stakeholder structure which functions as a check against one group's goals becoming dominant.

If incrementalism is conceived of as a normative model, its effects may become conservative rather than progressive. That is to say, gradual adjustment rather than major change becomes the ideal. Dramatic changes are regarded as disturbances in an otherwise stable process. The perception that decision-making *ought to* be carried out by gradual adjustment precludes calculated, rapid, and extensive changes within the organization (Sandberg 1976: Sec. 7.3.1).

It cannot be denied that decision-making in practice is often characterized by, and therefore can be described by, the concept of incrementalism. There exists, of course, even in the most autocratically governed organizations, elements of negotiation and compromise intermixed with the decision process. It is probably also true that decisions concerning goals at different levels vary with respect to the amount of incrementalism and rationalism. Etzioni (1968: 282ff.) has coined the concept "mixed scanning" for a process in which the most important decisions are reached after an analysis of, and choice between, different alternatives according to the rational means-ends scheme, while the less important decisions follow the incrementalist method.

To what extent can "incrementalism" and "mixed scanning" be considered alternatives to means-ends analysis? One can argue that both terms, in fact, reflect rationalistic processes, i.e., situations in which *different actors mobilize for different goals*. The decision-making situation can be interpreted as a confrontation between different goals, or in other words, as a more or less strong contradiction between different rationalities. In contrast to the attempts by the human relations school to distinguish between different rationalities at different levels in enterprises (where the use of concept such as "the logic of sentiment" implies that the employees are viewed as somewhat incapable of managing their own affairs), it seems important to distinguish between rationalities which are based on different interests. When the interests of management are confronted with the interests of the employees, a bargaining situation often arises which may be described in terms of "incrementalism." But neither "incrementalism" nor "mixed scanning" means anything radically new to the basic assumptions of rationalism.

The difference between, for example, Weber and Lindblom, is not that the former bases his discussion on rationalistic principles whereas the latter does not. Rather, the difference is that Weber isolates rational decision-making to *one* actor, whereas Lindblom tries to describe the decision which results from the interrelationship of *several* actors. The description in the latter case may coincide with Weber's analysis in the exceptional case when the different actors are in full agreement with one another on the goals of a possible joint program of action.

PROBLEMS OF METHOD

Concretization of Goals. One of the basic problems of the rationalistic model is its inability to formulate goals which are specific enough to allow the researcher to determine whether they have been reached or not. As I have argued above, the existence of diffuse superordinate goals is not a sufficient reason for rejecting the means-ends analysis.

The loose connection between superordinate goals and lower-level goals shows, however, that insufficient goal specification can have direct effects on values. There are no established neutral methods to logically deduce specific subgoals from ultimate goals. Thus, the application of means-ends analysis will always have consequences of an evaluative nature, even at lower levels in an organization. For example, it is naive to believe that politically elected representatives make choices concerning goals, whereas the tasks of administrators in an organization (e.g. the state apparatus) are only to implement these goals. As Edmund Dahlström, among others, has pointed out (1971: 66f.) the choice of means (subgoals) can never be conceived of as a completely neutral process.

Measurability, Effectiveness, and Efficiency. The discussion above directs our attention to another problem: that those who are entrusted with the implementation of a program may find the general goals so diffuse that they concentrate their work on activities which have easily and directly measurable results. There is a considerable risk that organizational activities will concentrate only on goals that are concrete and possible to operationalize, at the cost of goals that are more abstract and for which success criteria are less clear (cf., Etzioni 1964: 9).

Such a problem can become especially acute for organizations in the public service sector. For a long time, public organizations and government offices in Sweden have not been the objects of extensive efficiency controls. The justification for their existence has primarily been as the suppliers of needed services to the population, e.g., health care, education, child care, and local administration. The costs for satisfying public needs is a question which has become especially salient during the 1960s and 1970s, and which has acquired direct practional consequences for public organizations after the introduction of program budgeting and effectiveness auditing (see above, pp. 108-112). Accordingly, there is a certain risk that organizations for public services will emphasize economic efficiency criteria rather than more general measures of goal achievement.

The problem may be expressed in terms of *effectiveness* and *efficiency*, two terms which are conceptually separate. As Etzioni points out (1964: 8), "effectiveness" concerns the goal achievement of the organization, whereas "efficiency" represents the relation between a certain activity and the costs of its execution. Measurements of efficiency concern the costs of carrying out a specific task. Such productivity measurements can be implemented quite independently of any evaluation of the implementation of superordinate goals. That is, an organization may fulfill criteria of efficiency without being effective in goal-achievement terms. It is not, however, possible to conceive of an organization which fulfills criteria of effectiveness while at the same time being 100 percent inefficient. A certain degree of efficiency is a necessary but not sufficient condition for effectiveness.

For purposes of illustration, let us look at the following example. The effectiveness of the Swedish State Bacteriological Laboratory (SBL) concerns SBL's contributions to the improvement of public health. Among its responsibilities is the production of vaccines to prevent the dissemination of contagious diseases. One measure of SBL's efficiency is provided by the volume of vaccine which SBL is producing, and the costs of these operations (RRV 1970: 73). It is obvious that there is not a perfect fit between this one productivity measure and the demands of effectiveness put to the SBL and which are formulated in the statutes of the laboratory. If the SBL were 100 percent inefficient in its production of vaccines, its more general goal or promoting public health could not be implemented (assuming that vaccines are necessary for the public health programs).

Chapter 9

THE SYSTEMS PERSPECTIVE:

Problems and Shortcomings

Introduction

The emphasis that the human relations school placed on the informal system represented a reaction against the practice within the scientific management tradition of concentrating on the formal aspects of work distribution. The systems approach which owed much to the human relations tradition, meant a paradigmatic change in organizational sociology. It posed questions which, if answered, required a simultaneous consideration of *both* the informal *and* the formal system of organization. A new set of relevant questions developed: Which are the strategic parts of the system? How are these parts interrelated? By which processes is the adjustment of the various parts to each other achieved? Reciprocal relations, systems balance, and system adjustment were the new key words. One may perhaps argue that organizational theory has acquired its necessary synthesis in this process. Certain elements from the original, strongly "machine-directed" scientific management theory have been preserved. For example, its emphasis on the distribution and coordination of work will in all probability be continuous elements in social science analyses of organizations. The human relations school has so effectively pointed out the need for studying the social organization, informal group formation, communication, and information that its contributions will undoubtedly continue to be important to organizational theory. Finally, general systems theory has indicated the possibility of combining the two approaches in a common perspective, emphasizing the importance of studying the organization as a whole, its functions, balance, integration, and adjustment.[1] Is there, in fact, any reason to demand more? Is there any reason to search for alternatives?

I believe there is. In large measure, the systems perspective has managed to conceal the major point of rationalistic analysis: the thesis that *the organization exists to carry out tasks for the benefit of a mandator.* It has done so under the pretext of presenting a holistic analysis of the organization within the framework of open systems theory. The countercurrent, which has existed at various times, has had few possibilities of being heard over the pressures of these claims and ambitions.[2] Self-criticism among systems theoreticians has not been a particularly striking phenomenon.

In this chapter, I shall present some critical points related to the systems perspective. These criticisms are directed at the conceptual apparatus of systems theory, its views of organizational history, its propositions about dominance relationships in the organization, its basic thesis of inducement-contribution balance, and finally, problems related to its employment of the concept of "member."

The Conceptual Apparatus

The conceptual apparatus of systems theory is developed for the purpose of creating a general theory of so-called "vitalistic systems" (i.e., human organisms, groups, organizations, societies; see Blegen and Nyléhn 1969: 9ff.). (Cf. Buckley 1967: 4: "The major concern is with models of organization sufficiently general and complex, though built from simple units, to embrace behavior systems of any type—physical, biological, psychological, or socio-cultural.") The proponents of the systems perspective claim that it has the ability to interpret and formulate propositions concerning a multitude of different empirical phenomena of an open-systems character in terms of input, output, feedback, equilibrium, relative openness/closedness, environmental requirements, adaptation, energy input, energy transformation, etc.

The general adaptability of the systems approach is probably one of the main explanations of its wide popularity within the social and behavioral sciences. Another probable reason is its suitability for mathematical formalization by the use of differential calculus and set theory (see, e.g., Norrbom 1971: 7f.). Acceptance of the systems perspective is partly dependent on one's belief in the practical applicability of its conceptual apparatus. Partly it also hinges on one's confidence in the possibilities of creating a general, formalized theory using the aforementioned methods. On this point I wish to stress my own general scepticism. Organizational systems theory has, as yet, produced few, if any, formal-mathematical models capable of explaining and predicting organizational behavior.

The generality of the systems concept represents a considerable weakness. In their efforts to develop a general theory, the spokesmen for the systems perspective often extend the meaning of terms so far as to render them vague and impossible to specify in operational terms. Let me exemplify this by reviewing the use of the concept of energy in organizational systems theory. "Energy" in the systems tradition is logically connected with, among other things, the concept of efficiency.

ENERGY AND EFFICIENCY

Systems theory strives to measure the total energy input to an organization. If this cannot be achieved, the concept of efficiency becomes less useful, since efficiency is related to the organization's way of distributing the energy intake. As long as we stick to, for example, mechanical energy, the difficulties are not insurmountable, though still considerable. It is probably possible to construct useful measures of that energy which is generated when men and machines work on the material which is brought into the organization's production system. Also, other forms of physical energy which the organization employs may be measured, e.g., its import of electric energy.

A substantial problem is, however, that the efficiency of organizations can usually be only partially explained by measurable production factors. There remains a large amount of variation which is related to factors which are *private,* i.e., inherent in each individual, or which are produced when the individuals in the organization *cooperate* and interact. Let me illustrate with the following example.

Economists strive to explain the increase of the gross national product by, for example, adding up the increments in the amount of productive work accomplished plus the growth of physical capital. The summation of these measurable factors, however, explains only a limited portion of the total increase of the GNP (see, e.g., *SOU* 1966: 1, pp. 18-19). "Human capital factors," like the increase of knowledge, improved health, human creativity, and efficiency increases due to better organization, have to be included as a part of the unexplained residual (Schulz 1971). It is possible that a large amount of the difference between productivity in different organizations can be explained in a similar way.

How would a systems theorist measure the energy intake and energy transformation of an organization? Katz and Kahn explain, after a longer discussion of the problem, that a comprehensive measure does not in fact exist: the measure which may be used in estimating energy factors is primarily their value in money (dollars). And this, they say in a somewhat defeatist manner, "is not necessarily commensurate with energic input and output" (1966: 152). I find it easy to agree with them. It should be added that for many organizations which are not occupied with commodity production, the problem of measurement is especially difficult.

In his book, *Integrating the Individual and the Organization* (1964), Chris Argyris attempts to take into consideration propositions concerning "human capital" and human energy. The organization, he states, exists partially to utilize the "psychological energy" of the individual, energy which "is hypothesized to increase as the individual's experiences of psychological success increase, and to decrease with psychological failure" (P. 33). The problem of the operationalization of this concept, however, is solved somewhat too simply by Argyris. He frankly states that the existence of the concept of psychological energy "does not depend on its being located in the empirical world (as may be the case for physiological energy)."

> The acceptance of the construct of psychological energy will be a function of its (1) logical validity, which, in turn, is a function of its internal consistency as well as its relevance in a conceptual scheme and, (2) its power to help explain human behavior (1964: 22).

But neither (1) nor (2) is any argument for the empirical usefulness of systems theory and the concept of "psychological energy." One may appreciate a theoretical construction for its logical qualities. One may even agree that the concept of "psychological energy" is a possible partial explanation of the efficiency of organizations. However, as long

as it is not possible to determine the kind and amount of this postulated energy (like many other concepts in systems theory), the systems
perspective has not proved to be superior to, e.g., a rationalistic theory
based on goal evaluation.

THE DOCTRINE OF HARMONY

System-based theories of the enterprise and similarly, system-based
theories of work motivation, have been extensively discussed and criticized not only in social science but in political debates as well. The
critique has been largely directed against the harmony perspective of
the systems approach. For example, Krupp (1961: xi) uses the concept
"organization theory" (as distinct from "administrative design theory,"
i.e., scientific management) to include human-relations-in-industry,
small group theory, and expecially, the writings of Chester I. Barnard
and Herbert Simon. "Together these points of departure form a logically connected body of theory with a common emphasis founded in the
norm of cooperation and harmony. As a consequence, these theories
frame a managerial point of view in the traditions of philosophic conservatism and management engineering. Organization theory forms part
of a larger, more general, managerial interpretation of society."

Below, I shall briefly touch on some of the effects of the harmony
thesis. My purpose is not primarily to show how conflicts of interest
in the organization are concealed, as this follows almost as a matter of
definition. It is rather to point out the connection between the frequently loose concepts of systems theory and the manipulative consequences which can follow.

Argyris argues for the humanization of enterprises through the
abolition of authoritarian leadership, the introduction of more liberal
principles of enterprise management, increased codetermination, job
rotation, etc. (1964: 170 ff.). For these reasons, he takes a stand against
"the pyramidal structure" (i.e., a mechanistic type of organization)
and recommends a "healthy organization" (i.e., one with an organic
character; 1964: 133). This type of organization is characterized by,
among other things, the absence of labor conflicts (1964: 189-190).

The discontent of workers in enterprises is often channelled via
trade unions. The existence of such associations, however, is detrimen-
tal to organizational "health": "the introduction of trade unions tends
to develop stress within an organization at first" (1964: 131). But
unions are a mixed blessing also in the long run. If one attempts, as
Argyris has, to create an "organic" type of organization, trade unions

become an obstacle because of their pyramidal, hierarchic structure. For Argyris, the creation of a trade union is a method of adjustment for workers. However,

> the irony of this mode of adaptation is that the union also organizes itself by using the pyramidal structure. Now, the worker may become doubly dependent and subordinate (1964: 61).

The relationship between trade unions and management may be either good or poor. Poor relations are characterized by, among other things, the trade union ignoring the interdependence of relationships in the enterprise, and keeping management in the dark about its strategy (1964: 189). Good relations, however, have the property of keeping communication channels open, with both parties working towards constructive solutions. Argyris cites industrial research by William F. Whyte, summarizing Whyte's results by saying: "In terms of our model, we would say that the interdependence of parts by both parties was recognized, influence of the parts on the whole (labor-management system) was significantly increased, as was the time perspective" (1964: 190). The equilibrium of the system can thus be disturbed, first, by the employees' establishing an organization of their own, and second, by the use of traditional trade union means of influence.

It would be pointless to deny the main thesis that the equilibrium of the system is disturbed as a result of such processes. If one confines oneself to the view that the mutual interdependence of parts requires the absence of interest organizations, and that trade unions tend to be associated with conflicts ("a worker possessing favorable attitudes toward the union tended to have unfavorable attitudes toward work," according to one survey cited by Argyris; 1964: 63), the conclusion follows almost automatically: The balance is necessarily disturbed and the organization's "health" is threatened.

Finally, in this section a note is required on Argyris' view of the positive results that can be achieved through job enlargement, codetermination, and increase in the worker's responsibility for his job. Argyris quotes a study by Melman, showing positive results from the introduction of self-managing work groups. One of the advantages, according to Argyris, was that "under conditions of increased work responsibility, management was freed to focus more on marketing problems (and other problems with the environment). Also the need for foremen was greatly reduced and their work responsibilities become radically changed" (1964: 237).

Thus reductions in detailed control mean better resource management. Argyris expresses this as a gain in the effectiveness of the system as a whole. This view can be accepted as long as one avoids the question of what the mandator of the organization expects from the "system," and as long as the organization is not analyzed in terms of interests (or rationality/counterrationality). If one takes the latter approach, the question arises as to who benefits the most from increases in productivity.

I am not arguing that changes in the work organization towards greater autonomy for the worker, less supervision, job rotation, etc., are meaningless reforms. The humanization of work environment may be justified even if it does not involve any great step toward increased influence for the employees over the organization's management. It is important, however, that one does not confuse *quantitative* changes that increase work control with reforms that lead to a *qualitative* change in the basic power relations in the enterprise., i.e., a change of mandator. (More about this follows in Ch. 11.)

WALTER BUCKLEY: MICROTHEORY, MORPHOGENESIS, AND THE SYSTEM-AS-ACTOR

The perhaps most influential contribution to systems thinking in the social sciences during the last decade is Walter Buckley's *Sociology and Modern Systems Theory* (1967). In his book, Buckley attacks equilibrium and homeostatic-organismic models, such as the "social physics" of the eighteenth and early nineteenth centuries, and functionalist theory. He seeks to replace them with a model emphasizing dynamic processes of organization. He develops a theory which includes considerations of conflict, tension, and system-environmental interplay: "the process or complex adaptive system model."

> [This model] applies to systems characterized by the elaboration or evolution of organization; as we shall see, they thrive on, in fact depend on, "disturbances" and "variety" in the environment (1967: 40).

Buckley develops his theory by proceeding gradually from small, relatively uncomplicated elements to more complex and elaborated phenomena.

> This development proceeds from the micro-level of the *act* and the basic symbolic *interaction* process . . . to the more or less

stabilized interaction matrix referred to the *role* and role dynamics, to the complex of roles contributing to the makeup of *organizations* and *institutions* (1967: 82).

Elements are related to each other by means of *information*. Information is important, since it is the carrier of "meaning." Society, according to Buckley, may be described as "an organization of meanings" (1967: 92).

In general, we find that meanings are generated in a process of social interaction of a number of individuals dealing with a more or less common environment. Once generated, they act in the capacity of selective functions underlying the decision-making processes that make possible (but do not guarantee) organized social behavior (1967: 94).

In Buckley's model, the concept of *morphogenesis* is strategic. Morphogenesis refers to processes which tend to elaborate or change a system's form, structure, or state; i.e., biological evolution, learning, and societal development. This is in contrast to pattern-preservation or *morphostasis,* exemplified by Buckley as "homeostatic processes in organisms, and ritual in socio-cultural systems" (1967: 58-59). Strain and tension are natural, in fact essential, elements in morphogenesis: "We must view *tension* as a normal, ever-present dynamic agent which ... must ... be kept at an optimal level if the system is to remain viable" (1967: 160). Thus the main assumptions of consensus theory are questioned by Buckley.

Buckley has presented a critique of traditional, equilibrium-functionalist thinking, and an alternative model for the social sciences, which beyond any doubt will rank among the classical contributions. But, although critical of harmony and equilibrium assumptions, his model has certain problematic traits which limit its usefulness for the study of organization processes.

First, the basis of Buckley's model is behavioral *microtheory*, i.e., psychology and social psychology. Buckley commends, e.g., the exchange theories of Homans and Blau for the reason that they avoid "structural terminology and static categorization." Instead, "they have gone back to basics, starting from scratch with the basic interaction process" and ideas such as "Bentham's 'felicific calculus'" and "Adam Smith's laws of private profit and loss" (1967: 127). What Bentham and Smith did, among other things, was to revitalize the classical hedonistic notions of pain and pleasure. These concepts are paralleled in current stimulus-response theory by the concepts of "reward" and "cost." (One may question whether Buckley's model really represents a critical alternative to S-R theory, as he implies (1967: 95), or whether his theory is only a slight modification of it.) These concepts also constitute the basic building blocks in the Barnard-Simon-March theory of organization, i.e., the "inducement-contribution balance."

The problems connected with hedonistic, profit maximization assumptions—especially concerning their empirical testability—apply also to Buckley's model. Although starting "from scratch" is a quite common procedure in current organization theory, it is not necessarily a recommendable procedure. Whereas Buckley approves of Homans' theory because of its basis in psychological propositions (1967: 105-113), I believe that these very propositions represent fundamental obstacles to developing the theory into a logically strict and empirically fruitful scheme. (More about this will follow below, pp. 164ff.)

Second, one may ask whether the emphasis on small group processes does not, in fact, slant the theory towards *centripetal,* equilibrium-sustaining assumptions and towards an emphasis on stability and harmony in spite of Buckley's attempts to represent both centripetal and centrifugal tendencies in his theory.

The small group has provided an atomic unit for social science; and social psychology has aspired to become a science of precise measurement, cleared of normative constraints, proper in its use of rigorous methods (and it is hence attractive to system theory builders, who often have logical-positivist, unity-of-science ambitions; cf., Krupp 1961: 123). Buckley's theory is biased toward overstating the role of the social atom, and in doing this tends to overlook some of the very organizational conflict phenomena it attempts to model. (For still another another systems theory which is based on microtheory and reward-cost calculus, see Holstein 1974, esp. Vol. 5, sec. 1.4). To use Krupp's formulation:

> Small group theory and a psychological orientation may seriously understate the actual interdependence between members at any given organization level (plant slow-down), significant discontinuities (wildcat strikes), and codification (unions). Euclidean geometry is being used, perhaps, in a non-Euclidean world. Tying a theory of organization behavior to theories of individual motivation and decision (or to small group behavior) severely limits its predictive and explanatory capabilities (Krupp 1961: 166).

What Krupp stresses is the danger of losing sight of *collective organization* based on *common interests* among particular groups of actors *confronting* each other rather than cooperating; or, in other words, tendencies which are not only centrifugal but perhaps so centrifugal as to render the notion of *a* system fruitless.

It is easy to find formulations by Buckley which may cause the reader to question the "conflict-sensitivity" of his theory. For example, he states:

> Modern systems analysis suggests that a sociocultural system with high adaptive potential, or integration as we might call it, requires some optimum level of both stability and flexibility: a relative stability of the social-psychological foundations of interpersonal relations and of the cultural meanings and value-hierarchies that hold group members together in the same universe of discourse and, at the same time, a flexibility of structural relations characterized by the lack of strong barriers to change, along with a certain propensity for reorganizing the current institutional structure should environmental challenges or emerging internal conditions suggest the need (1967: 206).

One may ask: who sets the criteria for the "optimum level of stability?" According to whom do the "socio-psychological foundations of interpersonal relations" fulfill requirements of "relative stability?" According to what standards is there "sameness" in the universe of discourse? And how do we recognize the "suggestions" for reorganization by "environmental challenges or emerging internal conditions?"

Systems theory, however critical of earlier approaches it aspires to be, cannot escape from the fundamental idea of the system-as-actor and, thereby, from the implication that individuals or groups of actors in the system are subordinated to forces essentially beyond their control. Systems theory is biased towards underrepresenting human rationality; rather, it tends to attribute "human" characteristics to the system as a whole, i.e., it has an antropomorphic, or animistic, bias. Of course, independent action by subunits is assumed away already at the stage of defining the "system" as an *interrelation* of parts. Thus, the system is seen as the acting subject, adapting itself to internal and external requirements, and setting its own criteria for stability, flexibility, "optimum level of tension," etc.

This bias of antropomorphism is reflected, e.g., in the very title of Katz and Kahn's book, *The Social Psychology of Organizations* (1966); in the vast literature on "organizational psychology" and "organizational development" (see, e.g., Back 1972) and is a prominent feature in the writings of Chris Argyris (e.g., 1964).

How justified is the assumption of the system-as-actor when we deal with, e.g., the industrial enterprise? Are not the interests and resources vested in different groups in the organization, and the perhaps conflicting goals sought by them as actors, more fruitful starting points for organizational research? Does not the notion of the system-as-actor necessarily lead us to investigations concerning the conditions for the system's maintenance, thereby directing our attention away from the life-conditions of the people within it?

Although Buckley certainly has the ambition to present a systems theory which includes aspects of power, conflict, and tension, this ambition leaves meager results with regard to the reasons for and actual functioning of conflicts. Abstract, formal, and technological aspects of the system are stressed at the expense of the concrete problems which groups and individuals meet and at the expense of the reasons for organization that actors within the system may have, and the types of constraints which may limit attempts to organization. Buckley's theory is almost completely devoid of subject content; it is, to quote Krupp, very much a kind of "Euclidean geometry" in a "non-Euclidean world."

REIFICATION

When systems theory draws a parallel between men and materials (the concept of energy does not distinguish between these two kinds of production factors), it leads to consequences which are directly opposed to the liberal views of the human relations school, consequences which may involve a dehumanized view of man. Somewhat strangely, this appears very clearly in two books that deal with organization in which the humanitarian aspects would seem to be among the most important, i.e., hospitals. Let me exemplify with Eric Rhenman's *The Central Hospital* (*Centrallasarettet*, 1969), and Åke Asplund's *Health Care Administration* (*Sjukvårdsadministration*, 1973), which is a further development of Rhenman's theory.

Rhenman sees the hospital as a system of *components*. The components are, e.g., the different hospital departments, their wards and the service organs connected to them, and the various positions within these units (doctor, psychologist, almoner, work therapist, physiotherapist, etc.). Among other things, the behavior of the components is influenced by information. Bits of information which affect behavior are called *controlling impulses* (1969: 25; cf. also Rhenman 1967: 6).

The hospital may be described as a *controlled production system*, containing *administrative* and *productive units*. The administrative components have as their "sole task to . . . transform and transport information and thereby govern the flow of resources into and out of the hospital and the production within the hospital" (1969: 24-25). The hospital has two main products, out-patient and inpatient care (1969: 196). It offers a product assortment consisting of the different types of treatment and care (1969: 118). What is called production planning in industry is represented in the hospital by "intake planning and actual intake." Similarly, "production preparation" has a parallel in the hospital's decisions on treatment (1969: 198-199).

Rhenman recommends and employs himself "an industrial conceptual apparatus" (1969: 196) for the analysis of public organizations in general and, in particular, the hospital. This apparatus reaches its technological peak in Asplund's book on health care administration. Already in the headline of the introductory chapter, the points of association with Rhenman are clearly seen: "The Hospital—An Enterprise." Later on, Asplund presents a definition of his own of the systems concept of "component." According to him, a "component" may be "a group of individuals, a single individual, a group of machines, a single machine, or a combination of individuals and machines" (1973: 118). The most interesting components "are quite naturally those . . . which consist of individuals" (1973: 120). What properties do they have?

A component possesses, besides an inner driving force and an ability to receive impulses from the outside, a certain capability to perform, a capability which often is measurable. A component has the ability to carry out, e.g., certain arithmetical operations, to control in an acceptable way certain instruments during a certain time period, to carry out certain manual operations within a given time period, etc. (1973: 122).

Different types of individuals/components require different types of guidance and control. This is especially true of the components "problem solvers" and "program executors." The former have "an ability to solve certain problems on the basis of a limited access to information" and therefore, can be left on their own to some degree. The latter, however, have "an ability to act only on the basis of a very specific order" (1973: 122).

Thus the control of a hospital attendant or a patient (for all, according to the theory, are "components") is roughly comparable to the control of a somewhat complicated robot. A failure of control depends on faulty information exchange, a lack of ability of the component (cf., Simon's thesis of limited rationality) or, in Rhenman's formulation, "a lack of authority of the sender" (1967: 14). March and Simon (1958: 54) use the term "machine model" to describe scientific management's view of organizations. In the same way, the picture that emerges from the pages of Rhenman's and Asplund's books is also the picture of a machine. The hospital is described in terms of an industrialized and computerized production system, lacking in almost all forms of *human* relations. It is a system in which the main problems are to get the patients ready for treatment (prepare them for production), treat them (i.e., produce medical care), and put them on the transport line for completed products. Both books were written to be textbooks for the education of health care personnel and for politicians and administrators on local and regional levels. Hence, this narrow, productivity-inspired concept of efficiency may be expected to influence day-to-day medical care situations.

The Stakeholder Model and the Organization's History

The perception of the organization as a system, responsive to stakeholders' needs and striving toward equilibrium and adjustment to its environment, leads to a marked lack of interest in the history of the organization. Questions dealing with, for example, the emergence of the organization, its original initiators, the purposes for which the organization was once created—all of which may be essential for the understanding of the organization's present role and activity—are not considered to be strategic in a systems analysis. The function of the organization *in the presently existing total system* is emphasized at the cost of attempts to explain its present role partly against the background of its formation and development.

Of course, the lack of attention to these factors may be explained by the fact that the various authors do not judge the history of organizations as being particularly interesting for the problems they have chosen to concentrate on. However, when one realizes that a major portion of systems authors avoid this question,[3] one begins to look for other possible reasons. I believe the explanation is that the systems perspective simply functions as an obstacle against an analysis in historical terms.

March and Simon's theory, based as it is on assumptions about individual motivation, emphasizes the here-and-now factors relevant to organizational equilibrium. If we were to leave this psychological, decision-making problem-solving framework, we would enter quite another arena, i.e., "the world of strategic factors associated with combat in many fields of battle." But "the March and Simon analysis offers us few tools for this research and no hope of achieving this type of knowledge, particularly since their attempts to measure are restricted to carefully conditioned laboratory experimentation. They have ignored centuries of highly documented instances of economic, social, and political conditions for conflict taken from the concrete records of government and industry. If their analysis is correct there would never be a union" (Krupp 1961: 164).

Since the March and Simon theory has had an impact far beyond the American scene, let me exemplify what has just been said with a passage from Eric Rhenman's book, *Industrial Democracy and Industrial Management* (1968). In his book, Rhenman discusses the means and ends of the trade union movement. I have previously (pp. 117f.) extensively quoted Rhenman's model of stakeholders ("the flower"). Let me now cite the following sentences which contain an application of the stakeholder model.

The trade union movement is an organization, says Rhenman. Therefore, his general theory should be applicable to the trade union movement which, just like the enterprise, "can be regarded as having both a management as well as stakeholders."

The most important stakeholders are the individual member groups, another group includes the companies employing members. Such a suggestion may at first seem almost shocking. But it would be unrealistic not to accept that the unions are dependent on cooperation with the companies, just as the companies are dependent on cooperation with the unions (1968: 116).

This quotation raises the question of how general are the claims of the stakeholder theory. For which epoch or time period is this statement relevant? If it only concerned the beginning of the 1960s (when the Swedish original was written), it might have been explained by pointing to the then popular theory of "the end of ideology." The relative absence of political conflicts and strikes, plus the thesis of disappearing ideological differences, could have been a few of the reasons behind the quotation above.

Is this a reasonable interpretation? Hardly. I believe that a much more correct interpretation is that Rhenman claims *universal validity* for his model. Factors supporting this statement are, first, that March and Simon, from whom the stakeholder model is originally taken, do not mention anything about its possible limited historical applicability. There is no reason for them to do so since their theory is built on the general, temporally unlimited principle of inducement-contribution balance. Second, I have found no indication in any of Rhenman's other works, based on the stakeholder model, of modifications of this kind.

The stakeholder model has a static character. It describes the relationship between the stakeholders as largely permanent. In its approach to the relations between workers' organizations and enterprises, the model is somewhat naive. One cannot reasonably claim that the situation during, for example, the period around the turn of the century in Sweden, was characterized by the enterprises being dependent on "cooperation with the trade unions." On the contrary, owners attempted to combat these organizations, to prevent the further organization of the working class, and if necessary, to maintain production with the help of strikebreakers.

If one raises the question of the emergence and development of an organization, the systems perspective is prone to give a vague answer that points to these factors as being dependent on the needs of the larger surrounding system. If one sees historical analysis as essential for the study of organizations, these shortcomings of the systems perspective are too pronounced to ignore. The systems/stakeholder theory does not explain how stakeholders have come to be tied to the organization.

Authority Instead of Power

The general importance attached to balance and equilibrium criteria by the systems perspective results in rather diminished attention being directed to the differences in power between various groups and strata in the organization. In fact, the writers in the tradition very often avoid the concept of power altogether, preferring the term "authority" when they discuss relations between superordinates and subordinates in the organization. Briefly, the differences between power and authority are the following: In general, power has to do with the overcoming of resistance: within social science literature, there are many variations on this definition. Some authors determine power as the *actual* overcoming of resistance, whereas others define the concept as the *capacity* to do so. A much-quoted definition is Blalock's (1967), which treats power as a multiplicative function of resources and mobilization. In order for power to exist, a certain degree of both these elements is required. For example, the strike weapon alone does not create a strike. It has to be mobilized, i.e., utilized by some actor who is motivated to use it, who expects that he will have at least some success, and who has some concrete objective to achieve through his actions. Mobilization is motivated behavior. (I have summarized some sources concerning the concept of power in a previous writing; see Abrahamsson 1972: Ch. 12).

Blalock's definition stimulates questions of the following types. Who attempts to overcome whose resistance? Which resources for the overcoming of resistance do the parties in the conflict situation have? In which ways, and on what grounds, do the parties attempt to use (i.e., mobilize) their power resources?

The key concept of systems theory as it describes dominance relationships in an organization is *authority*. A detailed discussion of this concept may be found in Simon's *Administrative Behavior* (1957). His definition in turn, is based on Barnard's *The Functions of the Executive* (1968: 163 f.). (Cf. also, March and Simon, 1958: 99, 161, 167; Rhenman 1967: 16; and Ramström 1964: 35 f.) Simon defines authority in the following way:

> A subordinate is said to accept authority whenever he permits his behavior to be guided by the decision of a superior, without independently examining the merits of that decision (1957: 11-12).

Taken literally, this definition may seem almost identical to the concept of power. It obviously concerns a relationship in which the overcoming of resistance may become important, i.e., to get someone to accept authority. Note, however, that the criterion is *consent*. A subordinate "permits" his behavior to be "guided." Simon is eager to emphasize that the exertion of authority "is usually liberally admixed with suggestion and persuasion" (1957: 11-12). And: "Although it is an important function of authority to permit a decision to be made and carried out even when agreement cannot be reached, perhaps this arbitrary aspect of authority has been overemphasized" (1957: 12).

If the superordinate tries to force authority over a certain limit, i.e., the subordinate's "zone of acceptance," the consequence may be insubordination. What, then, is the "zone of acceptance?" It is that zone "within which the subordinate is willing to accept the decisions made for him by his superior" (1957: 133).

Which factors determine the scope of the zone of acceptance? Simon makes a new attempt at a definition based on the properties of different organizations. "A voluntary organization with poorly defined objectives has perhaps the narrowest range of acceptance. An army, where the sanctions as well as the customs are of extreme severity, has the broadest area of acceptance" (1957: 102-103). Note the subtle vocabulary. A "broad area of acceptance" represents a great *willingness* of the single individual to accept a decision. Thus, it does not primarily concern the use of *force* on the part of the organization, and "the sanctions as well as the customs" become means to extend the zone of acceptance of the single person, not primarily means for the organization to exert power.

The role of authority in organizations is to provide a basis for individual decisions, to give premises for the various actions and opinions of individuals (Simon 1957: 123ff.). In contrast to "power," the concept of "authority" implies that the individual actually is able to make a choice, i.e., between to accept authority or not. The essence of the power concept, i.e., the overcoming of resistance, explicitly includes cases when the conditions for submission may be completely determined by the party having the greatest resources. Or, somewhat simplified: the power concept directs our attention to the dominating part in a relationship, whereas the concept of authority emphasizes the importance of the subordinate's acceptance (cf., Krupp 1961: 101-105).

As an example of the interpretation of the concept of authority, let me cite the Swedish business economist Dick Ramström. In connection with Simon's definition, Ramström says that

> [it is clear that] authority, in contrast to what is usually assumed, is "delegated" from below upwards. Instead of assuming that authority is distributed hierarchically downwards by the management, we may say that it is the subordinates who provide authority for the superordinate by accepting his directives (1964: 35).

According to Ramström, the rights of the dominating part to exert influence becomes a kind of present from the subordinates. This may be seen as a reformulation of Simon's recommendation not to over-emphasize the "arbitrary" aspect of authority.

The choice one makes between these theoretical concepts depends on the general image of organizations which one considers to be the most important and fruitful. The concept of authority is intimately connected with the systems approach to organizations, and therefore with the claims made by the proponents of this theory. The representatives of systems thinking recommend themselves, as we have seen, sometimes by emphasizing their "scientific" approach. However, systems theory also lends itself fairly easily to purposes whose value to its user may be more ideological than "scientific."

The Inducement-Contribution Balance

One of the cornerstones of the systems perspective in organizational sociology is the notion taken from Barnard and Simon of the propensity of individuals to strive for a positive balance of rewards (surplus of "inducements" over "contributions"). This, in turn, is another formulation of the utilitarian doctrine of the individual's striving to maximize satisfaction and minimize pain. In the continuation of this section, I shall summarize some principal viewpoints which I developed in connection with a critique of George C. Homans' exchange theory (Abrahamsson 1970), viewpoints which are also relevant to the treatment of systems theory.

Homans emphasizes that the basis of all social science theory is psychological postulates. He states that these postulates are well known from learning theory, and are often used either explicitly or implicitly in common parlance among laymen. What are these postulates? The three most important ones are:

(1) If in the past the occurrence of a particular stimulus-situation has been the occasion on which a man's activity has been rewarded, then the more similar the present stimulus-situation is to the past one, the more likely he is to emit the activity, or some similar activity, now.

(2) The more often within a given period of time a man's activity rewards the activity of another, the more often the other will emit the activity.

(3) The more valuable to a man a unit of the activity another gives him, the more often he will emit activity rewarded by the activity of the other (Homans 1961: 53-55; cf. also, Homans 1967: 35-37).

Propositions (1) and (2) are variants of Thorndike's well-known "law of effect"; proposition (3) is primarily taken from elementary economic theory. Homans' most important point is that psychological and economic postulates are variations of one and the same general idea: "Both behavioral psychology and elementary economics envisage human behavior as a function of its pay-off: in amount and kind it depends on the amount and kind of reward and punishment it fetches" (1961: 13).

A major problem with utilitarian-hedonistic theory, as it is employed by Homans and March and Simon is that the concepts of reward and punishment (pleasure and pain) are extremely difficult to operationalize. The predictions one can make on the basis of the theory are of the type "in a certain situation the individual tries to maximize his profit, i.e., he will choose from a number of acts that act which is likely to give the largest reward and involve the lowest costs." This is, however, a rather vague prediction, since it remains to be specified which values the individual tries to maximize. Only when the statement has been specified with reference to these, and only when these values can be measured, is it possible to conclude whether the prediction was correct or not. Homans does not set any limits for what can be a value to a person. In fact, anything can be a reward. It is rewarding to husband one's resources; but it may also be rewarding not to husband one's resources (1961: 79-80). It is rewarding to be an egoist, but also to be an altruist (1961: 79). One achieves rewards by conforming, but also by not conforming (1961: 118). There are potential rewards in the fact that the price of a commodity is low, but also in that it is high (1967: 49). (For a longer discussion, see Abrahamsson 1970: 279-281. A recent extensive critique of exchange theory is given by Skidmore, 1975: 114-122). (It is remarkable that the hedonistic model is put forward by March and Simon, writers who otherwise are prone to emphasize the difficulty for the individual to predict and evaluate the results of his actions. If the person himself experiences these difficulties, it would seem that it would be even harder for an outside observer.)

Thus, the critique that may be leveled against the theses of inducement-contribution theory is not that it explains too little, but that it explains too much. In fact, there is no behavior of the organization's stakeholders which may *not* be interpreted in terms of inducements and contributions. According to the one, if a stakeholder chooses to remain in his relationship with the organization, this means that he perceives that the rewards he receives from the organization are greater than the contributions he gives to it. Analogously, if he chooses to withdraw his cooperation from the organization, this means he considers his contributions to exceed that which he can get from the organization.

However, the theory is remarkably silent about what actually *constitutes* rewards and contributions (and, even more importantly, what is not a reward or a contribution) and how the "balance" between these two factors should be measured. It lends itself easily to ex post facto explanations but is weak on predictions.

Sherman Krupp, besides stressing the tautological character of the inducement-contribution scheme (1961: 146), points to two difficulties connected with the empirical measurements of the utility balance. The first of these has to do with the appropriateness of indices of individual satisfaction which are used as operationalizations of inducement (or reward) surplus. Briefly, satisfaction indices are not dependent only on inducements and contributions, but also on the aspiration level of the individual. This level cannot be assumed to be fixed. On the contrary, it will change depending on, for example, intraorganizational conditions, and will affect the individual's perception of inducements. Krupp asks the rhetorical question, "What has satisfaction measured when the perception of inducement is altered by a human relations program?" (1961: 151). It would be wrong to assume that satisfaction in an organization is related to the same goals in two observation periods. And "if goals have changed, how can satisfaction be compared?" (1961: 150).

The second problem stems from the assumptions that March and Simon make concerning the utility balance. The employment of the concept is dependent on the following conditions:

- aspiration levels must be continuous, independent, and must change only slowly;
- environmental influences must be slight;
- the organization must be stable;
- large classes of people must have common values, yet they cannot influence each other (Krupp 1961: 154; cf., March and Simon 1958: 86-87).

"It is clear," says Krupp, "that these conditions can prevail only in the mind or the laboratory of the researcher" (1961; 154). Thus, what March and Simon try to do is to make their model consistent with reality by "trimming off the pieces that do not fit" (1961: 154-155).

Who is a "Member?"

In the literature on systems theory, one often finds the term "member" as a label for single actors within the system. Katz and Kahn (1966: 15) emphasize, for example, the risk inherent in the fact that an outside observer may equate "the purposes or goals of organizations with the purposes and goals of individual members." Ramström (1963: 23) describes the organization in March's and Simon's balance terms, and adds: "The members of the organization are willing to remain with it only to the extent that their contributions do not exceed the advantages they get from participating." Caplow (1964: 1) defines an organization as a social system with an unequivocal collective identity, an exact "roster of members," a program of activity, and "procedures for replacing members." Likert (1961: 97) cites studies according to which high-productive managers differ from low-productive managers by generally having more positive attitudes to "every member of the organization." Simon (1957: 102-103) discusses "the means the organization employs to influence the decisions of individual members" (i.e., division of work and establishment of standard practices).

This conceptualization of "member" is problematical in that, among other things, the formal aspects of membership are not clearly separated from the informal ones. The fact that the individual has a contract relationship to the enterprise, i.e., is an employee, tends to be associated with the assumption that he is also in general agreement with the organization's goals and values. "Member" imples that one actively takes part in, and gives support to, the organization in which he is working. However, formal employment (objective membership) should be distinguished from the degree of support and positive sentiments given to the organization (subjective membership).

The concept of member is used as a counterpart to thesis of balance between inducements and contributions, and gives increased strength to the harmony model of systems theory. The problems which one meets in using the term "member" are well illustrated by the introduction to one of the classical contributions to organizational sociology, i.e., Blau and Scott's *Formal Organizations* (1962). According to them, organizations may be classified by reference to prime beneficiary (the cui bono criterion). By the use of this criterion, they distinguish between four broad classes of organizations:

(1) mutual benefit associations (in which the organizational members themselves are the prime beneficiaries);

(2) business concerns (owners as prime beneficiaries);

(3) service organizations (e.g., hospitals, schools, etc., with clients as prime beneficiaries); and

(4) commonweal organizations (e.g., the police, fire protection, defense, etc., with the general public as prime beneficiary).

By using this interest group analysis, Blau and Scott's book separates itself from the mainstream of contributions to organizational theory. When they discuss the emergence of organizations and the role of organizational actors, however, they, as well as the writers mentioned above, run into the problem of distinguishing subjective from objective membership.

They state the purpose of their book in the following way:

This book is about organizations—organizations of various kinds, with diverse aims, of varying size and complexity, and with different characteristics. What they all have in common is that a number of men have become organized into a social unit—an organization—that has been established for the explicit purpose of achieving certain goals (1962: 1).

But from where does the initiative to organize emanate? And whose goals are supposed to be implemented? The following quotation points to the answer:

If the accomplishment of a task requires that more than a mere handful of men work together, they cannot simply proceed by having each do whatever he thinks needs to be done; rather, they must first get themselves organized. They establish a club or a firm, they organize a union or a political party, or they set up a police force or a hospital, and they formulate procedures that govern the relations among the members of the organization and the duties each is expected to perform (1962: 1).

The starting-point is that some persons organize *themselves*; those who have taken the initiative to organize are treated as the members of the organization. The continuation of the authors' discussion, however, takes a different turn. At the end of the quotation, the initiators' role is to formulate rules of procedure which govern the duties of themselves and others who now have enlisted in the organization. The original initiators have assumed the character of superordinates or employers, and it is clear that "member" in the latter version also includes a position in the organization which is subordinate and dependent. The "members" of a police force are seldom identical to the initiators.

Thus, there are reasons to be sceptical about the term "member" when it is employed by organizational writers. It often serves to conceal the fact that organizations are structures which have been deliberately constructed to meet the purposes of some major interest group or class (mandator), and that other "members" often have good reasons to be critical against these purposes (e.g., in the case when the mandator finds that the labor force is too large and decides that some should not continue as "members," but must be fired).

Summary

The systems perspective is of dubious value as a basis for a theory of organizations. First, it avoids or ignores aspects of power. To the extent that dominance relationships are discussed, the proponents of this perspective strive to see these relationships as arrangements in which one party voluntarily submits to the other's authority. Permanent contradictions have no place in the systems perspective. Furthermore, writers in the systems tradition have obvious observation problems when the issue of organizational history arises. The reason for this is simple: If the hypothesis of balance of interests is accepted as a theoretical premise, there exists no need to describe and analyze the development of possible *forced* associations of actors to the organization and/or conflicts between different parties. The harmony assumption also seems to lie behind the employment of the concept of "member," which frequently is used as a label for individual actors. The concept implies that those actors who are parts of an organization (i.e., who are objectively tied to it), also subjectively support the organization's goals. This is rarely the case with, e.g., coercive organizations (the military, prisons, etc.). Even in organizations where participation is in principle voluntary, there are usually large variations in the degree of subjective membership among the people working in the organization.

The fact that systems theory is based on assumptions of actors' needs for reward surplus (positive balance of exchange), and on other generally vague concepts makes it highly difficult to test empirically. Within organizational sociology and social psychology the hedonistic/utilitarian exchange theory still has to prove its fruitfulness for further research.

I have also put forward some other points of critique, although they are of a more marginal character. First, system concepts lend them-

selves easily to descriptions of a reifying nature, such as using industrial production terms for public organizations, as was the case with
hospitals. Second, the organic model, implicit in the systems perspective, may easily become biased in a manipulative direction, so that
"disturbances" which have their base in conflicts of interest are explained to hamper the organization's achieving full "health." Together
these reasons are sufficient for a rejection of the systems perspective
in organizational sociology. In the next Chapter I shall try to sketch
out an alternative model based on assumptions which are partly in
opposition to systems theory.

NOTES

1. A good summary of the major traits of the three traditions may be found
in W. G. Scott (1967).
2. Among these should be mentioned some works by Gouldner (1954a;
1954b; and 1959); Perrow (1967); and Woodward (1965).
3. "History" as an index word is absent from, e.g., Katz and Kahn (1966);
March and Simon (1958); and Rhenman (1968 and 1971).

Chapter 10

A PROCESS MODEL FOR THE
STUDY OF ORGANIZATIONS

Introduction

Rationalistic theory and the systems perspective are in contradiction with each other on several points, the most fundamental of which concerns the notion of why organizations even exist. The answer proposed by systems theory is that organizations fulfill various necessary *functions*. Organizations represent the answers to different needs of not only the surrounding macrosystem, but also of the different groups of stakeholders who, because of their relations to the organization, try to achieve a surplus of "inducements" over "contributions" (or at least an even balance between them).

The organization, or "vitalistic system," also has needs of its own. It strives to survive and to preserve the balance needed to guarantee adequate contributions from the participations. In this endeavor, the organization is dependent on its relations to the stakeholders. Organizational balance is disturbed to the extent that stakeholders abandon the organization in search of better alternatives. The organizational leadership (or the enterprise leadership, since the theory is most often applied to this kind of organization) acquires the role of an interest administrator or mediator.

The rationalistic perspective seeks the answer to the question of the organization's existence in its *tasks*. The organization is perceived as a goal-directed structure, established by some party for the explicit purpose of getting some kind of work done. The different parts of the organization are subordinated to this purpose. Thus, "balance" and "equilibrium" become relatively irrelevant concepts. To the extent that the parts do not fulfill their tasks, they may be exchanged for others. In direct contrast to systems theory, this exchange of parts does not necessarily involve a disturbance of the organization as a whole.

The antihuman consequences of the goals of Taylorism, to build organizational structures in which the individuals become little more than a complement to machines, have served for a long time as an argument rejecting the rationalist approach. Such arguments were further developed by the human relations tradition. Neither the negative consequences of the application of scientific management principles, nor the discoveries by the human relations researchers are, however, sufficient reasons for rejecting the rationalistic approach. The idea of the organization being established in order to carry out specific tasks for the benefit of some party need not exclude a recognition of the importance of the informal structural factors, nor a critical attitude against extreme division of labor and fractionalization of tasks. As I have tried to show above (pp. 157-159), also the systems perspective may be employed as a "machine theory" of organizations and may have the same reifying and manipulative consequences as scientific management.

It is true that the rationalistic perspective has some important shortcomings. Factors which limit rationality and which are related to conditions in the organization's environment are not adequately represented (p. 138). This perspective lacks an awareness of disturbances which may arise because of inner contradictions in the organization ("counter-rationality"; pp. 143-145). Furthermore, its methodological complement, the means-ends scheme, possesses several built-in limitations.

The discussion below is based on the notion that it is possible to compensate for these disadvantages while keeping the advantages of the rationalistic approach. It should be particularly emphasized that the notion of the organization as an instrument for the implementation of interests is coupled to the existence of *different* interests in society (e.g., those of employers and employees). Thus, for each organization it may be asked, "For *whom* are its decisions and action rational?"

Since organization, to use Schattschneider's phrase, is "the mobilization of bias" (1960: 71), it tends to weigh the making and implementation of decisions highly in favor of those who control the organization, i.e., those who use it as an instrument for mobilization. Thus, "the decision-making process may be rational only from the perspective of management" (Krupp 1961: 83). But what of the employees? Obviously, if private interests determine the "bias" of the organization, that organization cannot be used for the advancement of workers' interests. Two major strategies are available in this situation: to form a union and/or to fight collectively for being recognized as a legitimate mandator of the organization (i.e., to become part of the mandator group or to replace it altogether; "political participation," see Ch. 11). In other words, "it is rational to combine against the boss, Emperor, General, department head, bureau chief, or Dean" (Krupp 1961: 164). Organization is met by organization, rationality by counterrationality.

The process model to be developed below may hopefully serve as a starting point for the study of organizations, and as a basis for an analysis which clears away certain shortcomings inherent in rationalistic thinking. The model is developed to avoid the harmony assumptions of systems theory, its static perspective on organizations, and its general and diffuse conceptual apparatus.

Elements of the Model

(1) *Organizations have a history.* They are created by a certain group of mandators. They develop and grow under the influence of this mandator group, and are affected by various forces in the environment and by various "inner logic" factors (see Part I).

(2) *Organizations are the products of collective consciousness.*[1] They are the instruments for the interests of mandators; and they are rationally planned structures for the fulfillment of these interests. As Kenneth Boulding has pointed out, organization is "an expression of solidarity within the organized group, and . . . an expression of a lack of solidarity with those outside the organization" (1953: 10). The organization may strive toward integration, but integration of whom and for what purpose? It is important to recognize that the framework of an organization normally contains conflicting interests and opposing powers, the details of which are "shaped by the broader environmental forces in society." Thus, "an emphasis on the integrating aspects of organization is but one among many ways of viewing organization" (Krupp 1961: 169).

(3) *The mandator strives toward full rationality (optimization) but is forced by different circumstances to work at a lower aspiration level (satisfaction).* The mandator (or his representative in the organization, see below) cannot expect that plans which have been designed will be carried out wholly in accordance with the blueprint. The rationality is circumscribed partly by economic, technological, and political processes in the society (e.g., business cycles, development of machines and information systems, contradictions between conservative and progressive groups, state interference). It is also circumscribed partly due to the organized activities of other mandators (counterrationalities).

(4) *The mandator is usually not able to run the organization completely on his own.*[2] Even though a certain number of persons might have been sufficient for manning the organization when it started, this possibility usually decreases over time due to the growth of the organization and to modifications of external conditions. It is therefore a natural step that the mandator appoints a representative to handle the day-to-day activities of the organization. This representative is called the organization's *executive*. Motives for creating an executive are the need for a rational management of the mandator's time and his economic resources (the *economic* motive); the need for special knowledge to master different administrative and technical problems (the motive of *competence*); the need for long-range planning (the *continuity* motive); and the need to be able, if necessary, to quickly deploy the organization's resources in support of the mandator's aims (the *mobilization* motive).

(5) *The executive is usually appointed for the task of administering the organization.* In order to manage the organization's production, human resources as well as material assets are necessary. Therefore, the mandator and/or the executive hire a number of persons to carry out tasks at different levels and in different positions (officials and workers in staff and line positions). It is a problem for empirical research to define the executive independently of the rest of the labor force; more about this follows below.

(6) *The size and composition of the labor force (with regard to positions, offices, education, age, etc.)* vary depending on factors in the environment (material and social forces, competition from other organizations) and on the goals sought by the mandator and his representative.

(7) *The same factors also affect the structure of the organization,* i.e., the degree to which the organization approaches the mechanistic or the organic type (Ch. 7). The existence of a certain structure depends

partly on the plans by the mandator regarding production, personnel policy, etc., and partly on environmental factors which are difficult or impossible for the organization to control (market relations, legislation, etc.).

Items (1) to (7) are summarized in Figure 10.1, where I have also indicated those areas which I believe are the objects of the three primary types of organization theory, i.e., the theory of *bureaucracy*, *administration* theory, and *socio-technical adjustment* theory.

The theory of bureaucracy deals with the relationship between the mandator and the executive (see Part I). Administration theory analyzes the problems of the executive in its management of the organization's production. The two major areas of administrative theory are design theory, the development of ideas concerning optimum structure (cf., Taylor, Gilbreth, and various modern writers on e.g., staff/line problems and matrix organization), and theories of decision-making (e.g., Simon 1957; Cyert and March 1963). Socio-technical adjustment theory deals with problems which arise in connection with efforts by the executive to engage the employees in the organization's production. This area covers a great number of different theories which investigate the conditions for adapting human beings to technology, and vice versa. They concern, first, the psychological and socio-psychological preconditions for creating such adjustment. Second, they deal with the practical arrangements for improving the adjustment to work (self-managing work groups, job enlargement, job rotation, etc.). Well-known examples are Blauner (1964); McGregor (1966); Herzberg (1959); Friedmann (1955); Argyris (1964); Emery and Trist (1969); and Gardell (1971 and 1976).

In order not to unnecessarily complicate Figure 10.1, I have excluded those boxes and arrows which would illustrate the parallel processes for other interest groups. An important cause of the emergence of an organization is the existence of other organizations. The relations between employers and employees offer rich examples of this. Other organizations and their activities thus represent important conditions for the behavior of a particular mandator and his organization.

The Study of Organizations
as an Interdisciplinary Task

Systems theory is typically presented as, and claims to be, a truly interdisciplinary theory, by encompassing elements from the biological, behavioral, and social sciences. While recognizing the interdisciplinary

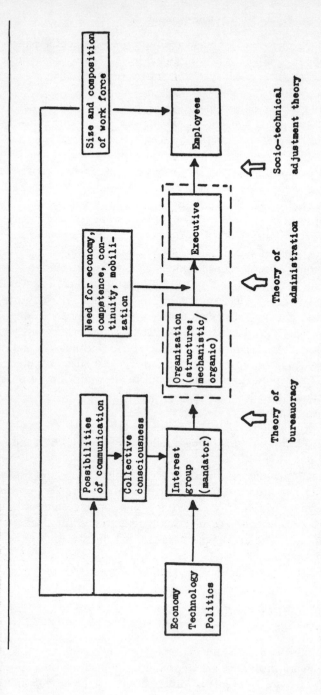

Figure 10.1: A PROCESS MODEL FOR THE STUDY OF ORGANIZATIONS

character of a theory as being of particular merit for the study of organizations, I believe that rationalistic models of the kind which has been outlined above offer at least as many advantages as systems theory. Consider, for example, the following research problem. Although hypothetical as presented here, it is a topic of great importance in the present economic and political situation in Sweden.

Traditionally, interest organizations have played a major role in the democratization of Swedish society. Cases in point are the role of the labor unions in the introduction of the 8-hour working day, old-age pensions, legislation for obligatory holidays, and solidary wage policy; the role of the workers' voluntary associations in the creation of a comprehensive system of basic and adult education; the influence of the abolitionist organizations on Swedish official policy on alcoholic beverages; and consumers' and housing cooperatives.

The growth of these organizations, and their gradually increasing fields of power and influence, also present some problems. As early as 1946, Gunnar Heckscher in his book *Staten och organisationerna* (*The State and the Organizations*) pointed out the tendencies to "free corporatism" that arose in the intersection between state and organizational power. Increasingly, the state had come to rely on the big organizations for achieving political consensus and obtaining the public consent needed to carry out various forms of legislation.

If anything, this role was further extended during the period after World War II. And as some writers have pointed out (see, for example, Elvander 1976; Westerståhl & Persson 1975), as various forms of interest representation develop, there is a danger that the fundamental principle of political democracy, "one man, one vote" will be eroded. To the extent that the organizations acquire direct influence in the political decision-making process, their members will gain an extra vote. This problem becomes particularly salient in public organizations (schools, hospitals, public-transport companies, etc.), which, according to the theory of parliamentary democracy, are to be governed only by the politically elected bodies.

If this is accepted as a legitimate problem for research, I believe that it can be fruitfully approached within the framework of a rationalistic, process-oriented model of organizations. Some examples of problems and questions for inquiry are presented below. I have chosen to structure the text with reference to three discipline areas (history, sociology/ political science, and law) and to two aspects of organizational relations (internal and external). I hope that the distinctions between the six alternatives that result from this scheme will become clear as the discussion proceeds.

Table 10.1

| | Relations | |
Discipline	External	Internal
History	1	2
Sociology/political science	3	4
Law	5	6

(1) *The emergence of labor organizations* as expressions of group/ class interests. The development of interorganizational linkages (for example, the association of individual trade unions) and patterns of corporatism (state-organization interdependence).

(2) *The historical development of mandator-executive relations* (in each particular organization), for example, tendencies to oligarchy, bureaucracy and power crystallization. To what extent are certain functions and tasks concentrated in specific posts and persons within the organization?

(3) *Conceptual/theoretical analysis* of doctrines of (a) parliamentary-representative democracy, and (b) organizational democracy ("industrial democracy," "economic democracy"). What are the possible points of conflict and agreement? What contradictions, if any, exist between the public as mandator to the state and parliament, and public employees as mandators to their trade unions)?

Empirical analysis of prevailing patterns of corporative relations. What influence can each particular organization exert on the state and the public representative organs? How do representatives of organizations look upon their role as defenders of particular interests, in contrast to the safeguarding of the public interest?

(4) *Mandator/executive relations.* What means do the members of the mandator group in a particular organization have at their disposal to control the executive? To what extent, and in what situations, are these means mobilized? How does the executive react in situations of internal/external cross-pressure (i.e., having to respond to demands from the mandator as well as from external forces, for example the state)?

Executive/employee relations. What means are used by the executive to control the employees and to secure compliance from them? What theories and doctrines are used to justify such control?

Mandator/employee relations. What latent and manifest conflicts, if any, exist between the mandator and the employees? To what extent, and on what grounds, do employees demand to be accepted as legitimate members of the mandator group? Does the mandator's definition of "organizational democracy" also include acceptance of employee representation in decision-making organs or is it limited to participation in direct production only (for example, through schemes of job rotation, job enlargements and other redesigns of the socio-technical system)?

(5) *Description and analysis of legal rules* concerning political democracy and organizational democracy. Analysis of possible contradictions in the intersection of these areas. Analysis of rules for employee influence in public and private organizations: to what extent do they differ, and to what extent do they *have to* differ, if the principles of representative democracy are to be upheld?

(6) *Description and analysis of rules* governing—or supposed to govern—the behavior of the organization's executive (such as goal formulations, procedural rules, rules limiting the executive's right to independent decision-making, rules resulting from the demands of external power centra). How do these rules vary between different types of organizations?

Some Problems

The application of Figure 10.1 in practical research leads to the following problems, among others.

(1) *Definition of "mandator."* I have identified the mandator of an organization in legal-juridical terms, i.e., as that person or group who has the formal right to appoint and dismiss the executive (see pp. 26-30). Two questions should be noted in connection with this. They concern, first, changes over time with regard to who is the mandator, and second, the difference between formal rights and actual power.

Changes over time. It is a quite commonplace occurrence that the original founder of an organization is not the same person or persons who currently form the mandator group. In turn, this means that the original goals may be far from identical to the present ones. Investigations of the composition of the mandator group at different periods of time may provide interesting insights into the conditions under which the executive works. Formal documents, protocols of board meetings, etc., are useful data for this purpose.

Formal right vs. actual power. An essential question concerns the mandator's actual possibilities for controlling not only the organization, but more specifically, the work of the executive. Quite often, the mandator's influence is primarily exerted in extraordinary situations. That is, he is usually content to follow the activities of the executive in a very general way, limiting his own role to interference "in the last instance," e.g., to deseat or replace the executive. This is largely the case of the relationship between shareholders and the management in privately owned capitalist enterprises.[3]

(2) *Operationalization of the model.* One of the problems here concerns the study of organizational effectiveness. To some extent, the activities of organizations are determined by the goals formulated by the mandator and by the means which organizations employ in implementing them. In order to investigate the extent to which the goals actually become implemented, it is necessary (as I have indicated, p. 145) that the goals be specific enough to allow determination of the degree of goal fulfillment. General and superordinate goals are of little use for this purpose, whereas goals at lower levels may be more easily operationalized. Furthermore, it is essential to investigate which definitions of effectiveness and efficiency exist within different groups in the organization, e.g., the executive, the mandator, and the employees.

Another problem concerns the delimitation of the executive. Like other employees, members of the executive (e.g., managers of private enterprises, high-level officials in voluntary organizations and in public bureaus) receive a salary from the organization for their work. How can one define the executive independently of the rest of the organization's labor force? One possibility is to begin with the fact that the executive group, being the representatives of the mandator, has a closer and more intimate connection with the mandator than other groups of employees. If this is the case, a sociometric criterion can be employed. Another possibility, which does not exclude the one just mentioned, is to base the definition on data concerning salaries and other benefits. Usually, persons in the executive have considerably higher salaries, more benefits, etc., than other employees. A third possibility is to examine formal documents, such as board minutes kept by the mandator. As a rule, decision about the hiring and firing of members of the executive are formally recorded.

One may object to the first two approaches on the basis that they contain a certain amount of arbitrariness. Sometimes even employees at the lower levels have close contacts with the mandator, and certain persons in high positions may not have any influence on the daily activities of the organization. The difficulty in defining what is the "management" of enterprises is, however, also a familiar problem within the systems-oriented approach (see, e.g., Rhenman, *Företaget och dess omvärld* (*The Enterprise and Its Environment*), 1971: 50).

(3) *Clients.* The model outlined in Figure 11.2 does not explicitly include clients and their interrelationships with other major groups in the organization. There is no simple way to introduce the client category. Clients may appear at two points in the organization sequence. First, they may be the mandators of organizations, or parts of the mandator group. One example is provided by the Yugoslav interest communities (see Ch. 13, esp. p. 217), i.e., associations of users and producers of public services, such as health care and education. The inhabitants of the commune fulfill the double role of being the mandators and the beneficiaries (clients) of these organizations. Second, clients may also appear at the right hand side of the diagram as the objects of the "production programs" of so-called treatment organizations. As such, they are subordinated to the executive and the employees.

For the taxonomically minded, it may be of interest to note that organizations may be classified according to the extent to which they include clients as legitimate members of the mandator group. Note in this connection the "therapeutic communities" and similar organizations such as Alcoholics Anonymous, which sometimes explicitly have this as part of their treatment program. The presence or absence of client alienation often hinges on the clients' being accepted as legitimate mandators of the organization.

(4) *Official and operative goals.* Critics of the rationalistic approach have argued, among other things, that organizations often abandon their initial goals, that the goals are too vague to serve as guidelines for empirical research, and that new goals often arise during the organization's day-to-day activities which often coincide badly, if at all, with the original purposes (and presumably also with the presently existing superordinate goals; see pp. 121-125).

The very process of abandoning initial goals is, in itself, an important object for study, and should not be seen as a reason for rejecting rationalistic approaches. If superordinate goals are too vague, there are usually more concrete goal indications at lower levels, which may be utilized for studies of effectiveness.. The emergence of new goals as a product and consequence of the organization's current work appears, however, to confront us with a considerable problem. If the executive gradually replaces all goals with new ones, our ability to determine the raison d'être of the organization is seriously impaired.

In answering this objection, I would like to refer to Perrow's distinction between official and operative goals. The official goals of an organization "are the general purposes of the organization as put forth in the charter, annual reports, public statements by key executives and other authoritative pronouncements. Operative goals, on the other hand, "designate the ends sought through the actual operating policies of the organization; they tell us what the organization actually is trying to do, regardless of what the official goals say are the aims" (1969: 369-370).

The official goals should be regarded as the general framework for the work of the executive which has been established by the mandator; the operative goals should be viewed as the ad hoc solutions proposed by the executive to handle those problems which arise in daily operations. If these solutions differs too much from the official goals, it is probable that the mandator will intervene to correct the executive. What is "too much" cannot be established beforehand. Rather, this determination is dependent on the judgment by the mandator himself of the fit between operative and official goals.

NOTES

1. The collective consciousness depends partly on the conditions under which each category of individuals lives and exists, and partly on the possibilities they have for establishing contacts with each other. These possibilities, in turn, are determined to a great extent by technological factors (e.g., the development of systems for communication).

2. In an article by Larry E. Greiner, "The Developmental Phases of the Organization," it is argued that the first critical decision concerning the development of a newly formed organization is "to find a strong administrator who is accepted by the founders." This is because the growing activities of the organization means that the founders "are charged with a responsibility for management that they do not want to have" (1974: 176).

3. An example is the following news item from *Aftonbladet* (December 20, 1974). "The executive director of Volvo, Pehr G. Gyllenhammar, 40, will meet his most difficult test when he is to confront the shareholders of Sweden's biggest enterprise at the annual shareholders' meeting. Influential shareholders will make him personally responsible for the drop of Volvo's business index. In 21 months, this favorite share of the Swedish people has decreased in value by 180 crowns." Gyllenhammar, however, weathered the storm and did not have to take the post as county governor in Gothenburg, which *Aftonbladet* had assumed to be a definite possibility.

PART III

PARTICIPATION, SELF-MANAGEMENT, AND
ORGANIZATIONAL DEMOCRACY

Chapter 11

ON SOCIO-TECHNICAL AND

POLITICAL PARTICIPATION

Introduction

One major feature in the political and social development in many European countries after World War II has been the widening of employee influence in industrial enterprises and, to a lesser extent, in public organizations. Important examples are the introduction of the Yugoslavian self-management system by the 1950 act (and subsequent constitutional amendments), the West German system of Mitbestimmung and joint consultation bodies (Betriebsräte; Betriebsverfassungsgesetz of 1952 and 1972), similar arrangements for labor-management consultations in Holland (Ondernemingsraad), acts of 1950 and 1971), France (comités d'entreprise, acts of 1945 and 1966), Norway (bedriftsutvalg, acts of 1945 and 1973), and Sweden (företagsnämnder, negotiation agreements of 1946, 1958, and 1966). (*SOU* 1975: 1, Chs. 2 and 3).

Although these examples certainly merit detailed attention, the purpose of this chapter is not to comment on the individual cases of the widening of workers' participation.[1] Rather, I shall deal with some general conceptual aspects which seem salient whenever the extension of "industrial democracy" or "organizational democracy" is concerned.

By *participation* I shall mean the involvement of employees in decision-making on different levels in an organization. Since decisions can have more or less wide ramifications, participation can have more or less deep-going consequences for the employees' power and responsibility in the running of an organization.[2]

Although the formulation "more or less" may seem to make participation a gradualistic concept, I do not believe such a contention to be theoretically fruitful, nor very useful for empirical research. On the contrary: Involvement in decision-making on the top level of organizations encompasses a qualitatively different role for the employees, compared to decision-making on lower levels. Below, I will argue for the notion that political participation (involvement in high-level goal setting and long-term planning) and socio-technical participation (involvement in the organization's production) most fruitfully should be seen as variables theoretically independent of each other. One implication of this is that possibilities of reducing workers' alienation should not be seen as depending on technological changes in the work process only. Both empirical and some theoretical arguments can be advanced to question the common view of the primary importance of technology to workers' alienation (put forward most eloquently by Robert Blauner).

Organizational Participation and Its Relevance to Societal Democracy: The Transition Problem

Participation in organization decision-making is commonly seen not only a means of reducing the relative power of the executive elite, but also as a way toward a more general democratization of society. This view is frequent among writers in the "radical democratic" school in political science, and developed by them as an attack on the functionalist, "democratic elite" school of thought (see Chs. 12 and 14 below). For example, Carole Pateman writes:

> For a democratic polity to exist it is necessary for a participatory society to exist, i.e. a society where all political systems have been democratized and socialisation through participation can take place in all areas. The most important area is industry; most individuals spend a great deal of their lifetime at work, and the business of the workplace provides an education in the manage-

ment of collective affairs that is difficult to parallel elsewhere. The second aspect of the theory of participatory democracy is that spheres such as industry should be seen as political systems in their own right, offering areas of participation additional to the national level. If individuals are to exercise the maximum amount of control over their own lives and environment then authority structures in these areas must be so organized that they can participate in decisionmaking (1970: 43).

If the notion of a widening of societal democracy through organizational participation is accepted, some questions remain, however. Are *all* kinds of participation in organizations equally conducive to societal democracy? Initially, this seems not to be the case, since only participation on a relatively high level involves the employees in issues that concern organizations and institutions other than their own. As I shall argue in Ch. 14, "democracy" should be construed as involving the maximization of two equality values: equality of influence on decisionmaking, and equality of economic and material resources.

Since the latter value cannot be reached without cooperation between organizations—where the resourceful agree to leave a relatively larger share to the less resourceful, e.g., through solidary wage policy and progressive taxation—it seems reasonable that participation in decision-making concerning solidary with other groups provides for more "education in the management of collective affairs" than decision-making strictly limited to the organization's internal problems. Thus, the issue of transition of participation from the organizational to the societal level is at least partly dependent on a distinction between various kinds of participation.

A further question concerns the issue of cui bono. Who is the prime beneficiary of a participative reform within an organization? Again the question of level of decision-making becomes salient. As many writers have pointed out, it is obvious that some participative reforms are being suggested by organizational leaders as a kind of defense, and as a way to quiet workers' demands for increased influence. For example, Blumberg (1968) attacks the proponents of neohuman relations models, such as inverted authority schemes, the "Y-theory," and T-groups, suggestions allegedly launched by theoreticians closely attached to private capital interests. His own view of participation, he claims, does not involve any calculations as to whether the increase of workers' involvement is economically profitable or not.

[We do not see participation] as a device to lower costs, to improve quality, to increase productivity, to undercut trade union or workers' demands, or to give workers the illusion of power without its actuality, the more easily to guarantee jealously guarded managerial prerogatives within the framework of private enterprise (1968: 129).

In a similar vein, Veljko Rus asks the question, "Where are those boundaries where participative management changes into manipulation with employee participation?" (1972: 169). Rus sees the safeguard against such manipulation in an equalization of participation possibilities within the organization, i.e., in a reduction of differences in knowledge between various worker strata, protection of the less privileged workers, and a deep-reaching decentralization of decision-making (1972: 171).

In my view, both Blumberg and Rus sidestep the argument that the initiators of "manipulative" participative schemes may not be the only ones profiting from them. (See also Palm 1974: 272.) In other words, T-groups are not necessarily bad because they have their root in a profit-centered managerial ideology. As is well known, all games are not zero-sum: and in the game of "industrial democracy," it may very well be that both capital owners and workers make some gain: the former by increasing their profits, the latter by getting a less alienating work environment. Thus, the fact that the productive efficiency in an enterprise rises as a consequence of, for example, a job enlargement reform, cannot be taken as the sole evidence for the reform being "manipulative."

A more fruitful task than trying to figure out whether a participative scheme is "manipulative" or not—more fruitful, since finding reasonable criteria of "manipulation" seems an almost hopeless undertaking—is to investigate the arguments for and against those kinds of participation that do *not,* in the short run, have any immediate effects on production but may be desirable to workers for *other* reasons.

As I shall argue below, this is largely the case of participation in high-level decision-making in organizations. Since the established owners usually have a double motive of resisting workers' influence at this level, it is here that the theory of participation, as a democratic strategy, is put to its real test. The double motive is, first, that high-level participation cannot as easily be showed to bring economic benefits; and, second, that such participation threatens the power positions of the owners with regard to their major goals and utilization of capital resources.

Below, I shall argue that *political participation*—i.e., participation involving the right to control the organization's executive—will have to be qualitatively distinguished from *socio-technical participation*, i.e., participation in the organization's production. I shall try to outline the characteristics separating the two forms, and to present arguments for their theoretical separation as variables independent of each other. The theory of participation has perhaps its most important basis in the Marxist concept of alienation. However, this concept may be used both in theories stressing the need for socio-technical participation, and in theories emphasizing political participation.

We shall examine one theory of the first kind (Robert Blauner's *Alienation and Freedom*, 1964). As I shall try to show, Blauner's pre-occupation with technology serves as a block to considerations concerning the possible de-alienating effects of workers' participation in high-level decision-making. In fact, he has to start out from a highly eroded and asociological version of the concept. Since Blauner's book has been highly influential in the debate on participation and industrial democracy, it is of interest to review its major implications.

Socio-Technical and Political Participation: Some Criteria and Comments

Figure 11.1 summarizes some major characteristics of the two kinds of participation. Political participation has its primary effect in extending the role for employees in management. If implemented, it will affect the relations between the mandator of the organization and its executive. To the parties involved the changes will manifest themselves concretely as alterations in the composition of the mandator group (or as the total replacement of the mandator). The change of mandator will put the executive under new kinds of demands, i.e., it will have to re-define its role to become representative of its new masters. Since the changes will involve the rise to power of (partly) different interests, the organization's environment will often become affected and will have to adjust to the new situation.

Socio-technical participation, on the other hand, extends the workers' involvement in production, i.e., in the implementation of decisions taken on higher levels. (Adizes [1973: 17] separates "the lowest level of participation" from higher levels by stating that on the lowest level the participant is "involved only with means," whereas on higher levels he participates in the design of policies and in the determination of organizational goals.) The organizational relations affected concern the

	Political participation	Socio-technical participation
(1) Primary effect of participatory reform	Extended role for employees in organizational management (including long-term goals)	Extended role for employees in production
(2) Organizational relations affected (see Figure 10.1)	Mandator/executive	Executive/personnel
(3) Operational criteria	Change in composition of mandator group	Change in production organization (e.g., self-managing work groups, job enlargement, job rotation)
(4) Mandator's demand on executive	Redefinition of representativeness	Reduction of production disturbances; increase in production
(5) Consequences to the organization's environment	Many	Few
(6) Major theoretical formulations[3]	Bureaucracy theory (J.S. Mill, Max Weber, Karl Marx) "Radical democrats" (P. Bachrach, C. Pateman)	Human relations (Roethlisberger and Dickson; Walker and Guest; McGregor; Argyris; Likert)
(7) Empirical examples	Yugoslavian self-management Sweden: the Meidner proposal	Sweden: the Volvo-Kalmar car factory

Figure 11.1

NOTE: **The Meidner proposal.** At the Congress of the Swedish Trade Union Federation (LO) in 1976, Rudolf Meidner and his associates presented a scheme for the gradual transference of executive company power to the employees. According to this scheme, a certain proportion of the profits of private companies is each year transformed into shares which are owned collectively by the employees. Depending on the amount of annual profit and the proportion of it which is converted into shares, employees would gain a majority on the company boards after twenty to seventy-five years.

The Volvo-Kalmar factory. In the Kalmar factory of the Volvo company, the assembly line has been abolished in favor of a system of permanent work groups, each in charge of a part of the assembly process. The groups are located around the periphery of the factory building, and supply of parts is from the center. Car chassis and bodies are individually transported to their respective assembly stations on easily moveable, computer-operated platforms. Because of this arrangement, the work teams are given a certain freedom in determining their own work pace, and job rotation within the group is facilitated.

interaction between the people directly involved in production, and their superordinates. The latter are rarely identical with the mandator, but rather, are people acting on the mandator's behalf: hence the term "executive/personnel."

The concrete changes take place in the organization of production: for example, through the formation of self-managing work groups, job enlargement schemes, job rotation, the introduction of joint consultation programs, etc. The demands which are put on the executive concern its role in maintaining and increasing production. Failure in this respect will cause the mandator to question the effect of the participative reform. Finally: The changes are primarily internal, they do not result in modifications of interests in the mandator group, and they do not affect the long-term goals. Hence they leave the organization's coalitions with other groups and organizations largely unchanged. The environmental consequences of increased socio-technical participation will therefore be few, if any.

On Theoretical Independence

It is a reasonable hypothesis—although still largely untestable because of the relative absence of experiments in workers' participation in high-level decision-making—that political and socio-technical participation may have effects (e.g., in reducing alienation) independently of each other. In other words, it may well be that high-level participation has positive effects on employees' involvement, even if nothing is done to change the technological job environment in the organization. If this is true, there is little ground for the gradualistic thesis that workers' influence has to be increased quantitatively step by step, starting "on the shop floor." Participation in management can then be motivated independently of shop floor participation.

Some evidence supporting this assumption may be found. Blumberg notes, for example, that results from the Hawthorne experiments show work satisfaction to grow as participation increases, in spite of the fact that technology was kept constant (1971: 83). Although "participation" was not used consciously as an independent experimental variable, it constituted a kind of hidden dimension: the traditional authority structure to which the workers were used to submit themselves was considerably attenuated during the experiments. Blumberg points out that variations in alienation closely followed the variations in participation (see esp. Ch. 3). As is well known, changes in the physical work environment were not related to variations in productivity. In my view,

Blumberg seems to be leaning a bit too heavily on these findings. As Carey (1967) has documented, the methodological shortcomings of the Hawthorne studies were considerable.

More convincing are the results from research in Yugoslav enterprises. As Veljko Rus states, it was a common belief among industrial sociologists until the mid-sixties that technology is the major independent variable which can explain variations in work satisfaction among employees. According to findings by Obradović and Supek this, however, seems highly questionable. In Rus' words, "technology is only one of the independent variables which influence the status of the employed." And he goes on:

> Obradović established that the degree of worker alienation (alienation in Marx's meaning of the word) is high and that there are no essential differences regarding the degree of alienation among workers engaged at different technological levels of production. This, then, means that all those determinants which are important for the social status of the employed or rather for the degree of their alienation do not, in general, depend on the technological factor (Rus 1972: 168-169).

Similar results attained by Supek serve to emphasize that "neither the possibilities of participation, nor participation aspiration" are hampered by a higher degree of technology or mechanization of work. Rus concludes, that "to date technology has not presented the basic limits for employee participation and . . . future technology will be even less able to limit this type of participation" (1972: 169).

How do these findings match the host of survey and experimental data (see Blauner 1964; and Argyris 1964) which underline the importance of, e.g., job rotation and job enlargement for the work satisfaction of employees? The explanation seems obvious: The results reflect the effects of *two different kinds of participation*. The Yugoslav research concerns participation in *management* (Supek, for example, measured workers' identifications with the self-governing system and their aspirations to control the staff, i.e., the organization's executive), whereas most of the research in the nonsocialist countries refers to participative schemes on levels *below* that of management. Here, the dependent variable being investigated is the workers' feeling of powerlessness, meaninglessness, social isolation, etc. (see pp. 193ff.). It seems wholly reasonable that technology should have effect on alienation *when technology is the only variable with regard to which the workers can hope for changes*. It seems equally reasonable that technology de-

Table 11.1

		Socio-technical participation	
		0	1
Political participation	0	1	2
	1	3	4

creases in importance when the workers do have the chance of deciding on how production should be organized to fulfill their own needs and the needs of the society at large.

What we wish to know, then, is the effect on alienation of *all* the four situations represented in Table 11.1. So far, the majority of empirical research findings concern changes of type $1 \rightarrow 2$. We know very little of what happens to workers' job satisfaction and organizational involvement in the other cases, i.e., $1 \rightarrow 3$, $2 \rightarrow 4$, and $3 \rightarrow 4$.

On the Erosion of the Theory of Alienation: The Defining Away of Political Participation

Robert Blauner's *Alienation and Freedom* (1964) has been highly influential in the social-scientific discussion on industrial democracy. In this book, the author attempts to explain the attitudes of workers toward their jobs by examining the basic characteristics of their technological environments. He finds 'alienation' to be especially high in industries characterized by mechanically controlled work rhythm, high-speed production, repetitiousness, and social isolation. A typical example of such industry is the automobile factory. In industries with process technology, e.g., chemical plants, workers have greater autonomy, freedom of movement, and more social contacts in work; hence alienation is lower.

Blauner's recommendations emphasize the need for less fractionalization of work, and a greater involvement in, and influence by workers over, their work situations. In the light of works by the human relations school and previous critics of the industrial environment (such as Georges Friedmann 1955), these propositions, however, are less original than Blauner's *theoretical* contribution. The importance of Blauner's work lies primarily in his tying together the Marxist theory of alienation with present-day work conditions in industry, thereby adding a new, seemingly left-radical touch to the American debate on the humanization of work.

> I have . . . attempted to demonstrate the usefulness of the alienation perspective in clarifying our understanding of the complexities of the modern social world. This idea, developed by Marx in his early writings, can be expressed in systematic concepts and propositions that raise important analytical, as well as sociopolitical, questions. . . . There is a need to fuse an empirical, realistic approach with the valuable humanistic tradition of alienation theory that views all human beings as potentially capable of exercising freedom and control, achieving meaning, integration, social connection, and self-realization (1964: 187).

In the course of Blauner's discussion, however, it becomes clear that although the workers may have the *capacity* of exercising freedom and control, he thinks there are certain kinds of freedom and control that they do not *want*. As a consequence, the concept of alienation becomes eroded. The original concept is deprived of its political aspects, and its socio-technical aspects are emphasized.

In his *Economic and Philosophical Manuscripts*, Marx identified three aspects of capitalist society which cause deep-going changes in people's work and social relations. First, private property and the fact that the means of production are privately owned and controlled. Second, the process of division of work, being a consequence of the development of productive forces. Third, the fact that human work has become a commodity subject to the laws inherent in the capitalist market system (Israel 1971: 56).

Blauner transforms the Marxist concept of alienation into four dimensions: the worker's feeling of powerlessness, meaninglessness, social isolation, and self-estrangement. (These, in turn, are adapted from Melvin Seeman.)

Marx	Blauner
private ownership	powerlessness
division of work	meaninglessness
labor a merchandise	social isolation
	self-estrangement

As has been noted by Israel, Blauner tends to transform a basically *sociological* theory into a *psychological* one (1971: 16, 264ff.). Especially important, to my belief, are the changes that the notion of power and influence of the working-class undergo in Blauner's treatment of 'alienation.' Let us look, therefore, a bit closer at Blauner's term "powerlessness."

Blauner states that "there are at least four modes of industrial powerlessness which have preoccupied writers on the 'social question.'" These four modes are:

(1) the separation of ownership of the means of production and the finished products;

(2) the inability to influence general managerial policies;

(3) the lack of control over the conditions of employment; and

(4) the lack of control over the immediate work process (1964: 16).

It would have been logical if Blauner had examined data of workers' reactions to all these four aspects. This, however, is not the solution he prefers. Instead, he advances as an initial postulate that workers *are not interested* in top-level influence in enterprises:

> It is my contention that control over the conditions of employment and control over the immediate work process are most salient for manual workers, who are most likely to value control over those matters which affect their immediate jobs and work tasks and least likely to be concerned with the more abstract and general aspects of powerlessness.

> The very nature of employment in a large-scale organization means that workers have forfeited their claims on the finished product and that they do not own the factory, machines, or often their own tools. Unlike the absence of control over the immediate work process, "ownership powerlessness" is a constant in modern industry, and employees, therefore, normally do not develop expectations for influence in this area (1964: 17).

Blauner is right, of course, in part of his argument. The very fact that ownership and high-level control is in the hands of private interests tends to hold back employee expectations for such influence. Data showing that workers fairly seldom demand such control can certainly be found (see, e.g., Blauner 1964: 18; Gardell and Dahlström 1966: 128). Yet the objections to the argument are obvious. Even if private ownership of industry is a "constant" in the major part of the Western world, this need not preclude that workers may develop *aspirations* to political participation, as a result of a rising class consciousness and

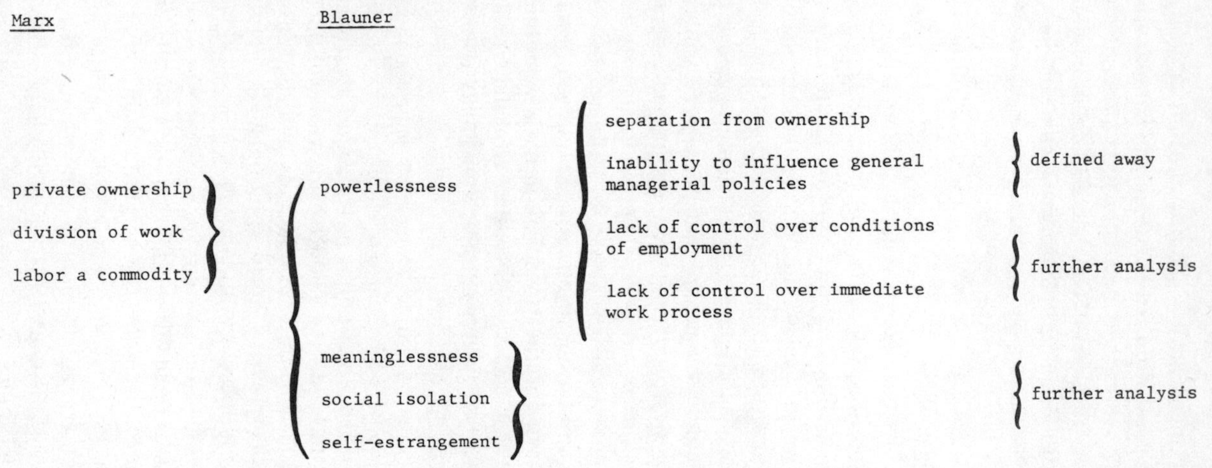

Marx

private ownership
division of work
labor a commodity

Blauner

powerlessness

separation from ownership

inability to influence general
managerial policies

lack of control over conditions
of employment

lack of control over immediate
work process

defined away

further analysis

meaninglessness
social isolation
self-estrangement

further analysis

Figure 11.2

political self-confidence (cf., Israel 1971: 265). Thus, it is quite conceivable that the workers could have made comparisons between today's "constant" (private ownership) and possible different conditions (social ownership) in the future, had Blauner cared to investigate the workers' political ideologies and aspirations. But the point is that Blauner's use of the concept and theory of alienation serves to define such questions away as being irrelevant.[4]

As we have seen, Blauner starts out by referring to the full concept of alienation, in which a mandatorial role for the working-class is a basic element. However, in the process of theoretical analysis, the concept becomes seriously eroded.

The aspects of alienation, serving as a ground for Blauner's empirical investigation, are primarily those tied to the technological characteristics of modern industry. Thus, the original concept is deprived of most of its political implications, i.e. those concerning the relations between social ownership/control and alienation. As a consequence of Blauner's analysis, the kind of participation which is emphasized as the primary means to reduce alienation is socio-technical, not political participation. (The "further analysis" with regard to the issue of control over employment conditions is scant and wholly subordinated to the analysis of differences in technological environments between different branches of industry. See esp. 1964, Ch. 8 ("Alienation and Freedom in Historical Perspective"), in which the role of organized labor is almost totally absent.)

NOTES

1. Since this chapter deals not only with participation in industries but in public organizations as well, "workers' participation" should be understood as including also employees in the public sector.

2. The literature on industrial democracy abounds with definitions of participation, ranging from very general formulations to specific statements concerning the necessity of social ownership of the means of production. As an example of the former, note French et al.:

Participation refers to a process in which two or more parties influence each other in making certain plans, policies, and decisions. It is restricted to decisions that have further effects on all those making the decision and on those represented by them (French et al. 1960: 3).

An example of the latter is provided by Marinković (1973 who sees it as "the basic meaning and the ultimate human goal of participation" that "the vast majority of direct producers not only participate in the process of production but also in the process of creating the forms of their community, in the management of this community's institutions, and in the disposition of and decision-making on how the means are to be used for their common needs." This, in turn, requires "socialized ownership and appropriate forms of acquisition and distribution" (pp. 184-185).

3. The most important theoretical contributions to the problem of relations between organizational mandators and their executives are given by the classical writers on bureaucracy (see Ch. 2). An important theme in writings such as John Stuart Mill's *Considerations on Representative Government,* Max Weber's *Wirtschaft und Gesellschaft,* Karl Marx' *The Civil War in France,* and Robert Michels' *Political Parties* is the problem of making the executive responsible to its mandator, prohibiting that the executive goes its own way and works for its own interests instead of those of its masters.

The issue of elite vs. participative rule reappears in more modern contributions to democratic theory, such as Peter Bachrach's *The Theory of Democratic Elitism* and Carole Pateman's *Participation and Democratic Theory* (see Ch. 12).

In contrast, socio-technical participation gets its theoretical formulations largely in books within the human relations tradition in sociology. The classical contributions are, of course, Elton Mayo's *Human Problems of an Industrial Civilization,* Roethlisberger and Dickson's *Management and the Worker,* and Walker and Guest's *The Man on the Assembly Line.* More recent works with roots in this tradition are, for example, Douglas McGregor, *The Human Side of Enterprise,* Rensis Likert, *New Patterns of Management,* and Chris Argyris, *Integrating the Individual and the Organization.*

4. It should be noted also, that contradictory evidence is not lacking, especially if we look at data in other western, industrialized countries. For example, a Swedish survey some years ago showed a majority of workers wanting greater influence not primarily in matters directly associated with production, but in issues such as appointments of supervisors, principles of promotion, long-term planning and investments (Karlsson 1969: 127ff.).

Results from a Norwegian survey also serve to question Blauner's postulate (Holter, in Thorsrud & Emery 1964). Contrary to Blauner's assumption, the very fact that high-level leadership is outside the workers' control does not seem to be a sufficient obstacle to workers' aspirations to gain such control. A high degree of working-class consciousness, trade-union and political organization (which is common in the Scandinavian countries) will reduce the ideological impact of private ownership and control.

Chapter 12

PARTICIPATION AND PROBLEMS OF

REPRESENTATIVENESS IN ORGANIZATIONS

I now want to expand the discussion somewhat to encompass the wider question concerning how participation in societal decision-making can be implemented. The debate on industrial democracy, in the two senses discussed in Ch. 11, has received considerable nourishment from the general, political science debate on democracy. This debate is highly relevant to questions of democracy and influence in organizations. Below I shall review two major lines of thought in this debate: the ideas represented by the so-called "democratic elitists" and those by the school of "radical democrats." The latter have defended participative rather than indirectly representative determinations of democracy. According to the "radical democrats," participation in local decision-making (e.g., within voluntary organizations and enterprises) trains the individual for assuming responsibility in wider societal decision processes. The value of the contributions by the "radical democrats" for the debate on democracy has been considerable. Some problems remain, however. This is especially true with regard to the consequences for both economic and material equality which follow from a participatory program. I shall discuss this in Ch. 14.

Participative and syndicalist principles have had perhaps their most important application in the Yugoslav system of self-management. In Ch. 13 I shall summarize some experiences of others as well as myself with this system. This summary will serve as an exemplification of the advantages that such a system may have for increasing participation. Further, it will be an exemplification of certain problems related to inequality and bureaucracy, which tend to remain in spite of energetic attempts to eliminate them.

Elitism and Participation: Democracy as Means and Ends

In general terms, democracy may be defined as the possibilities of citizens to freely take part, either individually or collectively, in the making of decisions that affect their lives (Gould and Kolb 1964: 187). But how is this "free participation" to be practically arranged? In this section, I shall briefly summarize two major theoretical traditions which deal with this issue. According to one theory put forward by Joseph Schumpeter (1966) democracy is primarily a means by which political decisions are reached. According to another school, represented by, e.g., Peter Bachrach, democracy is realized to the extent that the citizens participate in decision-making. From this viewpoint, participation becomes a goal in itself.

SCHUMPETER

According to Schumpeter,

democracy is a political method, that is to say, a certain type of institutional arrangement for arriving at political—legislative and administrative—decisions and hence incapable of being an end in itself, irrespective of what decisions it will produce under given historical conditions (1966: 242).

The prime political act by the citizen, therefore, is the election of representatives.

The democratic method is that institutional arrangement for arriving at political decisions in which individuals acquire the power to decide by means of a competitive struggle for the people's vote (1966: 269).

In various forms, Schumpeter's ideas have been reconsidered and empirically illustrated by several other American social scientists, such as S. M. Lipset, A. Campbell, G. Almond, and S. Verba. Thematically, the similarities between them could be expressed by saying that they all regard a certain amount of apathy by the citizens as a prerequisite for a well-functioning democratic system (or at least, they do not see apathy as inconsistent with such a system). According to these writers, the voters are not competent enough to understand anything except fairly uncomplicated political issues. The explicit task of the voters, therefore, is not to decide *what* the government should do, but rather *who* should make decisions on political matters (Campbell et al., 1964: 281). Intensive engagement in political issues by the mass of citizens may endanger the democratic system, since (according to attitude surveys carried out in the United States) the voters tend to be more intolerant than the elites to ethnic minority groups, and rank lower on "democratic creed" (results summarized by Lewin 1970: 67ff.).

In the views of this tradition, apathy is functional to the social system. This is a highly debatable point. It is just as reasonable to assume that apathy instead may harm the very base of democracy, since apathy has the effect of making intolerance and a dearth of "democratic creed" permanent. If the elite possesses a higher degree of "democratic creed," it seems essential to increase the degree of interaction between the elite and the mass. This conclusion, however, is rarely drawn. On the contrary, this emphasis on the positive functions of apathy tend to make it presented as the only safeguard against antidemocratic tendencies among the majority of the people. In other words, the people should be protected against its own, endemic, destructive tendencies by being assigned the limited role of electing political candidates. In such a system, the elites become the safeguards of the system, and the people themselves are viewed as a threat against democracy.

BACHRACH

This "theory of democratic elitism" has been strongly attacked during the last few years, in the United States by Peter Bachrach, in Sweden by Leif Lewin and Sten Johansson, in England by Carole Pateman (to take just a few examples). The critique is based to a large extent on classical liberal democratic theory as formulated by, among others, Jean-Jacques Rousseau and John Stuart Mill.

Classical theory

conceives the public interest in terms of both results and process. Thus public interest is measured by the soundness of the decisions reached in the light of the needs of the community *and* by the scope of public participation in reaching them (Bachrach 1969: 3).

Participation, then, is the main variable that separates the "radical democrats" from the "democratic elitists."

Bachrach strongly rejects the notion that apathy may be a sign of health in the political system. According to him, widespread participation is possible even though direct self-government cannot be implemented. Government *for* the people is necessary, but at the same time the government must make every effort to engage the voters in politics (1969: 6). Another writer in the same tradition who puts forward a parallel view is Lewin (1970). He defines democracy as "a form of government which is implemented to the extent that there is interaction between elite and mass in the political decision process." Interaction, therefore, should be maximized: "The theory of the positive functions of apathy has to be rejected already on the basis of definition" (1970: 228). As is evident, this statement can be seen as a reflection of the basic tenets of Mill's classical theory. Mill's views can be summarized in the following way:

(1) Only if all citizens participate in the political decision-making process can political decisions be guaranteed to reflect the interests of the mass of the people.

(2) Participation educates those who participate, thereby making them permanently able to defend their own interests.

(3) Participation develops the individual's personality, making the citizen aware that he is part of the total society, and making him feel that he is responsible not only to himself but to society at large (Johansson 1971: 7; cf. also, Pateman 1970: Ch. II).

Thus, participation theory challenges tendencies to centralism and elitism in politics. The critics of "democratic elitism" try to investigate the necessary preconditions and the possible methods for bringing about a greater amount of popular influence over political decision-making. See, for example, the suggestions by Lewin (1970: 237ff.) to establish direct contacts through telephone communications, computers, and television between the elite and the voters. At the same time, they are aware of the practical difficulties involved, particularly the complicated problem of establishing an information system which effectively transmits the opinions of the mass of the people to the elite.

In a society with a high degree of organization among the citizenry and a large variety of formal and informal associations, the possibilities of achieving this are naturally greater than in a society with a stricter division between elite and mass, and where the organizations are weak and therefore function poorly as mediators of the interests of various groups. A rather far-reaching decentralization of decision-making to organizations and various local interest groups is a major element of the plea for participation by the radical democrats. For example, Bachrach emphasizes the importance of including in the concept of "politics" that kind of decision-making which takes place in public and private enterprises. If people achieve a greater voice in these organizations, their interest for political issues in general will grow.

> For many individuals political issues and elections appear either trivial or remote and beyond the reach of their influence. Of a different magnitude are issues which directly affect them in their place of work, issues which are comparatively trivial, yet are overlaid with tensions and emotions that often infuriate and try men's souls. It is here—despite the legitimizing effects of bureaucratic forms—that the ugliness of man's domination of man is fully revealed, and it is here, consequently, that democracy must be established and put to use (Bachrach 1969: 103).

As we have seen (pp. 186-187) the theme reappears in Carole Pateman's, *Participation and Democratic Theory* (1970). The quotations from Bachrach and Pateman can be seen as reformulations of the third proposition in Mill's theory, i.e., participation in decision-making within industrial enterprises and local organizations will develop the citizens' responsibility for the society at large ("public spirit").

With regard to the Swedish situation, the same thesis has been put forward by Lars Erik Karlsson.

> If and when a general reform towards industrial democracy is put into effect, a multitude of social, cultural, and economic conditions outside of the enterprises will change. Status differences, now related to differences in occupation and income, will be reduced.

Theoretical schooling will become less prestigious, and manual occupations will grow in popularity. Consumption will become less conspicuous. . . . The change in the pattern of values will open up possibilities for extending social services, cultural activities, the protection of the environment from pollution, health services, and democratic organs for the scrutinization and control of consumer articles (1969: 201).

I shall return (Ch. 14) to issues concerning the relationship between internal democratization in organizations and the democratization of the social structure in general, i.e., the question of secondary effects of organized participation. Before that, however, let me comment on one of those factors which are among the most important for *restricting* participation: the increasing size of organizations. (The section below may be read as an addition and further comment to the discussion of "inner-logic"–factors in Part I of this book.)

Organizational Size and Participation

What are the consequences for participation when organizations increase in size, hierarchy, and specialization? One reasonable hypothesis is that participation declines and that the chances of creating value-similarity between members and leaders are also impaired. Some statistical data from different kinds of Swedish organizations tend to support this assumption.

Westerståhl, in his 1945 study of the Swedish trade union movement, pointed out "that the small local unions are often more active than the larger ones. In several cases, it is demonstrated that the members in Stockholm locals (i.e., relatively large organizations) have been particularly passive" (1945: 96).

Lindblad, in his survey of the Swedish Communal Workers' Union (1960), investigated the relationship between local union size and membership participation, and found a strong correlation. In locals with more than 1,000 members, 17 percent took part in the annual meeting of the local, and 9 percent in an "average meeting." In locals of size 30 or less, the corresponding proportions were 70 and 53 percent respectively (1960: 258, Table 44). It should be noted, however, that the larger organizations also had a greater meeting frequency, and that their work is delegated to subgroups more often than is the case in the smaller organizations. But in all likelihood, this does not compensate for the drastically smaller degree of participation, since the mobility among members who go to meetings is low. That is, roughly the same persons attend all meetings.

Similar data are given by Oskarsson (1963) who investigated membership participation in local 170 of the Swedish Metal Workers' Union during 1959-61. The local consisted of four suborganizations of varying sizes. Size and participation rates are given in Table 12.1.

The participation rate declines steeply with increasing organizational size. It cannot be disproved, of course, that the differences may be due to variations in, for example, social and geographical recruitment of the members, or in the kind of work and its organization in the various enterprises (e.g., a greater amount of shift-work in larger enterprises). A stronger hypothesis, however, is that size, hierarchy, expert dominance, and other factors related to the labor union apparatus tend to restrict participation. The larger the organization, the less chances there are for establishing direct interaction between all members. At the same time, the need for delegation of tasks grows because of an increase in the number of membership-related issues and because of extension of the organization's external contacts. Its political and economic role in the local community grows, and other organizations and power-groups become eager to profit from relations with it. To apply Tönnies' well-known dichotomy, its character of *Gesellschaft* increases at the expense of its role as *Gemeinschaft*.

Table 12.1

Suborganization	No. of Members Dec. 31, 1961	No. of Participants at "Average" Meeting	Participation Rate (percent)
Uddevallavarvets verkstadsklubb	2,657	100	3.7
AB Nordverks verkstadsklubb	213	25	11.7
Bilarbetarnas yrkesklubb	149	20	13.5
Uddevalla Gjuteri och Mek. Verkstads verkstadsklubb	67	18	26.9

Source: Oskarsson 1963: 504, Tables II and III.

The Raison d'être of Elite Rule: Efficiency

The last few decades have witnessed a continuous growth in the size and centralization of organizations. Prominent Swedish examples are the trade union movement and the cooperative movement (*Kooperativa Förbundet,* KF). In the trade union movement, small locals have been amalgamated and administratively centralized, a tendency which has been accompanied by the increasing power of union boards to appoint local union officials (Sunesson 1971: 123). In 1945, the number of locals within the Trade Union Federation (*Landsorganisationen,* LO) was 8,622. In 1974, the number had decreased to 1,897. The average number of workers per local was, in 1945, 128, and in 1974, 982 (Lewin 1977: 76).

The development of trade unions toward greater centralization has a clear parallel in the KF, where the concentration to ever bigger units was accelerated during the 1960s. In 1960, the KF congress agreed on a plan for "structural rationalization," which involved the reduction of local co-ops from around 600 to some 100. Again in 1964, the congress recommended a further reduction to between 20 and 40 local cooperatives (Elvander 1969: 80-81). For various reasons (most importantly, the active resistance to centralization by large groups of KF members), the actual concentration rate has been slower. At the end of 1971, there were 232 KF locals, a figure which two years later was further reduced to 200 (*Svenska Dagbladet,* August 30, 1974).

The main argument for centralization and concentration which has been put forward by KF leaders themselves is that of the need for administrative efficiency. A managing director of the KF in 1974 suggested further concentration to one large, unified enterprise for Sweden as a whole. The reason given was primarily economical:

I believe that the KF and the local co-ops in the end will become one big unified enterprise with the least possible duplication of administration. This will set free many millions of crowns for other purposes, says John Sallborg.

There are many members who, for completely understandable reasons, are against a further concentration of the co-ops and find it hard to accept some measures which have been undertaken from purely economic motives at different levels of our movement. But without commercial efficiency, it is not possible to pursue ideology (*Svenska Dagbladet,* August 30, 1974).

The defense of concentration in the name of efficiency may be reconciled rather easily with the vindication of the principles of representative democracy if the latter are understood as a *method* of decision-making (cf. "democratic elitism"). The chairman of the Swedish Trade Union Federation in the 1940s, August Lindberg, confirmed this at the 1946 congress of the federation. The statement was meant to be a defense of the veto paragraph of the federation's by-laws which put the right to decide on strikes in the hands of the federation and not, as previously, in the hands of its suborganizations.

Democratic freedom does not mean that the individual citizen has the freedom or possibility to exert direct influence on the decisions of the parliament. He has the right to elect representatives who speak and decide on his behalf. Representative democracy [has] been accepted also in the by-laws of the trade union movement. This form of democratic cooperation [is] perhaps the foremost proof of the maturation of the trade union movement. On grounds of principle, [it cannot] be maintained that the paragraph [is] in opposition to democracy. Instead, it is a question of the organization of work (Casparsson 1947: II, p. 498).

The counterarguments generated by advocates of participatory democracy are often based on assumption of hidden power-motives among organizational elites. For example:

In order to concentrate power to themselves, the elite often employs efficiency arguments. By combining smaller units into larger ones, executive personnel can be employed and administration be rationalized, thereby allegedly improving the conditions for democracy in small units.

Efficiency arguments, however, are often only a cover-up for power ambitions among the governing elite. Each mutual-benefit association that employs salaried officials runs the risk of developing into an economic enterprise. In democratic organizations as well as business enterprises, economic and democratic goals are in direct conflict, as the democratic ones emphasize membership influence and membership engagement (Karlsson 1969: 85-86).

It is not possible to establish empirically the degree to which "power ambitions" actually lie behind efficiency arguments. In all probability, the elites' recommendations to centralize organizational administration are normally motivated by a mixture of personal power strivings and a sincere ambition to serve the organization and its mandator.

From a democratic viewpoint, the most serious matter is perhaps not the elite's power hunger, but that such motives can so easily be *combined* with rational arguments in favor of leaving the daily business in the hands of a small circle of leaders. The elite can justify its position by saying that it is in the interest of all members that the organization be efficient, and therefore, power should be delegated to the executive.

It is hard to deny that centralization, concentration of resources, increasing expert functions, and administrative positions in the organizations very often lead to gains in efficiency, at least in the sense that the organization—to look back at Weber's concept of bureaucracy—gains in "Präzision, Schnelligkeit, Eindeutigkeit, Aktenkundigkeit . . . ." But as we have seen, the Weberian ideal-typical description of bureaucracy also contain another element, i.e., subordination. Bureaucracy has to be *dependent* on its mandator; bureaucracy is an instrument and an "animated machine." From this perspective, a self-indulgent administration is by definition an ineffective administration, for it does not act as a tool for its master but as a mandator for itself.

Here I want to refer back to the discussion on bureaucracy in Part I, pp. 23-26, and on effectiveness/efficiency, Part II, pp. 145-146. An organization may well meet criteria of productivity (i.e., be efficient) without being representative. Representative effectiveness has to do with the degree of relationship between actions undertaken and interests of the mandator, and thus requires a combined consideration of economic and democratic motives.

The answer to the question "Is centralization efficient?" must be given in this perspective. The real dilemma for an elite which strives to be democratic is the fact that the actions which it suggests in order to increase administrative efficiency—in good faith and in full awareness of the interests of the mandator—often have the immediate consequences of restricting organizational democracy. Lars Erik Karlsson's statement above is very much to the point. Economic goals are hard to reconcile with democratic ambitions. The contradiction, however, can perhaps be solved or at least mitigated. As I shall argue below, there is reason to expect that an increase in administrative efficiency strikes fairly hard at representativeness. But the reverse is probably not true: if representativeness increases, this may make the organization more efficient, especially in the long run, in its relations with other organizations and power-groups.

Some Limitations of Administrative Efficiency

Although it may be maintained that centralization, hierarchy, and expert influence in organizations contributes to their efficiency, there is also reason for the assumption that in the long run administrative efficiency will increase also as a result of participation among organization members. Both the Chinese example as well as that of Yugoslavia are well worth considering (see Chs. 2 and 13). The development toward new forms of work organization in the industrial sphere provides a further example worth contemplating.

It is not an exaggeration to say that the production patterns of Taylorism have strongly dominated the Western, as well as the Eastern, industrial countries during this century. The advantages of this system as it gradually appeared seemed obvious. By splitting up the work process into very short cycles containing a small number of body motions and by employing time-and-motion studies, new tools, and new physical lay-outs of plants, production could be drastically increased.

Today the situation is quite different at least if we look at the *theory* of industrial work organization. There is a growing insight that the gains in efficiency which are achieved by fractionization of tasks, may be counteracted in the long run by a greater rate of sickness and psychological stress among the workers. And so, the interest in sociotechnical participation schemes has rapidly increased both among labor unions and employers. Experiments with self-managing work groups, job rotation, hourly salary instead of piece-rate payment, etc., seem to promise something to everyone. For those who emphasize the need for the humanization of industrial working conditions, the results seem to provide good arguments. When workers are organized into self-managing groups they experience greater freedom and satisfaction; in addition, sickness rates as well as symptoms of psychological stress decline. Those who are affiliated with employers' interests, stressing that industrial democracy must be subordinated to profitability, can find consolation in the fact that work engagement as well as productivity figures often rise faster in plants and departments which employ new forms of work organization than in plants that do not use these new forms. (Summary of data from experiments with self-managing work groups at Norsk Hydro, quoted from Karlsson 1969: 166-169.) Pateman (1970: 66) reports on results from experiments of industrial democracy and participation, and says, "Here all the evidence indicates that not only will participation have a favorable effect on the individual in relation to the development of the sense of political efficacy, but that also it will not harm the efficiency of the enterprise, indeed it may increase it."

Chapter 13

YUGOSLAVIA: Participation

and Self-Management

What I have just said holds for reforms in a participative direction within fairly small social systems. Obviously, it is considerably more difficult to predict what happens to productivity and efficiency on the macrolevel, i.e., for society at large, if participation generally increases in all organizations. The example of Yugoslavia suggests that a widespread participation in societal decisions may well be achieved together with a high degree of productivity.

Some Background Notes

During the first postwar period, the Yugoslav Communists faithfully copied the Soviet economic system, and in many areas even tried to be more ideologically pure and orthodox than their Russian colleagues. The break with Moscow and Kominform in 1948 was not due to conflicts over economic principles; Tito and the Yugoslav Communists were judged by the Russians as liberal deviationists—where the fact that they were *deviationists* was probably more serious in the eyes of Stalin than the actual ideological content of their deviation. The Yugoslav left had come to power by its own force, without much assistance from the Red Army, and was determined to preserve its independence (Johansen 1967: 18-19).

The choice of a self-managed economic system and a market economy was partly a result of the struggle for independence from the Soviet Union. The constitution, prescribing that the enterprises should be governed by the workers themselves, although within a socialistic framework (an associationist-socialistic system; Horvat 1969: Ch. 1), was a logical consequence of these ambitions. Adopted on June 27, 1950, its main principles were formulated in the following way (article 1):

> The industries, the mines, and the enterprises within the fields of communication, transport, agriculture, trade, forestry and communes shall, as the common property of the nation, be governed in the name of the social community of working collectives, within the framework of the economic plan and on the basis of the rights and obligations prescribed by laws and statutes (quoted after Mandel 1971: 319; elements of central planning were gradually reduced during the years immediately following the adoption of this constitution).

Thus, the Yugoslav enterprises are not *owned* by the workers. The means of production is socially owned property, managed by basic organizations within the different areas of the economy.

After the acceptance of the constitution of 1950, development in Yugoslavia has deliberately been directed towards increasing the independence of the basic organizations. Table 13.1 illustrates the changes in the distribution of the total investment volume in Yugoslavia during the 1960s and early 1970s. In 1963, the federal social investment fund was discontinued, and in 1965 investments by the communes were cut to a minimum. As Table 13.1 indicates, the share of gross investments decided on by enterprises and banks increased from 30 percent in 1961 to well above 70 percent in the 1970s.

The continuously growing power of the banks is the most eye-catching feature of Table 13.1. Besides, the figures probably underestimate the real influence of the banks. Especially during the end of the 1960s the need for new investments in machines, buildings, etc., rapidly increased. Since the enterprises lacked investment capital of their own, they were forced more and more to rely on assistance from the banks (Flaes 1973: 118-119).

Table 13.1: Relative Share of Gross Investments 1961-1963 (percent)

	1961	1962	1963	1964	1965	1966	1967	1968	1969	1970	1971	1972	1973
Enterprises	29	30	28	26	29	39	33	31	28	27	27	30	32
Banks	1	3	8	31	36	39	45	47	49	51	51	42	40
Federal funds	37	30	27	7	3	6	9	9	9	9	—	2	1
Republics	7	9	10	9	4	3	2	3	3	3	15	14	13
Communes	18	20	20	21	20	7	6	4	4	4	—	4	5
Other	8	8	7	6	8	6	5	6	7	6	7	8	9
	100	100	100	100	100	100	100	100	100	100	100	100	100

Sources: 1961-70, Flaes 1973: 117
1971, Bilandžić 1973: 298
1972-73, Poduzeće-Banka, No. 2, 1974: 4

Self-Management at the Enterprise Level

The self-management system at an enterprise may be exemplified by the organization of the pharmaceutical company "Galenika" in Zemun, a suburb of Belgrade. The enterprise is one of the two leading companies in its branch in Yugoslavia. It has around 4,500 employees, producing pharmaceutical articles, semimanufactured products, and material for the production within other sectors of the economy (e.g., foodstuffs).

The enterprise is divided into ten sections, each one making up a *basic organization of associated labor* (BOAL). The members of each BOAL elect a workers' council. Each one of the ten workers' councils appoints five members to the central workers' council of "Galenika," consisting of fifty members. This elected executive committee has as one of its responsibilities to employ directors who are to lead the work in the ten sections.

PLANNING

A draft production plan for the enterprise is drawn up by the technical and administrative experts. Each worker receives a copy of the draft. Suggestions and comments are encouraged and collected, whereafter a new draft is written. The final proposal for the production plan constitutes the basis for negotiations between the BOALs within the various sections of the company. These negotiations concern decisions on the distribution of production tasks (which section produces what?), production volume and production financing. Decisions on the total production volume of the enterprise are taken on the basis of market surveys. The three most important instruments for the "harmonization" of interests within the enterprise are, (1) the general plan (as referred to above), (2) formal agreements between the BOALs to follow the plan, and (3) contracts regulating the relationships between the basic organizations. These contracts, among other things, include:

(1) specification of work and services to be performed;

(2) quantity and quality of the products;

(3) prices;

(4) the distribution of the collective income;

(5) rules for the delivery of products and services; and

(6) rules for sanctions in case the contract is not fulfilled.

Self-Management at the Communal Level

Although economic decisions more and more are delegated to the basic organizations, the need for local and regional coordination through planning is considerable. Tasks which require common decisions are, e.g., long-run plans for the development of the commune's production, the exploitation of land within the commune, housing programs, programs for environment conservation, and defense.

The three major interest groups within the commune are the workers' councils, the local communities, and socio-political organizations. Local communities comprise, e.g., people in a settlement, part of a settlement, or several interconnected settlements. The socio-political organizations are, e.g., the League of Communists of Yugoslavia (LYC), the Socialist Alliance, the trade unions, war veteran organizations, and the Communist Youth League.

Representatives of these three kinds of organizations elect delegates to three chambers in the communal assembly. They also appoint representatives in the so-called communities of interest which are responsible for carrying out tasks within the public sector (see below).

Delegates are elected on the basis of direct responsibility (they "shall act in conformity with the guide-lines received from their self-managing organizations" [constitution of 1974, article 141]); can be immediately recalled (article 142), have a duty to inform their basic organizations (article 137), and have a *limited term of office* (2 x 4 years in one and the same assembly; article 140). The delegates are nominated by the Socialist Alliance or the trade unions. The communal assembly elects an *executive committee* which, in turn, employs the public officials needed for the commune's administration. The executive committee suggests proposals on various issues to the communal assembly, and supervises that the different decisions are implemented by the administration. Figure 13.1 summarizes the main features of the representational system in a Yugoslav commune.

MAJORITY AND DOMINANCE RELATIONSHIPS

In the commune of Pančevo (in the autonomous province of Vojvodina) the distribution of seats between the three chambers of the communal assembly is the following one:

the chamber of workers' councils	90 seats
the chamber of local communities	40 seats
the chamber of socio-political organizations	40 seats.

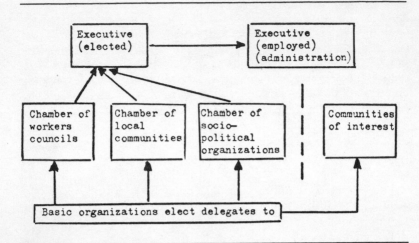

Figure 13.1

This may seem to involve the permanent guarantee of majority for the workers' councils. However, this is not the case, since the chambers do not vote together but each chamber on its own. The only occasions on which the votes are added together are at the election of the chairman and the executive council of the assembly, and when basic constitutional issues are decided upon (e.g., the fusion of two or more communes).

In actual practice, the numerical size of the workers' councils probably involves a certain political dominance. If the chambers are unable to reach a common decision, however, the socio-political chamber may ask that the issue be brought to the *general meeting* (see below). A proposal is carried if two out of the three chambers vote for it.

Discussions in the communal chambers reflect only to a part the political process in the commune. The demands for resources from the communities of interest are discussed—after being prepared by the communal assembly—at general meetings. These meetings are attended to by the delegates of the communal assembly, the representatives of the socio-political organizations, and the communities of interest. At these meetings the size of the annual budget for the public sector is decided upon, and basic decisions are taken regarding the relationship between public consumption and public investments.

THE COMMUNITIES OF INTEREST

The communities of interest for the public services are found in five primary areas, i.e., health care, education, culture, child care, and social assistance. They consist of representatives of (delegates from) two main groups. First, the personnel within each area, and second, the recipients of public services. Representatives of the latter group are appointed by the basic organizations. The representatives of the workers' councils have considerable influence over the resources allocated to the public sector (because of the taxes and fees paid by the enterprises to the commune). Thus, negotiations on the size and distribution of public spending are to a large extent held within the framework of the communities of interest.

As Figure 13.1 shows, representatives of organizations within the health care sector, education, etc., take part as ad hoc members when the communal assembly discusses issues that are relevant for the community of interest in question.

Participation in Reality: Some Data

So far, I have discussed the representational system as it looks according to the constitution. But how does the Yugoslav system function in actual practice with regard to participation? The available data indicate that between 20 and 25 percent of the active labor force take part as members of workers' councils or other basic organizations (Denitch 1974: 137; Barbić 1973: 24; for the period between 1950 and the first years of the 1960s, see Pateman 1970: 98). Because of the rotation system, most members of the labor force do their share in the management of their institutions during their active lives.

From a political viewpoint, the League of Communists, the trade unions and the Socialist Alliance exert a considerable influence, especially because of the function of the two latter organizations to nominate delegates for political posts. However, there seems to be a high degree of agreement among foreign observers that the electorate experiences a real freedom of choice between candidates. The candidates suggested often represent a wide spectrum of opinion. Also, the number of suggested candidates is usually much greater than the number of available posts. Finally, the voters have good possibilities, through their participation in the election meetings, of influencing the final composition of the list of nominees for political posts (see, e.g., Johansen 1967: 58; Burger 1973: 38; for figures on the proportion of candidates/posts, see Popović 1968: 121). One survey indicates that 45 percent of the electorate in four Yugoslav republics (Croatia, Macedonia, Slovenia, and Serbia) regularly take part in nomination meetings (Barbić 1973: 24). A comparison with the United States also shows that participation in political life is distributed over a greater number of activities (Barbić 1973: Fig. 1).

Problems and Contradictions

Problems of representation. The decentralization of decision-making, and the wide participation in basic organizations has the effect that decisions are generally well anchored in the actual needs and opinions of the citizenry. Like in every representational system, there is, however, a certain distance between the ideal of complete representativeness and the actually existing practice. The chairman of Pančevo's communal assembly, for example, expressed his concern especially regarding the difficulties of giving members in the basic organizations adequate information about the commune, i.e., information which is short, relevant, and easily understood. He also pointed to the problem of achieving the necessary majorities in the decision-making bodies at various levels. Decisions require a 51 percent majority, and at least half of the members in each body have to be present in order for a decision to be valid.

Strikes. In a system where the workers are at the same time employees and employers, strikes are an anomaly. Yet conflicts of this kind are not unusual. Between 1958 and 1968, about 2,000 strikes occurred in Yugoslav enterprises, the major part being small (i.e., involving few workers) and of short duration (one day or less). Primarily, they seem to be explainable as the outcomes of conflicts between the workers and the technical-professional personnel (managers and engineers in central positions; Jovanov 1974).

The role of the party (LCY). There are several signs to indicate that the gradual strengthening of the decision-making power of basic organizations is at the same time accompanied by measures to increase the influence of the League of Communists. The introduction of the socio-political chamber in the constitution of 1974 is a direct reflection of these trends. A prominent Yugoslav politician, Mijalko Todorović, explains the background in the following way:

> In an insufficiently developed and contradictory society, it is necessary to insure a synthesis of individual and general social interests, an integration of the momentary and the historic interest of the working class.

The Draft Constitution tries to solve this problem through the institution of chambers in charge of political-executive functions (1974: 36).

The need for coordination and planning of the activities within the basic organizations is emphasized in writings and public statements by prominent LCY spokesmen (see, e.g., *Second Congress of Self-Managers of Yugoslavia, 1972*). Finally, *measures against oppositional and dissident intellectuals* have become increasingly more common, and more severe during the autumn of 1974 and the spring of 1975. Eight sociologists and philosophers connected with the journal, *Praxis* (among them Mihailo Marković, Zaga Golubović, and Svetozar Stojanović) in January, 1975, were dismissed from their posts at the Faculty of Philosophy in Belgrade. Similar actions were taken against some social scientists in Ljubljana, among them the industrial sociologist, Veljko Rus. To a large degree, the attacks may be explained by the need felt by the party to strengthen its influence in order to compensate for the loss in power by central institutions such as the state and the federal investment fund. The *Praxis* groups is highly critical of the strengthening of organized political power (see Ch. 2, p. 44). Thus, the repressive measures against its members seem to be a consequence of the more general political and economic developments which I have just mentioned.

Economy and Efficiency

Real income per capita in Yugoslavia in 1964 was about four times as high as before the Second World War. During the period of 1957-1967, the gross national product increased by around 8 percent annually. According to the British journal, *The Economist* (1967), Yugoslavia during the postwar period had an economic growth roughly comparable to Japan's (Pateman 1970: 90).

It is, of course, possible that the growth might have been still faster in a traditional system of decision-making in industry. That hypothesis cannot be rejected. In the light of other results which suggest that participatory reforms within enterprises may increase productivity, it seems, however, less probable. In the long run an increase in participation within an organization will probably increase its efficiency as well, both in an administrative and a representational sense. It will become more representative of its members. The mandator's support for the executive will become stronger, and the organization's possibilities of enlisting the support from both administrators and members in crisis situations will grow. Probably, an emphasis on administrative efficiency will impede representativeness. An improvement of representativeness through increased participation, however, can probably be combined with an increase in administrative efficiency.

Chapter 14

ON PARTICIPATIVE AND
EGALITARIAN DEMOCRACY

To elaborate the hypothesis of the preceding chapter, a participative organization, besides being *effective* is often also an *efficient* organization. It may be assumed to increase its power vis-à-vis other organizations to the extent that its members are mobilized. Thus, a growth in participation will tend to be followed by positive effects externally as well as internally. Elite/mass interaction increases, and the organization becomes a better instrument for the representation of the mandator's interests.

However, this is also the dilemma of participation theory. It is suggested as a rationalization of the equalization of power, but to the extent that participation is implemented, it carries the risk of permanenting inequalities that already exist; indeed, they may be reinforced. To support this proposition, in this chapter I will look at some strategic elements in the theory of the "radical democrats," as represented by Bachrach's, *The Theory of Democratic Elitism* (1969). First, however, a short note of a more general nature.

To be a participatory democrat is easy. In fact, it need not involve more than some scepticism towards elite groups. In the most simple case, the participation thesis does not even require any specification as to how participation should be achieved, or in which organizations an increase in participation is most important. An increase in participation can be recommended without one saying anything about how the scarce resources in society should be distributed. This is especially evident when the question of organizational democracy comes up. Anyone can find examples of organizations, important to himself, in which interaction between the leaders and the members appears insufficient and should be increased. It is only when the role of an organization as an instrument for increasing the resources of one's own group vis-à-vis those of other groups comes under scrutiny that participation theory becomes highly problematical.

To illustrate this, let me quote a few passages from interviews with two prominent Swedes, one (Stig Ramel) being vice-president (1969) of the Swedish Export Association, an organization strongly connected with the interests of private industry. The other is Ernst Wigforss, a former minister of finance, and a well-known social-democratic ideologue. Both emphasize the need for participation in social decision-making: Ramel in an unspecified and general way, Wigforss speaking for the right of workers to take part in managing boards of industrial enterprises.

> *Ramel:* [The fact that Sweden is governed by elites] is one of our great problems. Many people feel themselves alien to decisions and far away from them. We have to create better forms of contact between those who make the decisions and those who are affected by them. I believe that greater decentralization both within enterprises and in political life is the right answer to this problem. (Quoted from Åkerman 1970: 175-176.)

> *Wigforss:* The long struggle of the workers' movement for voting rights and democracy have made many people forget that democracy is not only the question concerning the political organization of society. The quest for economic democracy is a natural outflow of basic democratic values. . . . To me, the great event during the last few years is the fact that the labor movement has become politically activated and demands solutions to these problems (*Tiden,* No. 7, 1974: 393).

Whereas Ramel and Wigforss agree on the need for participation, the former probably would object to Wigforss' way of *applying* the participation thesis which, as can be seen, concerns the redistribution of not only *political* power but *economic* power as well.

Both the attractiveness and the weakness of participation theory stem from its character of being apolitical, if by "politics" is meant the processes by which economic and material resources in society are distributed. And, as I will show below, the arguments of the "radical democrats" are partly based on that definition. For example, Bachrach denounces the concept of "equality of opportunity" and speaks in favor of "equality."

The main problem of participation theory is not how to implement it in various kinds of organizations. Suggestions for practical solutions to problems of participation abound in the literature, ranging from schemes for self-managing production units to designs for participation at all levels in an organization. (See, e.g., Pateman 1970: Ch. IV; Blumberg 1968; Argyris 1964: 59ff.) The main problem is to achieve a combination of sectorial mobilization through participatory reforms, and general democratization (in the redistributive sense). Solidarity *within* organized groups is not, of course, the same as solidarity *between* them. In other words, referring back to the three proposition from John Stuart Mill (p. 202) the defense of one's own interests (proposition 2) cannot easily be reconciled with the development of "public spirit" (proposition 3).

Or in Stojanović's formulation: "The illusion that societal self-management is equivalent to *complete* decentralization, and the naive belief that a self-management system can be created which is *predominantly direct*, is the theoretical back-side of particularistic self-management. As a consequence of such notions, comprehensive systems (such as the railroad net, the postal services, the electricity service) are torn to pieces. . . . Territorial units, especially the communes, are seen as self-sufficient and closed entities. Local autonomy [in Yugoslavia] has developed as local autarchy" (1970: 136).

The "radical democrats" are torn between, on the one hand, the thesis of the efficiency of participation and, on the other, the thesis of equality. We have seen how Bachrach and others argue for participation. But how does a "radical democrat" look upon equality? Bachrach's book, *The Theory of Democratic Elitism*, besides being an argument for better interaction between the elite and the mass, is also a plea for equality of political power. With great force he rejects the ideas by some "democratic elitists" (1969: 87) that "equality" primarily should be construed as equal possibilities for all men to reach certain positions. This is "equality of opportunity": but this is insufficient, since a true democracy requires equality with regard to the *execution* of power. To implement the latter type of equality, the traditional definition of "politics" has to be extended. "Politics" does not only concern the customary forms of government: it also has to involve decision-making in the private sector of society, and above all, in the giant industrial corporations. According to Bachrach, it is necessary to discuss seriously "the nationalization of one or a few corporate giants," like, for example, General Motors (1969: 102). Through such measures one may approach equality in the actual execution of power: and this kind of equality is essential to democracy.

> The crucial issue of democracy is not the composition of the elite—for the man on the bottom it makes little difference whether the command emanates from an elite of the rich and the well-born or from an elite of workers or farmers. Instead the issue is whether democracy can diffuse power sufficiently throughout society to inculcate among people of all walks of life a justifiable feeling that they have the power to participate in decisions which affect themselves and the common life of the community, especially the immediate community in which they work and spend most of their waking hours and energy (Bachrach 1969: 92).

Thus, to Bachrach the effective equalization of power is the final goal (see also his comparison of "democratic elitism" and participation theory, 1969: 100).

The question which Bachrach leaves without an answer (and this is true also of Pateman) concerns the origin of power. From where does it come? Society is characterized by large differences between groups with regard to their possibilities of using economic and material resources. The problem, according to Bachrach, is how to "inculcate among people . . . a justifiable feeling that they have the power to participate in decisions which affect themselves."[1] But how are underprivileged groups to be given that feeling unless they have something to decide on? Does not the *feeling* of having the power to make decisions come from the actual *command over resources*, the distribution of which one is entitled to determine?[2] If this is so, then the suggestions by the "radical democrats" to democratize decision-making is at best a necessary, but far from sufficient reform.

Democracy must concern the maximization of *two* equality values, i.e., *equality of influence on decision-making* (which has to do with reducing the distance between the elite and the mass), and *equality of economic and material resources*. Schematically, this is presented in Table 14.1.

Table 14.1

		Resources (economic, material)	
		Equality	Inequality
Participation (distance between elite and mass)	Equality	1	2
	Inequality	3	4

Starting from cell no. 4 (which characterizes the actual situation in most societies) the problem concerns how to approach the ideal state of cell no. 1. With all reservations due to the schematic representation, one may depict the difference between *participative* and *egalitarian* theories of democracy by saying that the former recommends the path 4-2-1, and the latter 4-3-1. According to participative theory, democracy (including economic equality) is best achieved through increased participation in local communities and organizations. In contrast, egalitarian theory maintains that democracy best can be implemented through the redistribution of economic and material resources. This, in turn, may improve the conditions for a heightened participation and greater interaction between the elite and the mass. (A host of survey data supports this assumption. See, e.g., the summary by Lewin on the relationship between socio-economic status and "efficacy," 1970: 246.)

Do we have to make a choice between the two theories? Not necessarily, if economic equality has the effect of improving the chances for participation. The problem seems to be to find practical ways for gradually approaching economic equality, taking due account of the mobilizing potentials of participation

Since economic equality can hardly be attained without any form of central controls, some "general interest" institution has to be guaranteed an influence. However, as was suggested above, this need not hold back participation; on the contrary, it may act as a stimulus for it. A more equal distribution of resources between organizations and groups can probably be achieved simultaneously with democratization and debureaucratization *within* them.

NOTES

1. The rest of the quotation reads, "and the common life of the community . . . ." As I have tried to show above, this is a persuasive formulation, since it presupposes something which has to be proved, i.e., that decisions which benefit the individuals themselves can be equated with decisions that are beneficial to the community and society at large.

2. Here Bachrach lacks in consequence. On the one hand, he recommends the nationalization of large industries. On the other, he maintains that the fundamental issue in politics "no longer relates to the problem of production or distribution but to the problem of power" (1969: 105). But it is hard to see how nationalization could be defended on other grounds than those concerning the control over "production and distribution." The power to make decisions cannot very well be a goal in itself. It has to be used in some way that *affects* production and distribution.

Chapter 15

POSTSCRIPT: The Struggle

Against Bureaucracy

To a very great degree, social life is organized life. The reasons to organize are obvious. Organization is a resource, a resource which can be used to reach common goals quicker, and to combat opponents who have competing goals. Very often, organization is *the* most important resource which a group may command. It is a resource which can be sufficient in compensating for the superiority—materially and economically—of a competitor.

Bad organization can often mean defeat. This is a truism. More interesting, however, is the fact that *good* organization can also lead to defeat, i.e., for the purposes, goals, and interests which were the original reasons that a group organized.

Every organized group needs administration: an executive which carries out the decisions of the group and which, in day-to-day activity, strives to implement organizational goals. The problem which has been the focus of this book concerns the ways and means to insure that the executive remains the administrator of group interests, to guarantee the executive's subordination to the mandator, and to prevent it from becoming a self-indulgent apparatus going its own way and becoming a bureaucracy.

The preceding discussion (see Part I, and Part II, Ch. 10, esp. Figure 10.1) suggests that the struggle against bureaucracy has to take place on two levels simultaneously.

(A) The dependence of organizations on *external forces* (economic, technological, and political) sets certain limits for the measures that can be taken against bureaucracy. Conversely, to the degree that organized groups of citizens can liberate themselves from the confinement of material and other factors, their ability to control and exert power over the executive is strengthened. The increase in economic productivity in organizations and in society at large creates the possibility of reducing working hours, and consequently of gaining greater freedom to organize for the improvement of working conditions. Economic development also provides the basis for the improvement of education and culture. In turn, these may become the foundation for a critique of the existing production relations, and for the rational and deliberate changing of these relations. Furthermore, economic development is a prerequisite for extending the resources of underprivileged groups, and for creating the economic equality which, in turn, contributes to the implementation of democratic rule.

Economic relationships which retard the development toward greater equality and a heightened quality of life, constitute the material bases of bureaucracy. Thus, the elimination of bureaucracy, in the long run, is intimately connected with the development of the productive forces.

(B) But bureaucracy also exists and is preserved because of factors which are *immanent* in the organization. Requirements concerning economy, competence, continuity, and mobilization automatically give the executive group a strong position. In the short run, and within the framework set by material conditions, the outcome of the struggle against bureaucracy depends on whether the executive group may be prevented from usurping the power of its special positions. How is this to be done?

I wrote in my commentary to Michels' book, *Political Parties,* that Michels primarily emphasizes the *form* of decision-making and ignores the *content* of the decisions involved. "It is quite possible that even a very small group in the leadership of the organization, because of good contacts with lower-level members, can reach decisions which are in good accordance with the goals and interests of the mandators/participants" (Ch. 2, p. 79). The only *guarantee* for this contact with the nonexecutive levels, and the only *safeguard* for this connection between the mandators' goals and the administration's day-to-day decisions, is a broad participation among all organization members in the governing of their own affairs.

I especially stress *guarantee* and *safeguard*. Elite responsiveness *can* exist even in a system where the participation of citizens in politics is limited to the election of representatives at certain intervals. But the less the citizens participate in politics, the more the "people" becomes dependent on the benevolence of the "elite" and its motivation to respond to popular will, and furthermore, people become dependent on having a well-functioning competition among the elites. A participative system decreases this dependency and provides the possibilities for continuous control of the executive.

The primary characteristics of such a system have been sketched out by Marx (in his comments to the Paris Commune, *The Civil War in France*); and Weber (*Economy and Society,* 1968: 289). The former, but not the latter, believed in the possibility of implementing these principles: a delegate system based on conditional mandates, immediate recall of delegates, information duty for delegates vis-à-vis their basic organizations, and rotation of mandates. It is true that the realization of such a system will meet great difficulties. Differences in education and interests among delegates would render some delegates more powerful than others. The requirement of continuity in organizational management constitutes a pressure not to make mandate periods too short, etc. But the participative system, in spite of these difficulties, represents a fruitful alternative for organizational leadership.

REFERENCES

ABRAHAMSSON, B. (1972) *Military Professionalization and Political Power.* Beverly Hills: Sage Publications.

——— (1970) "Homans on exchange: Hedonism revived." *American Journal of Sociology* (September): 273-285.

ADIZES, I. (1973) "On conflict resolution and an organizational definition of self-management." *Participation and Self-Management* Vol. 5. Proceedings of the First International Sociological Conference on Participation and Self-Management, Dubrovnik, December 13-17, 1972. Zagreb.

AIKEN, M. and J. HAGE (1968) "Organizational interdependence and intraorganizational structure." *American Sociological Review* (December): 912-931.

ALBROW, M. (1970) *Bureaucracy.* London: Pall Mall.

ARGYRIS, C. (1967) "Being human and being organized," in E. P. Hollander and R. G. Hunt (eds.) *Current Perspectives in Social Psychology.* New York: Oxford University Press.

——— (1964) *Integrating the Individual and the Organization.* New York: John Wiley.

ASPLUND, Å. (1973) *Sjukvårdsadministration.* Stockholm: Läromedelsförlagen.

BACHRACH, P. (1969) *The Theory of Democratic Elitism.* London: University of London Press.

BACK, K. W. (1972) *Beyond Words: The Story of Sensitivity Training and the Encounter Movement.* New York: Russell Sage.

BARBIĆ, A. (1973) "Citizen Participation in Four Yugoslav Republics." *Participation and Self-Management* Vol. 6 (see under Adizes).

BARNARD, C. I. (1968) *The Functions of the Executive.* Cambridge, Mass.: Harvard University Press.

BARNES, L. B. (1960) *Organizational Systems and Engineering Groups.* Graduate School of Business, Harvard University.

BENNIS, W. (1959) "Leadership theory and administrative behavior." *Administrative Science Quarterly* (December).

BERNTSON, L. (1974) *Politiska partier och sociala klasser.* Lund: Cavefors.

BILANDŽIĆ, D (1973) *Ideje i praksa društvenog razvoja Jugoslavije 1945-1973.* Belgrade: Komunist.

BLAU, P. M. and W. R. SCOTT (1962) *Formal Organizations.* San Francisco: Chandler.

BLAUNER, R. (1964) *Alienation and Freedom.* Chicago: University of Chicago Press.

BLEGEN, H. M. and B. NYLEHN (1969) *Organisasjonsteori.* Trondheim: Tapir Forlag.

BLUMBERG, P. (1968) *Industrial Democracy: The Sociology of Participation.* London: Constable.

BOALT, G. (1954) *Arbetsgruppen.* Stockholm: Tiden.

——and G. WESTERLUND (1953) *Arbetssociologi. Arbetsbetingelser och mätmetoder.* Stockholm: Tiden.

BOULDING, K. (1953) *The Organizational Revolution.* New York: Harper.

BUCKLEY, W. (1967) *Sociology and Modern Systems Theory.* Englewood Cliffs, N.J.: Prentice-Hall.

BURGER, W. (1973) "Public decision-making and self-management in an industrializing rural commune." *Participation and Self-Management* Vol. 6 (see under Adizes).

BURNS, T. and G. M. STALKER (1961) *The Management of Innovation.* London: Tavistock.

CAMPBELL, A. et al. (1964) *The American Voter.* New York: John Wiley.

CAPLOW, T. (1964) *Principles of Organization.* New York: Harcourt, Brace, and World.

CAREY, A. (1967) "The Hawthorne studies: A radical criticism." *American Sociological Review*: 403-416.

CASPARSSON, R. (1974) *LO under fem årtionden* I-II. Stockholm: Tiden.

Constitution of the Socialist Federal Republic of Yugoslavia (1974) Belgrade.

CROZIER, M. (1964) *The Bureaucratic Phenomenon.* London: Tavistock.

CYERT, R. M. and J. G. MARCH (1963) *A Behavioral Theory of the Firm.* Englewood Cliffs, N.J.: Prentice-Hall.

DAHL, R. A. (1970) *After the Revolution?* New Haven, Conn.: Yale University Press.

DAHLSTRÖM, E. (1975) *Den pågående kulturrevolutionära klasskampen i Kina.* Gothenburg: Department of Sociology (manuscript).

——(1971) *Klasser och samhällen.* Stockholm: Prisma.

——(1969) *Fördjupad företagsdemokrati.* Stockholm: Prisma.

——(1956) *Information på arbetsplatsen.* Stockholm: SNS.

DENITCH, B. (1974) "Självstyre och arbetarråd." *Tiden* No. 3.

DEUTSCHER, I. (1959) *The Prophet Unarmed: Trotsky 1921-1929.* London: Oxford University Press.

DJILAS, M. (1957) *The New Class.* New York: Praeger.

ELVANDER, N. (1969) *Intresseorganizationerna i dagens Sverige.* Lund: Gleerups.

——(1976) "Företagsdemokrati och politisk demokrati." *Organisationerna i det moderna samhället.* Uppsala: Almquist & Wiksell.

EMERY, F. E. [ed.] (1969) *Systems Thinking.* Harmondsworth: Penguin.

——and E. L. TRIST (1970) "Socio-Technical Systems," in F. E. Emery (ed.) *Systems Thinking* (see above).

ETZIONI, A. (1968) *The Active Society.* New York: Free Press.

——(1964) *Modern Organizations.* Englewood Cliffs: Prentice-Hall.

FLAES, R.M.B. (1973) "Yugoslavian experience of workers' self-management." *Participation and Self-Management* Vol. 6 (see under Adizes).

FRENCH, J.R.P., Jr., J. ISRAEL, and D. ÅS (1960) "An experiment in participation in a Norwegian factory." *Human Relations* Vol. 13: 3-10.

FRIEDMANN, G. (1955) *Industrial Society: The Emergence of the Human Problems of Automation.* New York: Free Press.

References [233]

GARDELL, B. (1976) *Arbetsinnehåll och livskvalitet*. Lund: Prisma.
––– (1971) *Produktionsteknik och arbetsglädje*. Solna: Seelig.
––– and E. DAHLSTRÖM [eds.] (1966) Teknisk förändring och arbetsanpass-*ning*. Stockholm: Prisma.
GERMAIN, E. [pseudonym for Ernest Mandel] (1969) *Om byråkratin*. Halmstad: Partisan.
GILBRETH, F., Jr. and E. GILBRETH CAREY (1972) *Cheaper by the Dozen*. New York: Thomas Y. Crowell.
GOULD, J. and W. L. KOLB (1964) *A Dictionary of the Social Sciences*. New York: Free Press.
GOULDNER, A. (1959) "Organizational analysis," in R. K. Merton, L. Broom, and L. S. Cottrel, Jr. (eds.) *Sociology Today*. New York: Basic Books.
––– (1954a) *Wildcat Strike*. Yellow Springs, Ohio: Antioch.
––– (1954b) *Patterns of Industrial Bureaucracy*. Glencoe, Ill.: Free Press.
GREINER, L. E. (1974) "Organisationers utvecklingsfaser," in Lennart Rohlin (ed.) *Organisationsutveckling*. Lund: Gleerups.
GULICK, L. and L. URWICK (1937) *Papers on the Science of Administration*. New York: Institute of Public Administration.
GUNNARSON, G. (1965) *Arbetarrörelsens genombrottsår i dokument*. Stockholm: Prisma.
HALL, A. D. and R. E. HAGEN (1956) "Definition of System." *General Systems: The Yearbook of the Society for General Systems Research* Vol. 1.
HARVEY, E. (1968) "Technology and the structure of organizations." *American Sociological Review* April: 247-258.
HEDBERG, B., S. SJÖBERG, and A. TARGAMA (1971) *Styrsystem och företagsdemokrati*. Gothenburg: BAS.
HEISKANEN, I. (1976) "Theoretical approaches and scientific strategies in administrative and operational research." *Commentationes Humanarum Litterarum* Vol. 39, No. 2. Helsinki.
HERZBERG, F., B. MAUSNER, and B. B. SNYDERMAN (1959) *The Motivation to Work*. New York: John Wiley.
HOMANS, G. C. (1967) *The Nature of Social Science*. New York: Harcourt, Brace, and World.
––– (1961) *Social Behavior: Its Elementary Forms*. London: Routledge and Kegan Paul.
HORVAT, B. (1969) *An Essay on Yugoslav Society*. New York: International Arts and Sciences Press.
HÅKANSON, K. (1973) *Socialism som självstyre*. Stockholm: Prisma.
ISRAEL, J. (1972) *Om konsten att lyfta sig själv i håret och behålla barnet i badvattnet*. Stockholm: Rabén och Sjögren.
––– (1971) *Alienation: Från Marx till modern sociologi*. Stockholm: Raben och Sjögren.
JOHANSEN J. O. (1967) *Titokratiet*. Oslo: Pax.
JOHANSSON, S. (1971) *Politiska resurser*. Stockholm: Allmänna Förlaget.
JOVANOV, N. (1974) *Radnicki strajkovi u SFRJ od 1958 do 1969*. Belgrade: SFJ.
KARLSSON, L. E. (1969) *Demokrati på arbetsplatsen*. Stockholm: Prisma.
KATZ, D. and R. L. KAHN (1966) *The Social Psychology of Organizations*. New York: John Wiley.

KNOX, T. M. [ed.] (1942) *Hegel's Philosophy of Right*. Oxford: Clarendon.

KRUPP, S. (1961) *Pattern in Organization Analysis*. New York: Holt, Rinehart and Winston.

KUPFERBERG, F. (1974) "Från Lenin till Breznjev." *Zenit* No. 1.

LANGEFORS, B. (1970) *System för företagsstyrning*. Lund: Studentlitteratur.

LASKI, H. (1930) "Bureaucracy." *Encyclopaedia of the Social Sciences*. New York: Macmillan.

LENIN, V. I. (undated) "On the party programme." Report delivered at the Eighth Congress of the Russian Communist Party (Bolsheviks), March 19, 1919. *Selected Works* Vol. VIII: 335-356. New York: International Publishers.

——— (undated) *The State and Revolution. Selected Works* Vol. VII. New York: International Publishers.

LEWIN, L. (1977) *Hur styrs facket?* Stockholm: Rabén och Sjögren.

——— (1970) *Folket och eliterna*. Stockholm: Almqvist and Wiksell.

LIKERT, R. (1961) *New Patterns of Management*. New York: McGraw-Hill.

LINDBLAD, I. (1960) *Svenska Kommunalarbetareförbundet: En studie i svensk fackföreningsrörelse*. Stockholm: Tiden.

LINDSKOUG, K. (1974) *Rationaliseringens institutionella-strukturella aspekt*. Gothenburg: Department of Sociology (manuscript).

LITTERER, J. A. (1969) *Organizations* 2nd ed., Vols. I and II. New York: John Wiley.

LITWAK, E. (1961) "Models of bureaucracy which permit conflict." *American Journal of Sociology* September.

LUNDQUIST, A. (1957) *Anpassning i arbetet*. Stockholm. PA-rådet.

LYSGAARD, S. (1961) *Arbeiderkollektivet*. Oslo: Universitetsforlaget.

MABON, H. (1973) *Organisationslärans utveckling*. Stockholm: M & B.

MANDEL, E. (1971) *Arbetarkontroll, arbetarråd, arbetarstyre*. Halmstad: Partisan.

MARCH, J. G. and H. A. SIMON (1958) *Organizations*. New York: John Wiley.

MARINKOVIC, R. (1973) "Participation and the decision-making process in the commune." *Participation and self-management* Vol. 6 (see under Adizes).

MARKOVIĆ, M. (1972) *Att utveckla socialismen*. Stockholm: Prisma.

MARX, K. (1976) *Capital* Vol. 1. Harmondsworth: Penguin.

——— (1933) *The Civil War in France*. London: Martin Lawrence.

MAYO, E. (1933) *The Human Problems of an Industrial Civilization*. Cambridge, Mass.: Harvard University Press.

McCLOSKY, H. (1958) "Conservatism and personality." *American Political Science Review* Vol. 52: 27-45.

McGREGOR, D. (1960) *The Human Side of Enterprise*. New York: McGraw-Hill.

MEIDNER, R. and A. HEDBORG (1974) "Den offentliga sektorns problematik." *Tiden* No. 2.

MERTON, R. K. (1957) "Bureaucratic structure and personality," in Merton, *Social Theory and Social Structure*. Glencoe, Ill.: Free Press.

MICHELS, R. (1958) *Political Parties*. Glencoe, Ill.: Free Press.

MOUZELIS, N. P. (1967) *Organisation and Bureaucracy*. London: Routledge and Kegan Paul.

NORRBOM, C. (1971) *Systemteori: en introduktion*. Stockholm: M & B.

OSKARSSON, V. (1963) "En metallfackförening och dess underorganisationer." *Statsvetenskaplig Tidskrift*: 494-519.

PALM, G. (1974) *Bokslut från LM*. Stockholm: Författarförlaget.

PARSONS, T. (1960) *Structure and Process in Modern Society*. Glencoe, III.: Free Press.

——— (1951) *The Social System*. Glencoe, III.: Free Press.

PATEMAN, C. (1970) *Participation and Democratic Theory*. London: Cambridge Uuniversity Press.

PELCZYNSKI, Z. A., "An introductory essay," in T. M. Knox (ed.) *Hegel's Political Writings*. Oxford: Clarendon.

PERROW, C. (1969) "The analysis of goals in complex organizations," in J. A. Litterer, *Organizations* 2nd ed., Vol. II. New York: John Wiley.

——— (1967) "A framework for the comparative analysis of organizations." *American Sociological Review* April.

POPOVIĆ, N. D. (1968) *Yugoslavia: The New Class in Crisis*. New York: Syracuse University Press.

POULANTZAS, N. (1975) *Political Power and Social Classes*. London: NLB.

PRESTHUS, R. (1962) *The Organizational Society*. New York: Alfred A. Knopf.

RAMSTRÖM, D. (1964) *Administrativa processer*. Bonniers.

RHENMAN, E. (1971) *Företaget och dess omvärld*. Stockholm: Bonniers.

——— (1970) *Centrallasarettet*. Systemanalys av ett svenskt sjukhus. Kristianstad: Studentlitteratur.

——— (1970) *God och dålig företagsledning*. Stockholm: Prisma.

——— (1968) *Industrial Democracy and Industrial Management*. London: Tavistock.

——— (1967) *Företaget som ett styrt system*. Stockholm: Norstedts.

RIZZI, B. (1939) *The Bureaucratization of the World*. London.

ROETHLISBERGER, F. J. and W. J. DICKSON (1969) "On organizational goals," in J. A. Litterer, *Organizations* 2nd ed., Vol. II. New York: John Wiley.

RRV [Riksrevisionsverket] (1971) *Effectiveness auditing*. Stockholm.

RUS, V. (1973) "The limits of organized participation." *Participation and Self-Management* Vol. 2 (see under Adizes).

SANDBERG, Å. (1976) *The Limits to Democratic Planning*. Stockholm: Liber.

SCHUMPETER, J. (1966) *Capitalism, Socialism, and Democracy*. London: Unwin University Books.

SCHULZ, T. W. (1971) *Investment in Human Capital*. New York: Free Press.

SCOTT, W. G. (1967) "Organization theory: An overview and an appraisal," in E. P. Hollander and R. G. Hunt, *Current Perspectives in Social Psychology* 3rd ed. New York: Oxford University Press.

SEGERSTEDT, T. T. and A. LUNDQUIST (1952) *Människan i industrisamhället. I: Arbetslivet*. Stockholm: SNS.

SELZNICK, P. (1957) *Leadership in Administration*. New York: Harper and Row.

SILVERMAN, D. (1970) *The Theory of Organisations*. London: Heinemann.

SIMON, H. A. (1957) *Administrative Behavior* 2nd ed. New York: Macmillan.

SKIDMORE, W. (1975) *Theoretical Thinking in Sociology*. Cambridge: Cambridge University Press.

SOU 1975: 1, Demokrati på arbetsplatsen.

SOU 1974: 39, Socialvården: mål och medel.

SOU 1967: 11-13, Programbudgetering.

SOU 1966: 1, 1965 års långtidsutredning.

STOJANOVIĆ, S. (1970) *Socialismens framtid: en kritisk analys*. Stockholm: Aldus/Bonniers.

SUNESSON, S. (1974) *Politik och organisation*. Kristianstad: Arkiv.

——— (1973) "Om begreppet byråkrati." *Häften för Kritiska Studier* No. 4.

——— (1971) *Stat och fackförbund i Sverige*. Stockholm: Department of Sociology.

TAYLOR, F. (1969) "Selections from 'Scientific Management,'" in J. A. Litterer, *Organizations* 2nd ed., Part I. New York: John Wiley.

THERBORN, G. et al. (1966) *En ny vänster*. Stockholm: Rabén och Sjögren.

THOMPSON, J. D. (1967) *Organizations in Action*. New York: McGraw-Hill.

THORSRUD, E. and F. E. EMERY (1964) *Industrielt demokrati*. Oslo: Universitetsforlaget.

TODOROVIĆ, M. (1974) "Report on the final draft of the SFRY constitution," in *Constitution of the Socialist Federal Republic of Yugoslavia*. Belgrade.

TOMASSON, R. F. (1970) *Sweden: Prototype of Modern Society*. New York: Random House.

TROTSKY, L. (1972) *Den nya kursen*. Kristianstad: Partisan.

——— (1969) *Den förrådda revolutionen*. Halmstad: Partisan.

WALKER, C. R. and R. GUEST (1952) *The Man on the Asembly Line*. Cambridge, Mass.: Harvard University Press.

WEBER, M. (1968) *Economy and Society* Vols. I-III. New York: Bedminster Press.

——— (1956) *Wirtschaft und Gesellschaft*. Tübingen: JCB Mohr.

WERIN, L. (1973) "Målstyrning contra alternativanalys–några lärdomar av traditionell ekonomisk teori," in Riksrevisionsverket, *Verksamhetsberättelse för budgetåret 1972/73*. Stockholm.

WESTERSTÅHL, J. (1945) *Svensk fackföreningsrörelse. Organisationsproblem. Verksamhetsformer. Förhållande till staten*. Stockholm.

———, and M. PERSSON (1975) *Demokrati och intresserepresentation–en principdiskussion*. Stockholm: Liber.

WHYTE, M. K. (1973) "Bureaucracy and modernization in China: The Maoist critique." *American Sociological Review* April.

WHYTE, W. H., Jr. (1956) *The Organization Man*. New York: Doubleday.

WOODWARD, J. (1965) *Industrial Organization: Theory and Practice*. London: Oxford University Press.

ÅKERMAN, N. (1970) *Apparaten Sverige*. Stockholm: Prisma.

SUBJECT INDEX